KU-383-894

Pluto Press Workers' Handbooks

Sue Ward

Pensions

What to look for
in company pension schemes
and how to improve them

Pluto  Press

First published 1981 by Pluto Press Limited
Unit 10 Spencer Court, 7 Chalcot Road, London NW1 8LH

Copyright © Sue Ward 1981

ISBN 0 86104 333 2

Cover designed by Colin Bailey

Photoset and printed in Great Britain by
Photobooks (Bristol) Limited, 28 Midland Road,
St Philips, Bristol

Contents

Preface

Unlike most books written on this subject, this is not intended as a book for experts. It is a handbook for shop stewards, union representatives and full-time officials, to assist them in understanding and negotiating company pension schemes. Despite its length, it does not cover everything: in particular the intricacies of taxation and administration have been left out, and in some places I have simplified complex processes in a way that may offend pensions professionals.

There is a mystique about pension schemes, sustained by many of those who have a vested interest in the pensions industry, who will no doubt dislike this book intensely. It is not an 'exposé' of the industry; but knowledge is power, and this book should help to redistribute that power towards the ordinary members of pension schemes.

My thanks are due to all those employers and pensions professionals who have unwittingly taught me so much over the last few years. Thanks are also due to the General and Municipal Workers' Union for allowing me to write this book, although the views expressed are my own and not necessarily those of the GMWU. I am grateful to the National Association of Pension Funds for allowing me to quote from their survey. They have asked me to make it clear that they have not been asked to comment on the use to which those extracts have been put, or on any views or conclusions drawn from them.

I should like to thank personally Myles White, Bryn Davies, Frances Bennett and Jim Moher for reading and commenting on the manuscript as a whole, and Michael Cunningham for the detailed help he has given on almost every word. Also Colin Lever, John Prevatt, Brian Mead and Don Warren for reading parts of the manuscript, and all my friends for listening to my moans on the subject for a year. And finally to my husband Michael, who had to live with me while I was writing it. The mistakes, of course, are entirely my own responsibility.

Sue Ward
August 1980

1.

Company pension schemes

Section 1: What is a company pension scheme?

'Company pension schemes' are agreements made by an employer to provide a certain amount of money

- when the worker retires, as a pension; or
- if the worker dies, as a lump sum; and/or
- as a widow's, widower's, or dependant's pension.

Nowadays, the amount of money to be provided is usually stated as a **fraction** (1/60th, 1/80th, etc), or as a **percentage** (1.66%, 1.25%) of the worker's wage. It doesn't have to be; it can be put in terms of a sum of money (£5 per year of service, for instance).

Not all pension schemes are negotiated – in fact, there are many employers who refuse to regard pensions as negotiable. But they will normally be

- written down, in a pension scheme booklet that anyone who is a member of the scheme should be given; and
- backed up by a **trust deed and rules**, which are legal documents.

Various names are used for these agreements. They can be called:

- **company** pension schemes; or
- **private** pension schemes; or
- **occupational** pension schemes; or
- **superannuation** – this is the name that is often used for local government, central government or nationalised industry pensions; or
- **retirement benefit** schemes – this name is used by a number of American companies.

These are all different names for the same thing. We are going to call them company pension schemes in this book, or just 'pension schemes'.

Who pays for them?

■ They can be paid for entirely by the employer, or
■ the employee can also pay a contribution.

Where does the money go?

■ Normally, it will be paid into a **fund** which is administered by **trustees**.

■ The trustees are responsible for investing this money – by doing it themselves (by buying stocks and shares and property), by getting a merchant bank or some other financial institution to do it, or by buying a policy with an insurance company.

In 1975 the Social Security Pensions Act, sometimes called the 'Castle Act' became law. Under this Act, all employed people must be either contracted **in** or contracted **out** of the State additional pension scheme. If you are contracted **in**, the State provides you with an additional pension on top of your basic one. If you're contracted **out**, your pension scheme does so. But you can also be contracted in, and have a scheme that 'rides on top'. Then you will get a pension from **both** sources.

If it is contracted **out**, there is a special set of rules a pension scheme must follow, and it is supervised by an organisation called the **Occupational Pensions Board**.

Whether it is contracted out or not, there are other rules laid down by the Inland Revenue (the tax people) about the maximum benefits a scheme can provide.

The rules, and the way pension funds work, are explained in detail later on. Although they may look very different and complicated, because of the various rules, *pensions are as much a negotiable item as anything else*, so far as we are concerned, though the employer may well think differently.

But you may have to treat pensions negotiations in a rather different **way** from wages negotiations, as explained in chapter 7.

Your employer may want you to think of the pension scheme as something he provides out of the goodness of his heart, as a matter of 'grace and favour' and therefore as something you have no business arguing about. Don't let this argument put you off. Even if your pension scheme is 'non-contributory', which means that the **employer** is making all the contributions, pensions are still your **deferred wages**.

If this money were not being put aside for a pension, it could be being added to your pay packet. You have a right to negotiate on pensions, just as you do on wages.

Section 2: Why should we negotiate company pension schemes?

In the past, trade unions have not taken much part in negotiating or running company pension schemes. Indeed, there has often been a strong wish **not** to become involved. This was for several reasons:

■ We have believed that pensions should be provided by the State, as part of the Social Security system. At the moment the State pension is far too small.

It has remained at 1/5th of the average industrial wage since the war, or about 1/3rd for a married couple. The TUC has been asking for years for the pension to be increased to 1/2 the average wage for a married couple, 1/3rd for a single person, but no government has done it.

■ Arising from this, many people have taken the view that, if we go for better **company** pensions for some, we will be contradicting the TUC aim of better **State** pensions for everyone. Even assuming the standard of living rises, there must be some limit on the amount of cash that can be distributed from the working population to the non-working population. At its simplest, there is certainly a limit on the amount that people are willing to see go in deductions from their pay packet, before they take it home. So the more we pay to company pension schemes, which at the moment give much more to the better off than to the poor, the less we may be willing to pay to the State, which gives the same basic pensions to everyone. By tying up so much in company schemes, we may well be making it impossible to achieve the TUC aim.

■ Pension schemes have been seen as basically a way of reducing a high paid person's tax bill, and therefore not something ordinary workers can or should benefit from. In fact, the tax relief on pension contributions, and the fact that pension payments are treated as earned rather than unearned income, means that even people on quite low incomes now get their tax bills reduced by being members of a pension scheme.

All these are strong arguments, and if we could redesign things from scratch, we probably wouldn't want to have company pension schemes, at least in their present form. We would probably rely far more heavily on the Government, although we might want to enforce an obligation on companies to look after their retired workers, but in a way that did not give extra privileges to some.

Pension schemes are also very *inefficient* at doing the job they claim to be doing. They work quite well for the very small group of people who

- stay 40 years with the same company,
- have their best real earnings at the end of their working life, and
- are never involved in a merger or takeover which means their pension scheme is stopped and a new one started.

They work **badly** for people who change jobs, for whatever reason, and for those who have a break in their working life, for instance in order to bring up children.

Those who are already well paid tend to have the most generous pension schemes, so that the system as a whole redistributes from the poor to the rich. And for many people they make promises which are to say the least misleading, because of the 'small print' which is kept deliberately obscure.

So why get involved; why have a workers' handbook about pensions?

We can't now avoid them. In 1975 the State went into 'partnership' with private pension schemes, so that whether we like it or not, all employed people now have an earnings related pension, whether from the State or their employer. Eleven million people are in occupational pension schemes, and the people who run them have a huge vested interest. If unions ignore the company schemes, millions of trade unionists will still be members of them, and management and the insurance companies will get away with more. So if we are going to put up with them **at all**, we ought to do the job properly, and **understand** what pension schemes are about, and get the best deal we can. This is what this book is intended to help you do.

Section 3: What can your pension scheme do for you?

The average life expectancy of a man at 65 is 12 years; of a woman at 60, 20 years. That's a long time to live on the State pension. But **also**, there are quite a lot of men and women who do not live until they retire. 30% of men and 12% of women die before they reach that age.

What about their position, and that of the families they are supporting?

■ It's all very well to say jokingly that you do not want to be worth more dead than alive. The wages your employer is paying are supporting not just you but also your family.

■ So there is a responsibility to provide for them if anything happens to you, the worker. (This applies as much to women as it does to men – your wages are still vital to your household.)

'But I'd prefer to have the money in my pay packet.'

A lot of people would – they'd rather not think about tomorrow anyway. You have every right to take that view as an individual, but if a pension scheme is actually *on offer*, you are giving the employer a free gift by saying this. He is willing to put an extra 5% or 8%, or whatever percentage it is, of your wages into the pension scheme, and you are telling him to keep it. You would not do that with ordinary wages!

A good pension scheme can be a good investment

Assuming that the money that is going into the pension scheme **might** be available to you in your pay, would it be possible to get a better return on your investment, if you had it in your hand, and

■ used it to buy Life Assurance, or

■ put it into a building society?

No, it wouldn't. But remember we are talking about **good** schemes – there are bad ones around that don't give you value for money.

A **final salary** scheme (see page 32), is as near an inflation proofed investment as you can get, at least if you stay in the scheme until retirement age. Why?

■ Because the pension you get when you retire is based on your **earnings when you retire** – not on your earnings when you contribute to the scheme.

Bill Jones, aged 25, earns £100 a week, and contributes £5 to the company's pension scheme. He feels it is a lot of money. But in the year 2020, when he retires, everyone is earning £1000 a week. His pension will be based on that, not on the £5 contribution.

There's a fuller explanation of how pension funds work on page 222. In this chapter, all that needs pointing out is that one of the reasons pension funds can do well on their investments is that they have a very privileged tax position (which is why the Inland Revenue is interested in their rules).

Pension funds **do not pay**
- Corporation Tax
- Capital Gains Tax
- Income Tax

on their normal investments. The only tax they do pay is Development Land Tax, if they develop a property commercially, and that is likely to be abolished soon.

Also
- contributions to company pension schemes get full tax relief, unlike National Insurance contributions which come out of your taxable income, although the employer still gets tax relief on his share of the contributions;
- when the pension is finally paid, it is taxed as **earned** income;
- the lump sums that often go with the pension, or are paid on death, are usually tax free.

You can be misled, if you look at your pension scheme booklet and see, for instance, that if you leave the company before you retire, you get your contributions returned plus a very low rate of interest. (Though, as explained on page 19, in the future most people will not get their contributions returned). This is **nothing to do** with the rate of interest your contributions have actually been earning. It's designed to keep the maximum amount of money in the fund, and it's in order to stop this that schemes these days are obliged to provide you with a deferred pension instead.

If you look at the benefits the scheme is designed to provide – the pension and the life assurance – and ask whether you could get the same result, taking account of inflation until you retire, from an insurance company, generally the answer will be no. For an older person, especially if s/he is not in good health, a pension scheme contribution may well be worth it for the life assurance alone.

We looked up a published table of insurance company rates, to see how much it would cost a man earning £100 a week to insure himself for £10,000 a year, which would be roughly twice his salary. The cheapest premiums were:

A man aged 30, in good health	£76.99	1.5% of salary
A man aged 45, in good health	£165.80	3.2% of salary
A man aged 50, in good health	£280.60	5.3% of salary

The rates for a woman would be a little lower, because women are expected to live longer.

Turn to chapter 8 for an explanation in more detail of why this is.

Pension schemes are not perfect – far from it. There are many which do not give a good pension, and **are** bad value for money, especially compared with the State scheme. **Most** pension schemes are not designed to cope with the sort of inflation we have been having over the last few years, and most of them give a poor deal to 'early leavers' (see page 19).

But because of the way it works, and the special tax privileges it has, a good pension scheme is an efficient way of saving for your retirement, and of insuring yourself and your family against the risk of death or long-term illness.

Section 4: Why do employers run pension schemes?

It may seem a mystery why the employer should bother. A good pension scheme is quite expensive – why does he not simply make the workers rely on the State?

Here is a quote from a students' textbook about pensions:

> The employee is helped to provide for his old age financially but the benefits are not one sided. An adequate pension scheme will assist an employer in his recruitment and retention of labour and enable him to dispense with the services of his employees in an orderly and humane manner as they age and contribute less to the profitability of the business. In addition, regular retirements mean easily visible openings for promotion.
> (from *Pension Schemes – design and administration*, CII Tuition Service, 1976)

This sums it up fairly well. Now that pension schemes are fairly widespread, it is necessary for an employer to provide one if
- he wants to show himself as a 'good' employer, or
- he is competing for labour with other companies who have pension schemes. This applies particularly with white collar staff, but increasingly also with manual workers.

These are therefore arguments you can use to persuade the employer to introduce a pension scheme, or to improve an existing one.

2.

The framework around company pension schemes

Introduction

Pension schemes operate within a number of sets of rules, and this chapter is designed to set these out. There are 4 main sets of rules to take into account.

- The State basic pension (section 1)
- The State additional pension (section 2)
- The rules about 'contracting out' (section 3)
- The rules the Inland Revenue lays down (section 4)

Section 1: The State basic pension

Most people will get this when they retire, and most pension schemes assume that they are going to get it. But some people don't get a State pension, or only get a reduced one, because they have not paid enough National Insurance contributions.

To get a full State pension, about 9/10ths of your **'working life'** must count as **'reckonable years'** for National Insurance purposes.

A 'reckonable year' is a year in which you have paid or been credited with either 50 stamps, under the old system, which ended in 1975, or contributions on 50 times the **lower earnings limit** (see page 11) under the new system.

Your 'working life' starts either when you are 16 – or, if you were already 16 in 1948, when the National Insurance system started, it starts in 1948. There are some people whose employment was insurable before 1948 – for them, working life started in 1936 or when they were 16, whichever came the later.

When you have worked out how many complete years there are in your working life, the table below tells you if you will get a full retirement pension:

Length of working life	Number of 'reckonable years' needed for a full pension
27–30 years	working life minus 3
31–40 years	working life minus 4
41 years or more	working life minus 5

If you have fewer 'reckonable years' your basic pension may be reduced – and if your reckonable years are less than ¼ of your working life, you get no basic pension at all.

The DHSS leaflet NP 32, **Retirement Pensions**, has a table on the back, which shows what percentage pension you will get. If you have any doubt about your own position, write to the local Social Security office.

What about married women?

A married woman paying the 2% contribution is earning **no** pension in her own right. She will be treated as a 'dependant' of her husband. The married woman's contribution is being phased out.

No one can now start paying at the 2% rate, but anyone who was already paying in May 1977 can go on doing so, until she is out of employment for 2 complete consecutive tax years – from April 1981 to April 1983, for instance.

Widows and widowers

For widows' pensions the contribution conditions are different. The wife qualifies for a widow's pension if the husband, in the tax year before the current calendar year, paid or was credited with contributions on 50 times the lower earnings limit (see page 11). You are credited with a contribution for any week you are receiving a National Insurance benefit, for instance sickness benefit.

Jack Smith dies in June 1982, that is, in **calendar year** 1982. The last tax year was April 1980 to April 1981. So, if his wife is to get a widow's pension, he must have paid or been credited with contributions on 50 times the lower earnings limit in 1980–81.

But not all widows get pensions, although (provided their husband has fulfilled the contribution conditions) they all get an **allowance** for the first 6 months, whatever age they are, and whether or not they have children. After 6 months, a widow over 50 receives a pension, and a widow with dependent children (up to age 16, unless they are still at school, or apprentices, in which case it is 19) receives a **widowed mother's** allowance.

When the children stop being dependent, if the widow is over 50 she also gets a widow's pension. If a woman is between 40 and 50 when she is widowed, or when she ceases to have dependent children, she gets an 'age related widow's pension', at a reduced rate, ranging from 30% at age 40 to 93% at age 49. If she is below 40, she does not get anything.

The State does **not** provide a widower's pension – a man left with dependent children must rely on supplementary benefit.

Retiring early

If you have to retire early because your health is too bad to continue working, you will probably find yourself depending on **invalidity** benefit from the State. This follows on from sickness benefit after 6 months, but it is paid at a middle rate between sickness benefit and retirement pension.

But if you retire early at your own request, or if your pension scheme has an earlier retirement age than the State one, you *cannot* draw your State pension early. If your pension is less than £35 per week, you may be able to sign on for unemployment benefit for 1 year, although they may offer you a job, and take away your benefit if you do not take it. After that, you will have to rely on supplementary benefit, if you cannot manage on your company pension.

There is a scheme called Job Release, by which you can get a weekly payment from the Government if you retire early, provided your job is given to a younger person taken from the unemployment register, but this is only available to men over 64, women over 59. The local Department of Employment will have details.

Section 2: The state additional scheme

The 'additional pension scheme' is also known as the 'Castle scheme' because it was brought in by Barbara Castle at the beginning of the last Labour government.

Its full name is the **Social Security Pension Act 1975**, and it was the **4th** attempt at producing an earnings related State pension scheme to go on top of the basic pension.

■ First was the Boyd-Carpenter scheme, introduced in 1961. This produced the **graduated pension**, which was very poor value because it was not inflation-proofed. This came to an end in 1975.

■ Second came the Crossman scheme, which never actually became law because of the 1970 General Election.

■ Third, Sir Keith Joseph brought out a scheme, which was actually passed as an Act, the **Social Security Act 1973**. It was not put into effect, because in 1974 it was swept away by Labour, who brought in the Castle Act in 1975 instead. (Bits of it did remain, though: the 'preservation' requirements, explained on pages 19–23, came from that Act, and the Occupational Pensions Board, which now supervises contracted out pension schemes, was originally set up to organise preservation).

■ Finally, the Castle Act. This did not come fully into effect until 1978.

The Conservatives, when in opposition, said they would not change the Act, so it may be that we shall have a few years *without* major changes in pension law. We shall certainly get ample warning of changes made: a long time is always allowed for a changeover, because of the large number of schemes involved (about 65,000) and because of the number of legal documents.

What does the Act say?

It's important to read this section, because, even if your company's pension scheme is contracted **out**, you need to understand the State additional pension scheme to know what you are contracted out **of**, and how the rules work. And if you're contracted **in**, this section will explain how your pension is worked out.

We all started contributing to the new State additional pension scheme in April 1978, and the first pensions were paid out in April 1979. You are contributing to part of the new scheme even if you are contracted out. But the first **full** pension will not be paid out until 1998.

People who are already pensioners don't get any credits under the new scheme – they stay on the basic pension. So the scheme does nothing for those who have retired, and not much for those coming up to retirement. Younger people will benefit most.

If you are contracted **in**, you are paying $7\frac{3}{4}\%$ contribution to the State scheme on all earnings up to £200 a week (at 1981–82 rates).

■ This £165 figure is the **upper earnings limit** – UEL for short.

■ It is about 7 times the **lower earnings limit** – LEL – but it may be rounded up or down to make a neater figure.

■ In turn, the LEL (£27 in 1981–82) is about the same as the State pension – again, rounded up or down.

If you are earning *less* than the lower earnings limit, you pay no contributions at all. As soon as you earn *more* than the LEL, you pay full contributions on all your earnings. If you earn over the UEL, you only pay contributions on your earnings *up to* that limit.

The **pension** changes each year in November, and the lower and upper earnings limits change in the following April – so there is always a 6-month time lag.

What about the employer?

He is paying 10.2% on all your earnings up to the upper limit. He also pays a tax of $3\frac{1}{2}$% of your earnings. Some employers try to give the impression that this is part of the National Insurance contribution, and should be taken into account if you're trying to get them to pay more to the pension scheme. Don't be taken in – it is a payroll tax which simply happens to be collected through the National Insurance system.

These contributions cover *all* your National Insurance benefits, short and long term. They're collected through the PAYE system ('pay as you earn' – the normal employee tax system) but you don't get tax relief on them. The employer does – they're treated as a 'business expense'.

The important thing about the lower and upper earnings limits is that it is only earnings between these that count for additional pension.

For each year you are in the State scheme, you get 1/80th of your *revalued average earnings* between the lower and upper earnings limits. The most you can get is 20/80ths – one quarter of your earnings between the limits. When you have been in the scheme more than 20 years, the averaging is done on your *best* 20 years.

Revalued average earnings is probably the most difficult point in this. The earnings figure for each year of your working life will be revalued by the Department of Health and Social Security (DHSS) to take account of the increase in national average earnings between the date they were earned, and the date you retire. The figures will be taken from your P60 tax form.

Susan Jones has contributed to the new scheme for 5 years. Her earnings in those years were £3000, £3300, £3600, £4000, and £4400. Over the 5 years, national average earnings have been rising by 10% a year.

So her earnings in year 1 are revalued by 46.4% to give a figure of £4392:
in year 2 by 33.1% to give £4392 again;
in year 3 by 21% to give £4386;
in year 4 by 10% to give £4400;
and not at all in year 5, the year she retires, as no revaluation is done on them.
These figures are added up and averaged, which gives a figure of £4388. This is then a figure for her earnings in *real* terms, as if inflation did not exist.

After you have been in the scheme for 20 years, all those years' earnings will be revalued to take account of inflation, and then the *best* 20 years are used for the averaging. This is particularly helpful to manual workers because in *real* terms their earnings tend to be highest in middle age. As they reach retirement, they cannot keep up with the piecework rates, or they go off shiftwork onto days.

Having got an average figure, the lower earnings limit (and if necessary the upper earnings limit too) are deducted.

We'll call the LEL £1196 (which is what it was in 1980–81) and therefore deduct that from £4388, giving £3192. Susan Jones then gets 5/80ths of that, which is £199.50 a year or £3.83 a week, which is added to her basic pension.

There are two important points to remember:
■ The calculation is done on all your PAYE earnings, between the lower and upper limits, not simply on basic pay. *But* it is based on your P60, i.e. the annual figure. So if you have a few weeks' poor earnings, because of layoff or bad weather, that will reduce the total.
■ If you are unemployed or sick (or receiving a National Insurance benefit for some other reason), you will be credited only for the basic State pension for those weeks. If you are unemployed for a whole year, you will be treated in the additional scheme as having £0 earnings in that year – so it will reduce the average when you finally reach pension age.

Home responsibility

Anyone who is at home looking after children under 16, for whom s/he is receiving child benefit, or looking after someone at home who is getting attendance allowance, or getting supplementary benefit because s/he is looking after an invalid, gets **credited** for those years. *But*

■ it is only for the basic pension; and

■ it is only for *complete* years. If you give up your job for this reason halfway through the year, you could find you have not earned enough to qualify for any additional pension, but do not get a credit either; and

■ theoretically it is available to both men and women, but in practice it is more complicated for a man to get it. A woman receiving child benefit will be automatically credited, whereas a man will only be credited if the benefit has been signed over to him as 'main payee'.

Widow's pension

The additional pension is payable also to widows, provided they are eligible for a basic widow's pension, and begins after the 6 months' widow's allowance runs out. It is based on the **husband's** contributions. If he dies before retirement, his widow gets the *whole* of his accrued additional pension added on to the basic widow's pension.

> Peter Williams dies in 1983, after the scheme has been running for 5 years. His widow gets the basic pension, because she is over 50, plus 5/80ths of his revalued average earnings between the limits.

If the husband is a dependent invalid, and the **wife** dies, then he gets a widower's pension. But there is *no* widower's pension for a healthy man, whether or not he has children, before retirement age.

After retirement, the pension becomes a **survivor's** pension. Whichever one of the couple dies first, the *other* inherits the additional pension. But the survivor cannot receive more than the maximum s/he could have had from the State anyway, if both of them had had earnings at the top limit.

> Eric Walters has an additional pension of £20, and his wife Joan has an additional pension of £10, earned in her own right. The most that anyone could have got out of the Castle scheme is £25. So when Eric dies, his wife inherits £15 of his pension, to bring it up to £25. If she died first, he could inherit only £5 of her pension. The Government takes the rest back.

Invalids

If someone is sick for more than 6 months, and therefore goes onto invalidity pension, then whatever additional pension s/he has earned is added on to that, for as long as s/he is an invalid. If s/he remains sick until retirement age, then it turns into a retirement pension.

Inflation

One of the basic ideas of the whole scheme is that pensions will be protected against inflation. Up to retirement, they are protected because the earnings on which they are calculated are **revalued**. After retirement, they are protected against increases in prices, by being increased by the **Secretary of State's estimate** of the rise in the Retail Prices Index. This means the Government, which thus has a chance to decide that inflation has been lower than other people think it has.

So what will this cost?

At present, the Castle scheme costs very little, because the pensions being paid out are very small. The **most** anyone, who retired in 1980–81 could get was £1.44 a week. But as the years go by, and the amount of pension increases, it will cost more, and the extra will come out of National Insurance contributions.

No one is going to grudge, surely, paying better pensions to old people out of our earnings. But we might question whether this is in fact the best way to do it. Some of the scheme's faults have already been pointed out, but here is a list of them:

■ It does nothing for people who are already retired, so they will always be poorer than the 'new' pensioners. In 1998, a pensioner aged 85 will only have about $\frac{1}{2}$ the pension of many pensioners aged 65.

■ Since it is earnings-related, if you are low paid at work, you will be low paid in retirement as well. Women will be particularly affected by this.

■ Anyone whose working life is interrupted, whatever the reason, will suffer for it when the pension is finally calculated. If you are made redundant and have difficulty getting another job, or if you are sick for a long time, your final pension may be lower, even if the interruption happened 20 or more years before retirement.

■ Although married women will be credited for the **basic** pension while they are away having children, they don't get any credit for the additional pension, so in many cases they will end up having a lower figure for their earnings over their working lives, and therefore a lower pension.

Section 3: Contracting out

When the Government was putting in the Castle scheme, it was faced with the question of what to do about the private schemes in which 11½ million people were involved. There would have been an outcry if they had simply closed them down, and it was too expensive, and too difficult, to take them over. Pension funds and long term insurance company funds together are now worth about £70 billion, and are growing every year.

So, instead, they went into 'partnership' with them. The people who run the pension schemes are a very powerful group indeed, and they struck a hard bargain with the Government. Chapter 8 goes into more detail about pension funds. Overall, the funds did a lot better than the Government out of the agreement.

As a result of this, a scheme can **contract out** of **part** of the Castle scheme, and provide its own pension instead. What does this mean?

■ The basic pension stays the same.

■ So do unemployment benefit and the other National Insurance benefits.

■ The 'contracted out' scheme provides an additional pension, under a number of fairly strict conditions.

■ In return, both you and the employer get a reduction (also called an **'abatement'**) of your National Insurance contributions.

At the moment, the **employer** gets a reduction of 4½% on his contribution, above the LEL, so he has to pay only 5.7%. You get a reduction of 2½% on yours, so that you only have to pay 5¼% – again, above the LEL.

So there is a total joint abatement of 7%, which is supposed to be enough to pay for a scheme which will give you almost the same benefit as the State would have done.

Over the next 20 years, this abatement will be reduced, probably in 5 year stages, to about 4% in the end. This is because the State scheme will become more expensive, as State pensions get bigger, and it will also become relatively easier for a company scheme to meet the contracting out conditions.

There is nothing to say that a scheme *has* to contract out. It is a question of what is best for any particular scheme. Many companies, including some very big ones, found it suited them better to contract *in* and carry on their scheme on top of the State scheme. For example:

- **GEC**
- **British Tissues**
- **British American Tobacco**
- **Laporte Industries**

Especially during 1977–78, a very 'hard sell' was done by many insurance companies and pension consultants. As a result, a number of schemes contracted out, that would have done better not to. In 1983 there will be a review of *all* the contracting out terms, and many of these schemes may well change their minds then.

Schemes that are contracted **out** have to get a certificate from the Occupational Pensions Board (OPB), which supervises them and ensures that they comply with the conditions. It also has a general responsibility to advise the Government about occupational pensions. This board is appointed by the Secretary of State, and has fourteen members. Five of them, just over 1/3rd, are trade unionists. The rest are from management, or are pensions experts. The chairperson is a retired civil servant.

Conditions for contracting out

- The scheme must guarantee that it will not pay a pension less than the State would have paid if the individual had been in the State scheme. This is called the **guaranteed minimum pension** (GMP for short). The guarantee has to be written into the rules, and must **override** any other rule. If the pension calculated on the scheme's normal formula falls short, the GMP is paid instead.

- There has to be a rule about 'solvency'. If the scheme should go bust (which hardly ever happens) the GMP will have **priority** over other debts. If a scheme *cannot* meet its obligations, the Government will pick up the bill – but only for the GMP.

- Because the State pension is calculated in a different way from most company pensions, the scheme must also meet a requirement called the 'requisite benefit' rule, which lays down the **minimum** amounts by which the pension can build up.

If you compare these minimum requirements with the Inland Revenue **maximum**, page 24, you will see that there is a good deal of room for negotiation between them.

So, a scheme has 2 main sets of conditions to fulfil: the 'requisite benefits' and the GMP. *Remember*, if the 2 give different results, it is the higher one that must be paid.

What are the requisite benefits?

The individual member's pension, often called the 'personal' pension, must build up at a rate of not less than 1/80th of **final earnings**. These can be calculated as

■ average annual earnings of the best 3 years in the last 10 or 13, or

■ average annual earnings in the last 3 years, or

■ earnings in the last year, or

■ earnings for the best year in the last 3 years,

or any other formula the Inland Revenue and the Occupational Pensions Board, who have to approve the rules of contracted out schemes, will agree to.

But this need not mean all earnings:

■ it can mean only **basic** earnings – which for many manual workers is well below what they expect to earn; and

■ a deduction can be made to take account of the State pension. This deduction can be anything up to 1½ times the lower earnings limit.

So pensionable earnings can be very different from your gross earnings.

> Harold Edwards has a gross wage of £100 a week. Of that, overtime and shift allowance are £30, so that is deducted leaving £70. Then 1½ times the LEL is taken off – £34 in 1980–81 – leaving him with **pensionable** earnings of £36.

As a way of simplifying things, the OPB have said that, if a scheme covers all earnings, it can build up at only 1/100th a year.

There is nothing to say that a scheme must make these deductions – they *may* do if they want. Many schemes do – and many of their members think they are earning a better pension than they really are.

There is also nothing, except administrative time, to stop a scheme working out its pension on the basis of revalued average earnings, as the State does. But very few schemes do this, as they claim that it is too difficult to organise, and for the members to understand.

Both the above are items which should be open to negotiation, which is dealt with in more detail in chapter 4.

What about the widow?

If a member dies before retirement, the scheme must provide a pension of ½ the member's requisite benefit or, if higher, half the GMP, which is then called the WGMP.

Schemes are allowed to get away with providing a good pension for the member, but only the minimum for the widow. They can also **use up** part of the lump sum that most schemes give as a death benefit, to buy an annuity for the widow (she has no choice in the matter). Again, it is a matter for negotiation to get a better deal than the minimum.

What happens to the other ½ of the widow's pension? The State takes responsibility for it, and adds it on to the basic pension book. If the scheme is actually giving a better pension than the State would, it makes no difference – the State still adds its ½.

The same principle applies when a member dies in retirement:

■ the scheme must provide only ½ a male member's pension to the **widow**, and

■ the State adds on ½ the GMP, regardless of what the scheme is actually providing, and

■ the State assumes that the private scheme is *not* providing a widower's pension – so if the wife dies first, the State pays all his pension automatically.

The company scheme has *no duty* to pay anything to a person who is an invalid. It may treat him/her as having left service. The *State* has the entire duty to pay benefit in this case.

What about inflation?

When a person has retired, the *company's* duty is to go on paying the pension at the same rate as when s/he retired. It need not make any increases – the State will do that. In practice, the State will add the increases onto the basic pension book, and the company's cheque can stay the same. But the State increases are only on the **GMP**.

Michael Fisher retires in 1990 with a company pension of £700, of which £400 is GMP. Over the next 5 years, the GMP increases, because of inflation, at 10% a year compound. This means the GMP is £644 in 1995. The company is still paying £700 – but the State adds £244 on top of Michael's basic pension to make up the difference.

What if you leave your job?

This is a complicated question, and it involves the Inland Revenue. It is simplest to deal with it here, and look at the Inland Revenue points here as well. But it will be useful to refer back after you have read section 4 of this chapter.

Most of us do leave our jobs sooner or later. Very few people stay 40 years in one job, or even with one firm. What happens to your pension then depends on 3 different sets of rules:

■ the Inland Revenue rules,

■ the Social Security Act 1973; this is Keith Joseph's Act, most of which was repealed, but not this bit, and

■ the Social Security Pensions Act 1975.

The **Inland Revenue** regards pension schemes as a way of reducing your tax bill, as indeed they are, especially for company directors and other highly paid people. If a person leaves his/her company and claims back his/her contributions, therefore, the Inland Revenue claim tax back at 10%.

But this is still quite a favourable rate, so they insist that a member must *really* have left before s/he gets the contributions back. They usually regard a break of at least 1 month as necessary to prove it. They don't find it easy to enforce, though, so schemes very rarely get into trouble if they try to fiddle it. *But* they may well put the individual in jeopardy in the event of dismissal or redundancy because his/her employment would be counted as starting from the day s/he 'rejoined'.

Next comes the Social Security Act 1973. This says that:

■ As from April 1980, if you are over 26 and with more than 5 years' pensionable service when you leave a company, you must have a **preserved** pension, or a transfer to another pension scheme, for the years after 1975.

■ You can still get your contributions back for previous years, but if you were contracted out of the old 'graduated' scheme, you may have a deduction made for that.

This Act applies whether or not you are contracted out. It applies to **any scheme** – including the old 25p a week, £5 per year of service, schemes that some companies still have.

Finally, there is the Social Security Pensions Act. This only affects **contracted out** schemes. It says that:

■ If you have more than 5 years' contracted out membership, whatever your age, your scheme *must* preserve or transfer your GMP, and revalue it to take account of inflation.

■ If you are in a contracted out scheme for *less* than 5 years, then the GMP *may* be preserved, or you can be bought back into the State scheme. This is done by the employer paying what is called a 'contributions equivalent premium' (CEP). He is allowed to deduct up to 4/7ths of the CEP from your contributions before he hands the balance back to you. This is called the 'certified amount'; the figure will change if the abatement changes in the future.

Fred White leaves XYZ Ltd after 1½ years. He gets a cheque for £12.53, which is made up like this:

Gross return of contributions	£36.35
Less 4/7ths of CEP paid to State	£22.43
Balance	£13.92
Less 10% Income Tax deduction on balance	£ 1.39
Final balance	£12.53

Fred is rather upset, because he had counted on having more back from the pension scheme. But it's no good getting upset with the company; this is what the law says.

So, most people who leave a company which has a pension scheme will have much less than they expect as a refund, if they get one at all.

What happens to the preserved pension?

We said above (page 20) that the scheme must preserve your GMP and revalue it. There are several different ways in which they can do this;

■ They can increase it by the same amount as national average earnings increase, each year between the date you leave and the date you reach State pension age. The DHSS will calculate, and publish, an **index** showing what the increase has to be.

■ They can pay a 'limited revaluation premium' to the DHSS, and increase the pension by 5% a year compound. The DHSS then pays you any extra to keep up with the index.

■ They can increase it by 8½% a year compound, regardless of what actually happens to the index. If it is less, then you still get the extra out of the scheme.

Whichever way is chosen, *only* the GMP is covered. The rest of your pension, if you've managed to negotiate a scheme better than the minimum, can stay the same. Or worse, the employer can use it up to pay for the revaluation of the GMP.

Jean Black leaves work at 55 with a *total* pension of £150, of which £100 is GMP, so she believes she has half as much again as the State would have given her, kept for her until she retires. Her GMP increases by 8½% a year. In 5 years, it is £150.36. So that is what she will get; the GMP only, with nothing on top for the extra contributions she put in.

But Jean had been in the pension scheme only since 1978, when contracting out started. If she had been there before that, and had earned pension before the Castle scheme was ever thought of, that could be used up too, to pay for the preservation of the GMP. Only when the 'escalation' of the GMP takes it above the amount that was there for the total pension does the company have to put any new money in.

No one will get less than the GMP. But because many companies have taken advantage of this arrangement, you can pay more contributions and still only get the same pension as you would have had from the State. What does *your* scheme do?

There are two extra complications:

■ Some people will have to have their GMPs preserved, because they have more than 5 years' service, but not the excess, because they are under 26. In this case, the Company can either insist on preserving (or transferring) all your pension, or it can refund your contributions for the excess, and preserve only the GMP.

■ If a GMP is transferred to a new scheme, the new Company *must* increase it in line with inflation, rather than at the fixed rate of $8\frac{1}{2}\%$. This may seem fair enough, but many pension fund managers object strongly to it, as too heavy a commitment, and will therefore not take over a GMP from any other scheme. So transfers are becoming less common, and more often you will be forced to take a preserved pension.

All these rules about leaving your job are very complicated. They might become clearer if you try to work out a few specific problems (answers are at the end of the chapter on page 27).

Mr A is 23 and has been with the company $1\frac{1}{2}$ years. He is in a contracted in company scheme. When he leaves:
   * *can he get any of his contributions back?*
   * *what will be deducted?*

Mr B is 28, and has been with the company 3 years. His scheme is contracted out. When he leaves:
   * *can he get any of his contributions back?*
   * *what will be deducted?*

Ms C, who pays the full rate of National Insurance contributions, not the reduced married woman's rate, intends to leave the company in 1984. She will have been in the scheme, which is contracted out, since it

started in 1978, and will be 24 when she leaves. There are 2 ways in which her pension can be preserved.
  * *What are they?*

Two other points that you need to remember are:

■ While you're still with the company, you *cannot* get your contributions back (unless there is a takeover or a merger, so that there is a technical break in your contract of employment, when it *may* be possible to do so), and

■ You don't get the value of the employer's contributions when you take a refund – and nor does he. They stay in the fund.

If your scheme is non-contributory, you have no contributions to come back anyway. What happens then?

■ If you fulfil the various conditions (aged 26 and 5 years' service, or 5 years' contracted out service whatever your age) your benefits are preserved or transferred.

■ If you don't, the company need not preserve any benefits.

Sex discrimination

One of the selling points made by Barbara Castle about her Pensions Act was that it gave equality in pension schemes between men and women. But in fact it doesn't.

What it did give was **equal access** to pension schemes. It says that

. . . membership of pension schemes, whether contracted out or not, must be open to both men and women on terms which are the same as to the age and length of service required for becoming a member, and as to whether membership is voluntary or compulsory.

A scheme must *not* discriminate except by 'category of employment'. This allows it to get away with a lot. It would be legal to allow foremen into a staff scheme, but not clerical staff. Neither the Sex Discrimination Act nor the Equal Pay Act apply to pension schemes.

Company X admits to its pension scheme people who are on its register of pensionable employees. Anybody earning more than £5000 is automatically on this register. Anyone earning less than £4000 is automatically excluded. People earning between £4000 and £5000 are admitted at management discretion. It so happens that most people earning between £4000 and £5000 are junior management (male) and senior secretaries (female). The men are put on the register, the women are not.

But if a company is making any difference in men's and women's **pay** because of the pension scheme, that would be against the law:

> Lloyds Bank paid men under 25 5% more than women. The 5% was then deducted as their contribution to the pension scheme. Women were also in the scheme, but made no contribution. The Employment Appeal Tribunal decided this *was* discrimination, and the case has now been referred to the European court for a further ruling.

There is also nothing to stop a scheme discriminating in the **benefits** it provides. Most schemes have a lower retirement age for women than for men, because that is what the State does. Only a few schemes give a widower's pension on the same basis as a widow's pension. And some give a *lower* pension for women than for men, or charge women a higher contribution than men. It's all legal. There were proposals under the 1974–79 Labour government to change this, but nothing happened.

Section 4: The Inland Revenue

We've seen the **minimum** level of pension a company is allowed to provide, and still be contracted out. Now we must look at the **maximum**. This section is aiming to give a broad outline of what the rules allow. The finer details will come up in the sections on particular items. To find out **all** the details you need to read a book called *Occupational Pension Schemes* (IR12), published by the Inland Revenue. (See book list, page 260, for details). It's very boring, but essential; get your branch or shop stewards' committee to get a copy, and to go on the mailing list for the amendments that come out every so often. It's normally called the 'Practice Notes' and we will be referring to it quite a lot.

Very few pension schemes, especially for manual workers, actually reach the maximum. If yours does, it will be *expensive*, for you or the company or both. Don't assume that just because your scheme is not as good as the Inland Revenue allows, it's no good.

These are the main things the Inland Revenue will let you have:

■ A **personal pension** of 2/3rds of your final earnings. This is whether your scheme is contracted in or out. It covers all pension schemes of which you have been a member. If you would end up with **more** than 2/3rds, the scheme is not allowed to pay it to you.

■ A widow's, widower's, or dependant's pension of 2/3rds of the member's own pension, had s/he lived until retirement date with no change in earnings. (That is, if a person dies at 45, the 20 **prospective** years (for a man, or 15 for a woman) of service which would have been put in before retirement may be taken into account, as well as the years s/he has actually done.

■ Children's pensions of up to 2/3rds of the member's prospective pension also. But the **total** of any widow's or dependant's pensions must not come to more than the member's own pension would have come to.

■ A **death benefit** (also called 'life assurance') of 4 times the member's final earnings. This will usually be paid at the discretion of the trustees of the scheme, in which case it is tax free.

■ A pension on **early retirement** due to ill health, taking account of all actual *and* prospective service (that is, the years the person could have done if s/he had not been ill).

As you will see, these all add up to a pretty good pension scheme. The details in the Inland Revenue book take up about 90 pages, and are being added to all the time as they think up new rules and change the old ones. There are a few other important points that they lay down:

■ **Contributions**. For a scheme to be 'exempt approved', the employer *must* make some contribution, but there is no rule about how much or how little. The employee is allowed to contribute a maximum of 15% of his/her salary per year. (You may think that no one would want to pay that much anyway, but quite a lot of highly paid people do, because it benefits them as far as tax is concerned).

■ **Commutation**. This means **using up** part of your pension to buy a lump sum when you retire. You are allowed to do this to end up with a maximum lump sum of $1\frac{1}{2}$ times your final year's wages, and this is tax free. Some pension schemes, like the Civil Service scheme, have a lump sum built in, and the $1\frac{1}{2}$ times restriction also applies to them. You would not be allowed to commute any of your pension to take the total above that magic figure. It's **less** if you have been with the company less than 20 years.

■ **Retirement age**. The Inland Revenue will let a scheme have a retirement age of anywhere between 60 and 70 for men, or 55 and 70 for women, without creating problems. If a scheme has a lower retirement age, they will look at it specifically, and may restrict the benefits. But if they feel there are good reasons for earlier retirement (as with airline pilots, for instance) they may not bother.

How does the Inland Revenue ensure that schemes keep to all these rules?

There is a special section called the Superannuation Funds Office (SFO) which does nothing else. They work very closely with the OPB (see page 17), and in fact have a Joint Office in New Malden, Surrey. Any new pension scheme, and any change made in an existing one, must be submitted to this office for approval.

The Old Code and the New Code

The law about pension schemes is very complicated, and needs tidying up every so often. The last time this was done was in the Finance Act 1970. This consolidated all the previous Acts, which were called the Old Code, and made some alterations. It then became the **New Code**.

Any *new* scheme which started after 5 April 1973 had to be approved under the New Code. All existing schemes, if they were amended in any way, had to be reapproved under the New Code. And by 5 April 1980 *all* schemes, even closed ones with just a few members, had to be reapproved. This has meant a lot of detailed work, and is one of the reasons why administrators have been making minor detailed changes in schemes. It's also the reason why some Old Code schemes have been wound up altogether (and it may be one of the excuses that administrators have used for not giving enough information).

Informing the members

The Inland Revenue lays down some basic rules as to what you must be told about the pension scheme. You have a right to 'particulars of all the essential features of the scheme which concern [you]', which means:

- the main benefits,
- arrangements, if any, for increasing pensions once they start being paid,
- the legal constitution of the scheme,
- the level of contributions from the member and how they will be collected (but no figure need be given for the **employer's** contribution),
- details of who administers the scheme (there must always be a particular person or company that is 'the administrator'),

■ and details of who are the trustees of the scheme.

This is in section 22.10 of the Practice Notes. If you have any trouble getting this information, you could try quoting this section.

But what if a scheme is not approved?

It's very much in the members' interest to make sure their scheme is approved. If it is not, then

■ there's no tax relief on your contributions,

■ *and* the employer's contribution is added to your earnings, and taxed as *your* earned income.

> Bob Jones's employer contributes 10% on his behalf to an **unapproved** pension scheme. Bob earns £100. But the employer's £10 (10% of £100) is added to that when Bob's tax is calculated. So he is taxed as if he is earning £110.

So it's pretty important to get your scheme approved. The result of this is that the rules they lay down are **unbreakable**, for all practical purposes, unless you get specific permission. If you want something unusual, and you have a good reason, it's always worth trying to get that permission. But if you want for instance to go over the 2/3rds limit, it's not even worth trying.

Mr A   *Yes, he can get his contributions back. The only deduction will be 10% income tax.*

Mr B   *Yes, he can get his contributions back, but his share of the CEP (contributions equivalent premium) will be deducted as well as the 10% income tax.*

Ms C   The company can either:
a. preserve all her pension, or
b. preserve the GMP, and refund the contributions left over on the rest, again, with the 10% deduction.

3.

Types of pension scheme

Introduction

Before dealing with the many different clauses and variations that you get in pension schemes, it's as well to understand the different **types** of scheme. This chapter explains them in broad terms. The finer details are in chapter 4.

We're also dealing in this chapter with **integrated** pension schemes – which means taking something away from your pension because the State gives you something – but it will have to come up later again as well. We're taking them after **final earnings** schemes, because they are the sort that tend to be 'integrated'. Then we will go on to the other types of scheme.

There are 5 types of pension scheme, which are:
- final earnings (section 1, page 32)
- career average earnings (or salary grade – section 2, page 36)
- revalued average earnings (section 3, page 38)
- money purchase (section 4, page 39)
- flat rate (section 5, page 40)

The vast majority of schemes are of the **final earnings** type – 95% at the last count, according to a survey done by the National Association of Pension Funds (NAPF) in 1979. If your scheme has been negotiated or renegotiated in the last few years, it's almost certainly final earnings, but not definitely. So the first thing is to work out what type your pension scheme is. Find your scheme booklet (which it will be helpful to have beside you while you're reading the rest of this book as well), and in most booklets there will be a list of 'Definitions', probably near the front. If this mentions:

- final pensionable earnings, or
- final pensionable pay, or
- final pensionable salary, or
- retiring pensionable pay/earnings/salary, or
- final remuneration, or
- retiring pay/earnings/salary, or
- final pay/earnings/salary,

or a phrase which means the same, then your scheme is a final earnings scheme. If there is no list of definitions, then look in the rest of the booklet – some of them are very oddly arranged – and see if there is a page which says 'How to calculate your pension', or something similar, and look for the same words there.

So now, turn to page 32 to read about these schemes. There is no need to read about the other types of scheme, unless they particularly interest you.

If, having checked right through, you're sure it's **not** final earnings, then it might be one of the others.

Career average earnings schemes are much rarer. They are also called **salary grade** schemes. Again, look at the definitions in your booklet. Do they say anything about 'pensionable earnings' or 'pensionable pay' or words of that sort, *without* including the term **final** anywhere? If so, it's quite likely career average earnings. If you can't tell from the definitions, *and* to double-check anyway, find the paragraph which says 'How your pension is calculated' or something similar. If it says something like

A unit of pension for each year's contributory service from joining the scheme up to 24 July before the normal retiring date. The units vary according to the salary grade in each year, as shown in the table on page . . .

or

The total pension at normal retirement date is the total of the pensions thus earned by each year's service.

or there is a table like this

Salary/ Wage class/ grade	Annual salary/wages				Yearly pension from normal retirement age for each year of membership	Member's yearly contributions	Life assurance payable on death before retirement age
A	Not exceeding £1100				£12	£31.20	£1000
B	Over £1100 but not over £1300				£16	£41.60	£1200
C	,, £1300 ,, ,, ,, £1500				£20	£52.00	£1400
D	,, £1500 ,, ,, ,, £1800				£24	£62.40	£1600
E	,, £1800 ,, ,, ,, £2100				£30	£78.00	£2000
F	,, £2100 ,, ,, ,, £2400				£36	£93.60	£2200
G	,, £2400 ,, ,, ,, £2800				£44	£114.40	£2600
H	,, £2800 ,, ,, ,, £3200				£52	£135.20	£3000
J	,, £3200 ,, ,, ,, £3600				£60	£156.00	£3400
K	,, £3600 ,, ,, ,, £4000				£68	£176.80	£3800
L	,, £4000				£76	£197.60	£4000

then it is a career average earnings scheme.

But look out for any mention of 'revalued' or 'indexed' anywhere. If you find this, it's probably the next sort of scheme.

As a slight variation, it may say that 'your pension is £1 for every £2.50 of contributions' or something similar. That's also career average earnings. But take care, because a lot of final earnings schemes also have a guarantee about the pension you get back from your contributions. Make sure you haven't missed a *final* anywhere.

If you've decided it definitely is career average earnings, turn to page 36 and read that. But when you've finished it, you should look at pages 32 and 38 as well (final earnings and revalued average earnings schemes) because they give you a much better pension and you ought to try to change your scheme to one of these.

What if you have come across the words 'revalued' or 'indexed' in your booklet, among the definitions? Then you may be in a **revalued average earnings** scheme. But they're very rare, so don't jump to the conclusion you're in one. Look for a phrase like 'revalued earnings' or 'revaluation factor' and some mention of the Retail Prices Index.

Or there may be some statement like

> The pension is based on your earnings for your whole working life uprated to take account of inflation.

Or it may be expressed in terms of contributions, like this one:

> Your yearly pension on retirement at your normal retiring date will be £1 pa for each £2 that you contributed to the scheme, increased to take account of changes in the Index of Retail Prices up to your normal retiring date.

(This of course is very similar to one of the examples given above under the last type of scheme. The key words are in the last clause.)

If you're convinced it's one of these, turn to page 38.

No luck so far? Then maybe you're in a **money purchase** scheme. These have been making a bit of a comeback recently, and are being sold by a number of insurance companies. Does your booklet say something like

> The amount of tax free cash benefit on retirement at age 65 if male or 60 if female will depend on the age that contributions commenced, the number of contributions paid, and the bonuses declared by the XYZ Insurance Company. The leaflet at the end of this booklet gives examples of the cash benefit on retirement assuming full contributions are paid throughout membership and that the XYZ current bonus rates are maintained at their present level.

or

> For each member of the plan his contribution and the company's contribution on his behalf will be paid into an individual account with the ABC Life Assurance Society. The society will invest these monies so as to obtain interest and capital growth. The earnings will then be credited back to individual accounts by way of interest and bonuses and will be entirely tax free.

Then it's money purchase and you need page 39. But read pages 32 and 38 as well, to give you ideas about a better scheme.

Not that either? The final possibility, then, is a **flat rate** scheme. This ought to be fairly easy to spot, because it will say, for instance:

> Benefit is £20 pension per year of service . . .

or

> Pension is 10p per week for each year you have been with the company.

A few schemes put it in a more complicated way – for instance, the London Brick Company says:

> The maximum benefit payable by this scheme is £3000 and can be attained after 27 full calendar years continuous service with the company at the rate of 3/80ths for each full calendar year of service, that is £112.50 per full calendar year.

If you're in any doubt, look for a *money* figure per year of service, without 'estimated' or a similar word in front of it. Turn to page 40 for an explanation of these schemes – and also read pages 32 and 39 for details of a better sort of scheme.

Two further points:

■ Any of these types of scheme can give you a pension, a pension plus a lump sum, or a lump sum alone. Only a final earnings or a revalued average earnings scheme can be **contracted out**.

■ If your scheme appears to be career average, money purchase or flat rate – before you rush into denouncing it, check that you have the *up to date booklet*. It may sound very obvious, but personnel departments have been known to hand out old booklets, and the slips of paper that amend them have been known to get lost! So make sure you're acting on the right information.

The different types of scheme are outlined in detail below.

Section 1: Final earnings

This is really simple, but it is often made complicated by the way it is set out. There are 3 things to take into account:

■ your **final earnings** – what you are earning when you reach retirement age, or when you die or retire early,

■ your **pensionable service** – how long you've been in the pension scheme, and

■ the **accrual rate** – the rate at which the pension builds up.

The accrual rate will be a fraction, or a percentage, of your final earnings. It might be 1/80th, or 1/60th, or 1/45th, or some other figure. For each year you are in the scheme, you collect one of these fractions. So after 5 years you might have 5/80ths, or 5/60ths, or 5/45ths. Then you *divide* this into the final earnings, and there's your pension.

Jo Evans has final pensionable earnings of £3000. Her scheme's accrual rate is 1/60th. So for each year she is in the scheme, she accrues £3000 ÷ 60 = £50
As she has been in the scheme 10 years, she gets 10 times that (that is, 10/60ths), which is £500.

Sometimes you have both a fraction and a percentage in the same booklet. The most common accrual rates are:

- 1/45th   = 2.2 per cent
- 1/50th   = 2.0 per cent
- 1/56th   = 1.8 per cent
- 1/60th   = 1.67 per cent
- 1/70th   = 1.43 per cent
- 1/80th   = 1.25 per cent
- 1/90th   = 1.1 per cent
- 1/100th = 1.0 per cent

One important point to note is that, because it's **final** earnings, you can't know how much your pension is going to be when you retire. Before then, you can only estimate it, based on your **current** earnings and what you think is going to happen to inflation.

Integration

This means that a certain amount is deducted 'to take account of the State pension' before your company pension is calculated. It can be done in several ways:

■ Your scheme can deduct something from your earnings before it uses them to calculate your pension. It will usually be a figure related to the lower earnings limit (see page 11), or to the State pension for a single person, which is more or less the same. It might be

* 1½ times the lower earnings limit, or
* the same as the lower earnings limit, or
* ¾ of it, or
* a fixed money figure, perhaps based on what the pension was a few years ago.

How does it work?

Harold Smith has final earnings of £6000. But his pension scheme is **integrated**, so that an amount equal to the lower earnings limit is deducted from them, before his **pensionable** earnings are calculated. The LEL is £1196.
£6000 minus £1196 = £4804
He has been in the scheme 10 years, and it is a 1/60th scheme. So he gets 10/60ths of 4804 = £800 pension.

■ Or your scheme can build the integration into your pension, so that for each year you are in the company scheme a fraction of the State pension is deducted. It's usually worked out so that when you have worked for the maximum number of years in the scheme, the whole of the State pension is deducted.

This then means you have to do a *second* sum – having worked out the company pension for each year, you then have to deduct the appropriate slice of the State pension, before you get the final result. For example:

> Jack Smith's scheme gives 1/60th pension, minus 1/40th of the lower earnings limit, for every year he is in the scheme. His final pensionable earnings are £6000, and the LEL is £1196 a year. So his pension for each year of service is:
> £6000 ÷ 60 = £100) minus (£1196 ÷ 40 = £29.90) which comes to £100 minus £29.90 = £70.10 for each year of service, or £701 after ten years of service.

Large numbers of **contracted out** schemes are integrated, including a lot, on the hourly paid side, which only just meet the minimum requirements.

Contracted in schemes

These are also often integrated, although there are some of them that just ignore the existence of the State scheme altogether (mainly senior management schemes). Some only integrate with the basic pension, but others take the **additional** pension into account as well. There are many variations on this, but there are 3 main ways:

■ **Loose integration:** you make a rough estimate of what the State additional pension will be, and deduct that when you calculate each person's pension. So for instance, the Revlon scheme booklet says:

> The intention is to provide a total retirement income (plan + State) of 70% of final pay for a member who has completed 40 years' service. This is achieved by the formula below. A member who completes less than 40 years' service will receive a smaller benefit. Your pension from the plan will be:
> 1.75% of final pay for each year of pensionable service, less 2.5% of the final basic component for each year of pensionable service, less the final additional component.

and when you turn to the list of definitions, you find that the final additional component means

> 1.25% of the excess of final pay over the final basic component for each year of pensionable service subject to a maximum of 20 years to count.

Why is this complicated procedure only a rough calculation? Because it's based on final earnings, not average revalued earnings, as the State scheme pension is. Turn to pages 12–13 if you can't remember how the State scheme pension is worked out.

■ **Tight integration,** which some companies have adopted, means that they keep their own records, and revalue the average earnings of their employees themselves. C & J Clark, for instance, do the same calculation as the State, and then deduct that amount from the pension before they pay it.

■ A third method of integration for contracted in schemes is even more complicated. This is integration by the **accrual rate**.

Armstrong Cork bases its calculations on the fact that the State scheme builds up to a maximum of 20/80ths. So for anybody with more than 20 years to go to retirement, the effective accrual rate is not 1/80th, but a smaller fraction. For anyone with 40 years to go, it is 1/160th. So Armstrong Cork has a different accrual rate for each 'age of entry' group. It's also different for men and women, because of women's earlier retirement.

Men		Women	
Age at 6 April 1978	Pension rate %	Age at 6 April 1978	Pension rate %
25 & under	1.045	25 & under	0.956
26	1.029	26	0.935
27	1.012	27	0.912
28	0.994	28	0.889
29	0.976	29	0.864
30	0.956	30	0.837
31	0.935	31	0.808
32	0.912	32	0.777
33	0.889	33	0.744
34	0.864	34	0.708
35	0.837	35	0.670
36	0.808	36	0.628
37	0.777	37	0.583
38	0.744	38	0.534
39	0.708	39	0.480
40	0.670	40 & older	0.420
41	0.628		
42	0.583		
43	0.534		
44	0.480		
45 & older	0.420		

Integration is going to crop up again in chapter 4, 'Negotiating improvements', particularly on pages 95–100, where we deal with the reasons for it, and the problems it can cause.

Section 2: Career average earnings

The basis of a career average scheme is that all your earnings, throughout your working life, are added together and then averaged to work out your pension. This isn't quite as stupid as it sounds; it was a method of calculation developed in the days before inflation really took off, when earnings in money terms could go down as well as up. There are 4 ways in which it can be worked out:

■ The first takes 3 things into account:

* your average earnings: the total amount you've earned with the company from the year you start to the date you retire divided by the number of years you've been there;

* your pensionable service: the number of years you've worked for the company;

* the accrual rate: the rate at which your pension builds up.

The accrual rate will be a fraction, or a percentage, of your average earnings. It might be 1/80th, or 1/60th, or some other rate. For every year you're in the scheme, you collect one of these fractions, so after 5 years you have 5/80ths, or 5/60ths, or whatever. Then you divide this into the average earnings, and that's your pension.

> Ghulam Mayet retires at the end of 1979. He has had earnings over the last 5 years of:
> 1975 £2000
> 1976 £2400
> 1977 £3000
> 1978 £3400
> 1979 £4000
> Added together, these make £14,800. So his average earnings are that figure divided by 5 = £2960.
> Now you divide that again by 60 (the **accrual rate** in his scheme) = £49.30, and multiply by 5, which comes to £247.

■ The second method is in fact almost the same mathematically, but it looks different. This is to say that the pension is, for instance, 1% of total earnings, or 1/80th of lifetime earnings. If you look at the sum above, you'll see that we have divided by 5, and then multiplied by 5 later on. This method shortcuts that – you simply add up all the earnings and then divide by the accrual rate, and there's your pension;

In Ghulam Mayet's case £14,800 ÷ 80 = £247

■ The third method is really a variation on the other 2, but expressed in terms of a proportion of the contributions paid in, rather than a proportion of earnings. The booklet will say something like 'you receive £1 pension for every £2.50 paid in contributions'. You need then to find the contribution rate, and you can work backwards from that.

James Curran's contribution rate is 5% of earnings. 5% of his total earnings of £14,800 is £740. For each £2.50, he is given £1 pension, so £740 ÷ £2.50 = **£296**, and that's his pension.

The final variation is the **salary grade** system. In this, the scheme members are divided into grades or 'classes' each covering a specific range of earnings. An example of the sort of table that's drawn up can be seen on page 30.

In each year, a member is credited with a 'brick' or unit of pension that depends on his/her current earnings, and is fitted into bands according to the company's salary structure. The final pension depends on how many 'bricks' you have accumulated, and how much they are worth.

John Wadham joins his company at a salary of £1200, and gradually gets promoted through the salary grades, as in the example on page 30. His pension will build up like this:

For, say, 2 years in class B = £32 (£16 × 2)
          3 ,,   ,,   ,,   C = £60 (£20 × 3)
          5 ,,   ,,   ,,   D = £120 (£24 × 5)
          4 ,,   ,,   ,,   E = £120 (£30 × 4)
          6 ,,   ,,   ,,   F = £216 (£36 × 6)
         10 ,,   ,,   ,,   G = £440 (£44 × 10)
         10 ,,   ,,   ,,   H = £520 (£52 × 10)
                              ────
          Total pension   £1508 p.a.
                              ────

What all these versions have in common, of course, is that they do not give a good pension, because they take no account of inflation. With high interest rates around, they tend to be cheap for the employer to run (which is why he will have carried on with the scheme). If you are stuck with this sort of scheme, then before looking for any other improvements, you need to get it changed to a final earnings or a revalued average earnings scheme. And you should try to ensure:

■ that the changeover is backdated as far as possible, and paid for by the **employer**. It's his fault that it hasn't been changed before for something more suited to modern conditions; and

■ that, over the first few years after the changeover, a check is kept on people retiring, to see that no individual is worse off because of the change. The only people likely to be are those with short service, whose earnings have fallen in money terms in the few years before they retire. If there is anyone affected (and with current rates of inflation there will be very few) they should get a pension calculated on the old rather than the new method.

Section 3: Revalued average earnings

If you've read chapter 3, you'll know that this is the method by which the State calculates the additional pension. It's possible for a private scheme to calculate in almost the same way, though without a computer it's very laborious. The only difference is that the Inland Revenue will only allow you to calculate in line with the increase in *prices*, not earnings. How does it work?

■ First, your earnings are listed for all the years that you've been in the scheme;

■ next, each year's figure is increased by the amount prices have increased since the earnings were paid:

■ then, the earnings figures are averaged, and

■ *then* the pension is calculated from them, on the basis of the accrual rate (the fraction of earnings by which you build up pension year by year), and the number of years you've been in the scheme.

On page 36 we used the example of Ghulam Mayet, whose earnings were averaged over 5 years. We'll use the same example here, with his earnings being averaged **after** being revalued:

In 1975 he earned £2000. Since then, prices have gone up 85%. So that figure is now increased to £3700.
In 1976 he earned £2400. Since then prices have gone up 60%. So that figure is increased to £3840.

In 1977 he earned £3000. Since then prices have gone up 40%. So that figure is increased to £4200.
In 1978 he earned £3400. Since then prices have gone up 20%. So that figure is increased to £4080.
In 1979 he earned £4000, but this is the year he retires, so this figure is not increased.
Then all these increased figures are averaged. Adding them together gives you £19,820, which divided by 5 gives you a pensionable earning figure of £3964. He then gets 1/60th of that for every year he's been in the scheme – as he's been in it five years, he gets £3964 ÷ 60 × 5 = £330 pension.

You'll notice that in real terms – in the amount that the money will buy – Ghulam's earnings actually went **down** in the last couple of years before retirement. This is quite common for manual workers, especially in heavy industry, where for example they can't keep up the piecework rates, or they go off shifts. This particular type of pension scheme can therefore have considerable advantages for them, which is why the State uses it. The **disadvantages** are:

■ it's difficult for an ordinary person to work out, and

■ it's difficult for the company to work out, unless they have access to a computer, and

■ for people on incremental scales (e.g. staff workers) who expect to get their best earnings in *real* terms shortly before they retire it doesn't give as good a pension as a final earnings scheme would.

Section 4: Money purchase

The idea of 'money purchase' is to relate the pension you get in the end *directly* to:

■ the contributions you pay,

■ the contributions your employer pays, and

■ the interest they earn.

The pension you get does not relate at all to your earnings – simply to the amount that has been put in, and how well it has been invested. Schemes like this are usually run by insurance companies, who in selling them to the members make optimistic statements about the amount of interest that will be earned. The same method is used if somebody who is self employed, or who has no pension scheme in his/her company, takes out an individual policy.

The younger you are, the more pension your contributions will earn, because they have longer to build up interest.

Four people join the same company at the same time, and the employer promises to buy pensions from the MNO Insurance Company. He will put in £100 a year for each of them.

Martin Smith is 25. £100 a year for him until retirement date gives a pension of £3100.

Bob Ede is 35. £100 a year for him gives a pension of £1720.

Jim Winter is 45. £100 a year for him gives a pension of £830.

Mario da Costa is 55. £100 a year for him gives only £300.

You might expect the pension for the person with 20 years' service ahead of him to be $\frac{1}{2}$ that of the person with 40 years – but in fact it is only just over $\frac{1}{4}$. This is one of the major disadvantages of this scheme – it gives a poor deal to the older person.

Others are that:

■ It throws the risk of inflation, and of a bad return on investments, onto the individual. In a final earnings, or revalued average, scheme, at least some of the risk is thrown onto the employer, because he usually agrees to meet 'the balance of the cost'. This is right, because this is the business he's in – he's far better equipped to cope with it than the individual pensioner is after s/he's retired. In a money purchase scheme, the employer's liability is **fixed** – the risk of having to live with a bad pension is thrown onto the member.

■ You cannot calculate what pension you will finally get, even by estimating it based on your current earnings. It depends in most cases on the bonuses declared by the insurance company.

■ It makes it difficult for anyone to retire early. The penalties for taking your pension before they are expecting you to are heavy.

That said, if an employer is prepared to put a reasonable amount of money into it, a money purchase scheme with a respectable insurance company is better than nothing. Some employers are very neurotic about having an 'open ended' commitment, and will not concede a final earnings scheme. A scheme like this, provided the amounts going in are large enough, can be a fallback proposal.

It's also perhaps worthwhile with very small employers, or ones where the future is not secure, if you can't get anything better.

Section 5: Flat rate

Unlike the other types of scheme we've dealt with, these are extremely simple – that's the problem.

A flat rate scheme booklet will say something like 'For every year you are in the service of the company, you will get £x pension.'

> John Laing Ltd's scheme booklet says:
> **Your pension**: at normal pension date, your 65th birthday, (60th for women), you will be entitled to receive your plan pension. The pension you will receive will be £18 for each year of pensionable service you complete, with a proportionate amount for part of a year.
> **Example**: if a member were to retire at normal pension date after completing 30 years and 4 months pensionable service, he would receive a pension of $30\frac{1}{3} \times £18 = £546$ a year.

Sometimes these schemes are also set up in such a way that management has discretion about whether to pay the pension or not.

The disadvantages of this sort of scheme are:
- it will usually give a very low pension,
- it does nothing to protect even that pension against inflation, and
- it takes no account of your actual earnings.

There are only a few schemes like this still actively operating. But many companies have flat rate schemes still lurking in the past – and even those who now have a good pension scheme may well have a very small deferred pension from this sort of scheme. You cannot get it out before retirement date (unless you leave, and often not even then), because of the Inland Revenue rules. But you might be able to get it increased, to take some account of inflation. Chapter 4 goes into detail on this (section 8.2, page 109).

Section 6: Lump sums

Any of these types of scheme can provide
- a pension only, or
- a pension and a lump sum, or
- a lump sum only.

If your employer won't provide a full pension scheme, or if you're trapped in a bad scheme and can't get rid of it, it might be more use to you if the money is paid as a single **cash sum**, when you retire. Getting a very small pension merely reduces the amount of supplementary benefit you can get.

The Inland Revenue allows you to take a cash sum on retirement of not more than $1\frac{1}{2}$ times your final year's earnings, provided you've done 20 years' service or more. There's a scaled down rate for those with fewer years. This is then **tax free**. There are a number of schemes of this sort.

> The BSR cash benefit scheme gives you 3/80ths of your final earnings for each year of your service, to a maximum of 40 years. So this is a final earnings scheme.
>
> London Brick gives a lump sum of £3000 if you have been with them 27 years or more. For each year below that, it builds up at £112.50 a year. So this is a flat rate scheme.

This sort of scheme has the advantages of
■ simplicity;
■ people like to have a lump sum in their hands when they leave; and
■ it can be useful where there are a lot of part timers, who could not earn enough to be able to get a pension worth having.

But in any scheme you can get the lump sum arrangement – either by reducing the pension or automatically (see chapter 4, section 9, page 113), so the attractiveness is not that great. The **disadvantage** of a lump sum scheme is that, because of the Inland Revenue limits, you are not allowed to have a very good scheme based on this principle. So for a better overall package, you are going to *have* to take some of the benefit as pension.

4.

Negotiating improvements

Introduction

This chapter is designed to help you look at your pension scheme and decide what changes you want, and then to give an idea of how to set about getting them. You should look at chapter 3 first, to find out what sort of scheme you're in, because some of these points don't apply to some types of scheme.

The chapter is divided into a series of sections, each covering one area of the pension scheme, so that you can use it easily. *But* remember that you're supposed to be dealing with a **package**. It's not much good getting a really good personal pension, if the person who doesn't live to retirement leaves a miserable pension to his/her dependants.

Chapter 6 gives you some idea about how a claim is built up, and the sort of thing you need to think about when you are setting your priorities.

First of all, though, we're giving a list of the basic words used in scheme booklets, and what they mean. This won't cover all the different bits of jargon that you will find, but we hope it will deal with the main ones. It's arranged in the order that most booklets are organised in (but not all), and the numbers refer to the sections later in this chapter

1. Eligibility. This means **who can join** the pension scheme. It covers how old you have to be, how long you have to have been with the company, which grades or groups of employees are allowed in, and whether the scheme is compulsory, voluntary or at the discretion of the employer.

2. Normal retirement age (NRA), or **normal retirement date** (NRD). This means the age the scheme assumes the members are going to retire at. It need not be the same as the State retirement age, though it often is.

3. Pensionable earnings (or **salary**). This means the amount of your earnings that counts in calculating your pension. Sometimes it will be all your earnings, sometimes only parts. For instance, shift premiums might not count. Sometimes it will be your earnings minus an amount that equals the State basic pension, or more. Other names for this are:

■ benefit earnings (or salary), or
■ scheme earnings (or salary).

If your scheme is a **flat rate** scheme (see chapter 3, section 5, page 40), it won't have a definition of pensionable earnings in the booklet, because it won't need one. Nor will *some* money purchase schemes.

4. Final pensionable earnings (or **salary**). This means the amount of earnings that are used to calculate the pension when you come to retire, or when you die. It is often an **average** of pensionable earnings figures over a number of years, but it can be just 1 year. Only a **final earnings** scheme (see chapter 3, section 1, page 32), will have this.

5. Pensionable service. This means the length of employment that is counted towards your pension. It may be all the complete years you've been paying into the scheme, or it may be the years and months. There might be some time before you were contributing which counts as pensionable service. This section will also tell you the maximum number of years you can build up in the scheme. This word 'service' is not one trade unionists like, but as it is almost universally used in pension schemes we're sticking to it.

6. Contributions. This will tell you **how much** you have to pay to the scheme, and whether it is a fixed amount each week, or varies when your earnings vary. Sometimes the booklet will also tell you how much the employer is paying.

7. Accrual rate. This means the rate at which your pension **builds up** for each year you are in the scheme. It might be expressed as a fraction, such as 1/60th, or as a percentage, e.g. 1.66%. In a **final** earnings scheme you are building up, say, 1/60th of your final pensionable earnings for each year of pensionable service.

In an **average earnings** scheme you are building up 1/60th, or some other fraction, of your average pensionable earnings, averaged over your *whole* working life, each year in the scheme. It might be a **career** average scheme, which means your actual money earnings are averaged, or it might be a **revalued** average scheme (like the State scheme), where your earnings are uprated to take account of inflation.

Either a final earnings or an average earnings scheme may also be **integrated** to take account of the money available from the State. This is explained under 'Integration' in chapter 3, page 33, and section 7 of this chapter goes into the pros and cons of it.

8. Past service entitlement. This means any extra benefit you are entitled to because you were in an old scheme, or because you were given credits for years before the scheme started, or because your scheme was merged in a takeover and you carried over some entitlement.

9. Commutation. This means turning your pension into a **lump sum** when you retire.

10. Early retirement. This means retiring at **any age** below the scheme's normal retirement age (see item 2 above). It can be because of **ill health** (also called **incapacity** or **disability**) or because of **redundancy** (also called 'in the interests of company efficiency' – see also chapter 9, section 3, page 255, or it may be **voluntary** (or 'at the member's own request').

11. Late retirement means retiring at any age after the normal retirement date.

12. Death benefit. This can mean either all the benefits payable on death, or it can mean only the **lump sum**, which can also be called **Life assurance**.

13. Widow's/Widower's (or **Spouse's**) **Pension**. This means what it says. Occasionally it is called an **annuity**. There are two sorts of pension: where the member **dies in service**, i.e. when s/he is still working for the Company, and in the case of

14. Death after retirement, and the rules tend to be different for each.

15. Escalation. This means the amount by which the pension is **increased** each year once it starts. Some schemes will have a fixed percentage written into the rules. Others will say that the pension will be 'reviewed'.

16. Leaving service. This will explain your rights and the choices you have to make when you leave the company, other than on early retirement.

17. Temporary absence. This means what happens when you are off sick, or away having a baby, or on an extended holiday (or even 'doing work of national importance'), so far as your pension is concerned. It should explain whether you have to continue your contributions, or can pay them when you come back to work, and what happens to the benefits if you die while you're away.

18. Alteration, amendment and **termination**. This will say what your rights are if the scheme is wound up or changed; and probably also say that the company reserves the right to wind it up or change it.

19. Miscellaneous clauses. Most booklets also have a section near the end of extra points. They may include

■ Life assurance continuation. This means that the insurance company will give you favourable terms if you leave the company before the age of 60, and want to take out life assurance privately.

■ Assignment. This will be a warning that you must not 'assign', i.e. give away your legal rights to, your benefits.

■ Evidence of health. This will explain when and if you need a medical examination before coming into the scheme.

20. Additional voluntary contributions (AVCs). These are extra payments you can make to build up your pension faster. Not all schemes have a provision for this.

Trustees. These are the people who are actually **in charge** of the fund, and supervise the benefits that have to be paid. Sometimes the booklet will actually name them, but other times there will just be a general statement about them. Getting members appointed as trustees is very important to the unions, so we have put this in a separate chapter (chapter 7, section 1, page 202) along with the question of negotiating rights in general.

If your scheme booklet doesn't have all these sections (or if you have trouble getting hold of a booklet at all), don't be too surprised, but put 'proper communication' down on your list of negotiating items. Far too many companies are secretive about their pension schemes. Remember – it's *your* deferred pay.

In the following sections, we cover:

■ what you must have, for instance under any rules about contracting out;

■ the maximum you can have (the Inland Revenue rules);

■ what schemes tend to provide, and what improvements you can reasonably expect to get; and

■ what arguments to use in negotiating, and what sorts of objections the employer may raise.

In some sections we have also given an idea of the costs – *but*

A warning on the costs: we felt it would be helpful to give some idea on these, but *don't* use it as any more than a very rough rule of thumb. There's an explanation of how pension schemes are funded, and how the costs are calculated, in chapter **8**. If you read this, you'll understand why the costs in different schemes can vary so much. So the figures given in this chapter are *only guidelines*.

All the cost figures are given in terms of **percentage of payroll**, because that is how the employer will usually express them. If you want to know how much any particular item might cost *your* employer, you need to know the payroll cost for the last year, and then you can convert the percentage figures into cash. Sometimes the employer will let you see the figures the experts he employs have worked out, but not often; you should always try to get them.

Note: we've quoted in a number of places the NAPF 1979 **Survey**. This is an annual survey done by the National Association of Pension Funds, which is an organisation to which a large number of pension schemes (or rather, the managers of pension schemes) belong. Each year for the last 5 years, the NAPF have issued a questionnaire to their members, and then published the answers. The 1979 survey, published in 1980, covered 1190 schemes, 6 million people. As there is no compulsion on anyone to complete the questionnaire, it is probably the better, or at least the more aware, scheme managers who do so. But for all practical purposes the sample can be regarded as representative.

Section 1: Eligibility

The legal requirements

We have already looked at the **equal access** rules, on page 23. These only deal with giving the same access for men and women. Other than this, a company may limit its pension scheme to any 'category of employee' it wants, or

- it can provide a special scheme for one person, or
- management can select particular people.

There are some restrictions on company directors and partners, but they need not concern us.

If you are to be made to join a pension scheme, you have a legal right to know, under the Employment Protection (Consolidation) Act section 1, the following (the numbering is that of the original):

1. (1) Not later than 13 weeks after the beginning of an employee's period of employment with an employer, the employer shall give to the employee a written statement in accordance with the following provisions of this section.

(2) An employer shall in a statement under this section

(a) identify the parties;

(b) specify the date when the employment began;

(c) state whether any employment with a previous employer counts as part of the employee's continuous period of employment and, if so, specify the date when the continuous period of employment began.

(3) A statement under this section shall contain the following particulars of the term of employment as at a specified date not more than 1 week before the statement is given, that is to say . . .

(d) any terms and conditions relating to . . .

(iii) pensions and pension schemes.

In ordinary language, this means that if membership of the pension scheme is **compulsory** it *must* be stated in the 'particulars' of your job. Usually this will be done briefly and refer to the scheme booklet or the rules. (You have a **legal** right to a statement of particulars, although many employers don't give one).

If the scheme is voluntary, there is no legal right for it to be mentioned, though it usually would be.

The maximum you can have

Since there are no restrictions, the scheme *may* also admit the widest possible group of employees. It can let in everyone, from the age of 16 and the day they join the company, until they reach the scheme's normal retirement date (NRD). A scheme is not allowed, however, to admit a new member who is over NRD.

Negotiations

There are enormous variations between schemes, as to who they let in, at what age, and how long they have been with the company. To try to keep things simple, we've subdivided the rest of this section into;

1.1. Category of employee

1.2. Earnings qualifications

1.3. Upper age limit

1.4. Entry ages

1.5. Length of service

1.6. Anniversary dates

1.7. Part timers

1.8. Compulsory or voluntary membership

For each item, we've looked at what schemes tend to provide, and what improvements you can achieve; and then at the arguments you can use, and what the employer will say. At the end of the section, there's a note on the main principles behind your arguments on a particular item.

1.1. Category of employee

Typical arrangements and possible improvements

Some pension schemes are open to both staff and manual workers; according to the NAPF survey, 43% of all schemes. (According to the same survey, 47% of schemes provide extra benefits for 'senior executives'). Many others, though, restrict membership to, for instance;

- staff but not manual workers;
- monthly paid staff only;
- monthly paid staff, senior foremen, hourly paid staff who have been with the company a certain length of time;
- staff, and those manual workers who have been granted 'staff status' at the company's discretion.

Or there may be 2 or more schemes in the company, covering different groups, with the members, and the company, paying different amounts; the manual workers' scheme will usually be the lower standard.

In general, we should be looking for **harmonisation**, so that everybody in the company is covered by either the same pension scheme, or identical ones. This need not mean only one **fund** – there can be good reasons for retaining two separate funds:

- because you may want different definitions of pensionable pay (see page 63):
- because some people have frozen benefits under old schemes, which are administratively easier to deal with in this way;
- because the company is making payments for the works members' past service pension, which it is helpful to keep separate from the staff scheme.

There may well be some additional costs, over and above those of having more people in the pension scheme, if a staff scheme is opened up to manual workers. When the actuary works it out, s/he may decide that the company will have to pay *more* per manual worker into the scheme than it does for the staff. This could be because:

■ there is a larger proportion of women among manual workers than staff. As women retire earlier and live longer, it is more expensive to provide for them:

■ the manual workers are, on average, older than the staff. It is more expensive to provide a pension for an older person, because there is less time ahead for the contributions to build up interest.

There are other factors, though, which partly balance this by *reducing* the cost per manual worker. They tend to have a shorter life expectancy. That is, they have more accidents, and more chance of contracting chronic illnesses, before they retire, and after they retire they die sooner.

If it appears that it is going to cost a lot more to have manual workers in the scheme, try to find out why. It may be that the employer is adding in other costs that should really be separate, or that the scheme hasn't been adequately financed in the past and he's taking the opportunity to put it right.

In one way, there is almost bound to be an extra cost in the first **few** years, though. When a scheme starts, or is opened up to a new group of people, the people who volunteer will usually be the older ones. But if the scheme then becomes a condition of employment for new entrants, this problem does not last long.

One problem with harmonisation, or with achieving the right to enter the staff scheme where there has been no scheme before, is the level of **members'** contributions, which will almost invariably go up.

> At Massey Ferguson, the agreement to phased harmonisation means that the works employees' contribution will go up from $4\frac{1}{2}\%$ to the staff rate of $5\frac{1}{2}\%$.

It's worth working out exactly what it will cost, taking tax relief into account, for a few typical people, so that this can be discussed with the membership before you put in the claim.

> Thus, an increased contribution of 1%, for a person earning £120 a week, would mean an extra £1.20 a week out of the pay packet. But if you take into account that you *don't* pay 30% income tax on this, the real cost is reduced by just about 1/3rd to 80p extra a week.

It will be important to be able to make a definite statement when the employer asks, 'Are you sure your members want this?'

A manual union making a claim for harmonisation with the staff would be sensible to discuss it with the staff unions, and get their agreement. There may be difficulties if the staff feel that the manual unions are eroding their differentials. The manual unions might be able to point to other areas – use of the canteen, or holiday entitlements – where differentials have gone without damaging the staff. At least, there should be agreement between the unions that the staff will not actively oppose the works claim.

The best you may be able to get from the company is a commitment to 'move towards' harmonisation between staff and works conditions, with or without a definite date being put on it. If so, you will need to make sure the commitment isn't lost sight of in future negotiations.

Possible arguments and responses

The issues on admission to the pension scheme, or harmonisation of existing schemes, are the same as the arguments for staff status in other areas, like sick pay or holidays.

A quick summary of these arguments is that:

- everyone is important to the company. It can't get along without its manual workers, any more than it can without its managers;
- differentials in terms and conditions are outdated, and against trade union policy. The differentials should be in terms of **money**, not anything else;
- the perpetuation of a 'them and us' atmosphere is bad for the company and bad for industrial relations.

The employer's response will essentially be about cost, because he will often be putting a lot more into the staff scheme than into the works one. He may also say that

- better pensions are a 'traditional' fringe benefit for staff which he does not wish to disturb: if there have been discussions between staff and manual unions on this, and harmonisation is a **joint** policy, this argument will be much weaker;
- that he does not think manual workers value pension schemes as staff do. You can point out that, if this were true, you wouldn't have raised the issue at all.

1.2. Earnings qualifications

Typical arrangements and possible improvements

Some schemes only allow in people with earnings at or above a certain level.

Unicorn Industries Ltd have a 'higher benefit' scheme, into which they allow only those with weekly earnings of 3 times the lower earnings limit or more. In 1980–81 this meant £69 a week.
Initial Services Ltd similarly let in people with weekly earnings of 3 times the LEL or more.

In the second case, the company justify it by saying that since the scheme is **integrated** (see pages 33 and 95–100), it would not be worth the while of the lower paid to join. Unicorn do not have this justification, and produce no particular reason; they have twice reduced the qualification level, which started off at 7 times LEL, and with luck it will soon disappear altogether.

Any limitation of this sort should be opposed on principle. The *most* the company should be allowed to do is to make the scheme voluntary rather than compulsory for people earning below a certain amount.

Possible arguments and responses

The essential argument here is that, whether intentionally or not, these provisions tend to discriminate against women, since they are usually the lower paid. (As pension schemes are not covered by the Sex Discrimination Act, there is no *legal* case here, but there is a strong moral one).

They put as much into the company as anyone else – so why should they be excluded from the benefits? It is likely to be bad for industrial relations on other matters, if the groups who are kept out feel resentful of the fact, as they have every right to. You might also suggest that it puts the pension scheme in a bad light if it looks like a tax fiddle for the higher paid.

The employer may say

■ that the scheme is not worth it for the lower paid – in which case he should redesign the scheme, to make it worthwhile for everyone, or

■ that he cannot afford to bring everyone in – in which case you will need to start arguing about how much he can afford to give everyone a fair deal. (See page 77 for some of the arguments you can use on the question of costs.)

The unions' argument, that the only differential should be on wages, not conditions, applies here as it does in questions of staff/works differentials.

1.3. Upper age limit

Typical arrangements and possible improvements

Pension schemes very often exclude anyone with 5 years or less to go to retirement, i.e. over 60 for men, over 55 for women. A contracted out scheme is specifically allowed to exclude them, even though they will be in the same 'category of employment' as everyone else. The reason for this is simply cost. The older you are, the more expensive it is to provide either pension or life assurance.

There is no reason why the employer should be allowed to get away with this. We should work on the principle that if someone is fit for work, s/he is fit for the pension scheme.

At the least, older entrants ought to have life assurance coverage. And if you're negotiating a new scheme, or one to take the place of an existing one, it is important that *existing* employees of all ages are allowed in, even if there is to be an exclusion for older new entrants.

Possible arguments and responses

The arguments you can use are:

■ If the employer is claiming to provide a benefit for all his workers, he should not be able to exclude a few people just because it is inconvenient for him, i.e. expensive, because an older person costs more to ensure and provide a pension for than a younger one.

■ The worker is going to need the life assurance most at this stage, and find it most difficult to get elsewhere.

■ More and more in the future, a person who changes jobs at a late stage will have earned a pension in a previous job, which will either be preserved, or transferred with him/her, *if* the new scheme would accept that person. If s/he is excluded from a scheme for the final few years, the pension will be even less inflation-proofed than would otherwise be the case.

■ Very few people close to retirement age are ever taken on in new jobs, so the total cost will be very small, even if the cost for any one person is quite high. If the employer has taken someone on who is close to retirement, it's for a good reason, like a particular skill. So the employer ought not to exploit him/her.

1.4. Entry ages

Typical arrangements and possible improvements

Pension schemes are **allowed** to let in anyone from the age of 16, but there are very few that do.

Reads Ltd, and Imperial Tobacco, are a couple of examples, but the most common entry age is probably 21, and schemes have ages ranging from 18 to 25.

Ideally, 16 should be the entry age, but since there tends to be a very high turnover of young people in jobs, and most of them are not at all interested in pensions anyway, age 20 may be more realistic. But you should seek life assurance coverage for anyone who's too young to join the full scheme, with the employer paying for it. This is now quite a common provision – Hoechst Ltd is just one example. Alternatively, you could ask for voluntary entry to the full scheme below the compulsory age level, so that at least those who are interested in their pension can join.

The younger the entry age, the more important it is for the leaving service provisions (see page 156) to be properly worked out.

Possible arguments and responses

Specific arguments for reducing the entry age are:

■ Young people may well have dependants: if not a spouse and children, then possibly a parent who would have to pay off the HP on the motorbike or the stereo if anything happened to their son or daughter.

■ One needs to be in a scheme from an early age to get full benefit from it, because so few people do stay 40 years with one company, and because a **woman**, in particular, needs to be in the scheme from the age of 20 to be able to get a 2/3rds pension.

Arguments the employer may use are:

■ The young aren't interested, and won't thank you for putting them into the scheme, if it means they have to pay contributions (this would not apply if the scheme is non-contributory). No one's very interested in pensions when young – as in the old Pearl Assurance advert, you have to be middle aged before you really start worrying.

■ They will leave quickly and there will be an administrative problem of sorting out a lot of small pensions, and these may not give value for money when they finally come to collect them, because of inflation.

■ The scheme has a maximum number of years for which you are allowed to build up pension, and if you work for the company for longer than the maximum, you don't get any further pension. *But* there's often no need to have a maximum (see section 5.2, page 74), so you should then argue on this point.

If you have to fall back on asking simply for life assurance for those too young to join, the only argument the employer can really use is administrative problems. Cost hardly applies, because the cost of insuring the life of someone under 20 is tiny.

If the employer says that a large proportion of young people leave very quickly, you should first of all ask for evidence of this, from research in personnel department records. It may be a myth that is not borne out by the facts. If it *is* borne out, then, outside the pension scheme negotiations, you ought to be looking at the reasons for this. Are they being given all the worst jobs, and little training?

The employer may say, on this and other issues, that the insurers are restricting him. Insurance companies are often seen as distant organisations with rigid rules you can't argue with. This *isn't* the case. If they want the business enough, they will send a representative to a meeting, and they can be asked to give as full an explanation as you want of the various restrictions they impose. If *they* don't want the business, you can probably find an insurance company that does. (But beware of the hard sell.)

Many insurance companies do 'package deals' designed for different types of workforce. Standard Life, for instance, have a series of 'Stanplans'. You may agree with management that it's worth taking one of them, with all the restrictions imposed, because asking for variations would put up the cost too much, and/or create administrative problems. But whether to take one or not should be a matter for negotiation, not a 'take it or leave it' attitude.

1.5. Length of service

Typical arrangements and possible improvements

How long should you have to work for a company, before they bring you in to the pension scheme? There are any number of variations, for instance:

APV Ltd makes staff and *skilled* hourly paid join on the day they join the company, but semi skilled or unskilled hourly paid 'will be required to join on 1 May or 1 November immediately following the

> date on which you first become eligible and have completed 3 months' service with the Company.'
> Tarmac Roadstone ask for 2 years' continuous service before you can join their works scheme.

Any scheme should provide life assurance from the day you join the company. If there really is a problem of a lot of people staying for a very short time, or perhaps of seasonal workers, then a waiting period for the **pension** is acceptable, but it shouldn't be longer than one year. And there certainly *shouldn't* be different waiting periods for different groups of employees.

Possible arguments and responses

There's a straightforward financial argument you can use here, in opposition to that of the employer. If, by letting people in to the scheme sooner, he cuts down the turnover of employees, it will pay for itself. Suggest that he works out the cost of recruiting and training a new person, and therefore what he will save if he can cut staff turnover down by a few percentage points.

You can also point out that it is especially unfair to people who have had a pension scheme in previous employment, to force them to have a gap in their entitlement. As pension schemes become more common, this will increasingly be the case.

As we suggested in section 1.2, if the employer insists there is a serious problem of people leaving very shortly after they come to the company, it ought to be looked at separately.

1.6. Anniversary dates

Typical arrangements and possible improvements

Many schemes, particularly smaller ones, let new people in on only one date in a year, usually the same date on which new rules come into force, contribution rates change, etc. This is called the 'anniversary date' and will often be 6 April, to coincide with the beginning of the tax year, but it can be any other date.

This will be the date at which premiums to the insurance company are fixed, which is why new entrants will be allowed in then. There can be a genuine problem of administrative cost for the smaller scheme, which makes this necessary, but again, life assurance coverage should be immediate. This may well mean negotiating a change in the policy held with the insurance company, but in general they won't object to the extra business.

If possible, you should ask for entry dates at least twice a year, and you shouldn't accept both a long waiting period *and* a rigid entry date.

Possible arguments and responses

The argument here is that the employer is penny pinching. He is saving a fairly small amount by inconveniencing a few people quite a lot. These 'small print' clauses can also devalue the scheme in ordinary members' eyes. If someone joins the company shortly after the anniversary date, and then finds that, instead of waiting 1 year to join the pension scheme, s/he must wait nearly 2 years, s/he won't think much of it. So the money the employer is putting into the scheme to prove how enlightened he is will be wasted.

1.7. Part timers

Typical arrangements and possible improvements

Many schemes let in only 'permanent full time staff'. What this actually means varies a good deal from company to company, or even within one company, at different plants. Getting a clear definition of what it means will often be a useful first step in discussions.

Other schemes will say that they:

■ let in those who work over x hours per week, or

■ let in those who work, say, between 16 and 25 hours a week on a voluntary basis, but impose an absolute cutoff below that, or

■ let in people however short the hours they work, and adjust the benefits on a pro rata basis.

Izal Group make it a condition of employment when you reach the age of 21, and after 6 months' service, and are working more than 25 hours a week. Part time employees fulfilling these conditions and working more than 16 hours and less than 25 may join if they wish. Temporary employees, or those working less than 16 hours a week cannot join. Ofrex Group make it a condition of employment for everyone working over 16 hours with 2 years' service; and anyone working over 8 hours, with 5 years' service, *may* join.

In theory, all part timers should be allowed into pension schemes, or at the very least those to whom the Employment Protection (Consolidation) Act applies, that is, people who work 16 hours a week or more, or 8 hours a week after continuous employment of 5 years or more. But particularly with an integrated scheme, the benefit that they get can be very small. A reasonable compromise is to say that:

■ anyone who the company defines as part time should be covered for life assurance, however low their earnings;

■ those working over 16 hours a week should be brought into a non-integrated scheme on the same basis as anyone else;

■ for an integrated scheme, a deduction should be made pro rata.

If the company will not agree to this, then at least try to ensure that those working over 16 hours have the chance to join if they wish. You'll also need to look at those whose hours fluctuate around the defined limit, for instance because the company frequently asks them to do overtime. Sorting out a definition may lead you into a lot of *other* discussions with the company (for instance, are this group being exploited by being given part time conditions but being asked to do more than part time work?). On the pension side, the most practical approach is probably to look at the *average* number of hours done over the year, and take that as the definition.

Possible arguments and responses

What you'll have to counter here is the assumption by many employers that part timers are working only for 'pin money' and are not concerned with fringe benefits like pensions. If this was ever so, it certainly is not true for many people today. The majority of part timers are women (40% of employed women work part time, as opposed to 2% of employed men), and they may be

■ married with children;

■ looking after an elderly or disabled relative; or they may be

■ single parents; or

■ wanting financial independence from their husbands.

None of these factors means that they will take the job less seriously. They will simply be *unable* to work full time. But their income will nonetheless be vital to keep up the family's standard of living, and the family will suffer considerably if that income is lost. The Diamond Commission found in 1978 that it was the extra income provided by the **wife** that kept many two parent families off the poverty line.

Employers take on part timers, and perhaps arrange special 'twilight shifts' because it is convenient for them to do so. Partly this is because it means they can use machinery more intensively, but it is

also because they feel part timers can be used as a 'reserve army' of cheap labour, who can be given fewer fringe benefits, are less likely to make a fuss about working conditions, and can be laid off if orders drop, with less trouble from the unions than if they were full timers.

Sadly, in the past this has tended to be true. The unions have tended to treat part timers as marginal. But this is much less so now, and the pension scheme is one area where the change should come. By paying lower overheads on one group of workers, the employer is under-cutting the rest of the workforce, and he should not be allowed to do this.

1.8. Compulsory or voluntary membership

Typical arrangements and possible improvements

The law is that, when a scheme starts, whether it is completely new or replacing an existing one, you cannot normally be compelled to join the scheme if you are already working for the company. However, your legal protection is weak, because if the employer simply starts deducting contributions, and you do not protest very quickly, you will soon be **deemed** to have accepted the change in your terms and conditions.

A reasonable employer, though, ought to accept that no one already in the job should be made to join the scheme. But what about new workers, who come after the scheme comes into force? Should they be made to join?

A lot depends on how good or bad the scheme is, and what you think the chances of improving it later are. On balance, it's probably better that a scheme that gives value for money *should* be a condition of employment. This is because

■ it reduces the average cost for everyone, as younger employees are much cheaper to provide a pension for than older ones;

■ it is 'being cruel to be kind'. The young worker would probably prefer to have the money in his/her wage packet at first, but later on s/he will regret not having joined. So will his/her family, if anything should happen to that person.

If after discussion you and the employer agree that it should be voluntary, however,

■ a person should be allowed to join at any point while s/he is working for the company, not just when s/he starts, and

■ you need to be confident that local management, or whoever deals with new workers when they start, explains the scheme properly, and

■ if the shop stewards consider the scheme is worth joining, **they** should also be telling the new worker about it, and making sure s/he returns the application form.

Possible arguments and responses

An employer who offers a voluntary pension scheme may genuinely believe in giving people freedom of choice to decide whether to join or not. **Or** he may be hoping that women and manual workers will not bother to join, so that the scheme will really only benefit a small number of 'career grade' staff.

He may say that

■ he doesn't want to compel someone who feels that s/he can't afford it, or who isn't interested, to join;

■ if a person doesn't feel s/he is going to stay with the company, it will be in his/her interests, as well as the company's, if they don't join the scheme.

Arguments for making the scheme compulsory all depend on the scheme being a good one.

■ The individual may wish to spend his/her money, rather than put it into a pension scheme, but what about the dependants for whom it is partially provided? Should s/he have the 'freedom' to reject financial protection for them?

■ The point at which a person has the most financial commitments, like a mortgage, children at school, heavy HP, is the time when a pension scheme is *most* necessary, in case anything happens to that person. It is in his/her own interest to be forced into the pension scheme, however annoying it may be at the time.

■ Non-joiners will be undercutting their fellow workers, if they reject the money the company is prepared to put into the pension scheme on their behalf. (In fact a voluntary scheme gives an incentive to the company to undersell the scheme to save money.)

■ The scheme is cheaper *per person* when it is compulsory. If it is voluntary, it is naturally the older person who tends to join, and this pushes up the average cost.

1.9. Conclusions

The essential issue underlying all the items in this eligibility section is that **you** will be trying to bring the widest possible group of people into the scheme, while the employer is trying to keep down the numbers allowed in.

■ Your argument should be that, if the employer believes the scheme is a good one, and worth paying for, then it is worthwhile for everyone, not just a select group.

■ The employer's objection, whether he actually admits it or not, is usually going to be the cost. The scheme may be cheaper *per head* if it takes in a larger group, but there will be a larger bill.

Each person allowed into the scheme is paying perhaps 5% of his/her earnings to the pension fund. On top of this the employer is paying perhaps 10%. So if the scheme at the moment has 50 people earning £100 a week in it, the employer is paying 10% of 50×100, which is £500. If another 10 people, earning the same amount, join, the cost might drop to $9\frac{1}{2}\%$ of each person's earnings. So the employer will then be paying $9\frac{1}{2}\%$ of 60×100 which is £570.

Whatever the employer is paying, it will come out of the profits of the business, which are created by the **whole** workforce, so a particular group is being subsidised by the rest, if the scheme only allows in a narrow group of people.

Section 2: Normal retirement age

What a scheme must have

Any pension scheme **must** have a fixed 'normal retirement age', though this may be different for different categories of people. If a scheme is contracted out, then whatever the *scheme's* retirement age, it must be able to guarantee that at the State retirement age of 65 for men, 60 for women, it will not pay less than the GMP.

What the Inland Revenue allows

The Inland Revenue will let a scheme have a retirement age of anywhere between 60 and 70 for men, 55 and 70 for women, without creating any problems. If a scheme has a lower retirement age, they will look at it specifically and *may* restrict the benefits.

Typical arrangements and possible improvements

Most manual workers' schemes have a retirement age of 65 for men, 60 for women, like the State. The NAPF 1979 survey (table 27) showed this:

Retirement age	Males				Females			
	Staff schemes	Works schemes	Com-bined schemes	All schemes	Staff schemes	Works schemes	Com-bined schemes	All schemes
	%	%	%	%	%	%	%	%
Over 65	—	1	1	1	—	1	—	—
65	82	96	86	86	5	3	10	7
Under 65 but over 60	8	1	3	5	1	—	—	1
60	10	2	10	9	93	96	88	91
Under 60	—	1	—	—	1	1	1	1
Total	100	101	100	101	100	101	99	100

The goal of most of the unions is a retirement age of 60 for men, but don't be surprised if you don't achieve it for a while yet. Very few manual schemes have reached the goal. Some that have, or have got part of the way, are:

> British Airways: 63 for general staff, (55 for pilots and cabin crews)
> Imperial Group: 60
> ICI: 62
> S & W Berisford: 62

Lowering the retirement age is an expensive prospect, although just how much it would cost in any particular company depends on the proportion of men to women on the payroll.

> Massey Ferguson calculated in 1979 that it would cost £1.29m annually, 3% of payroll, to bring this in.

If you can't achieve a reduced retirement age for everyone, it may be possible to go towards it, at least for the longest serving people, in other ways. These are dealt with in the section on voluntary early retirement, 10.2, on page 123.

Even if you think it unlikely that you will achieve a reduced retirement age, you may wish to include it in your claim each time, to show it is not forgotten.

Possible arguments and responses

It is union and TUC policy that men's retirement age for the

State pension should be brought down to 60. But this is unlikely to happen in the near future, not least because of the cost, which would be several billion pounds a year. (Although there is the argument that an earlier retirement age would reduce unemployment, it is doubtful how many jobs would actually be filled by younger people, and how many the employer would just get rid of.)

If retirement age is changed it will probably cause a major upheaval, and would need to be phased over a number of years. So if we want a male retirement age of 60, we cannot sit back and wait for it to come from the State – we must set out to achieve it in our company pension schemes.

Other arguments you can use are:

■ What's good enough for the bosses is good enough for you. The management with whom you're negotiating are quite likely to have a male retirement age of 60 in *their* 'top hat' pension scheme (that is, a scheme restricted to directors and very senior management). It would certainly be helpful to find out.

■ There might be advantages in productivity you can point to, especially if the job is heavy. Retiring people at 60 may push down costs in other areas.

What the employer will say:

■ Truthfully, it *is* expensive. If you get an age 60 retirement in one go, you'll probably have to agree to freeze any other major improvement to the scheme in that negotiating round.

■ 'Why should I be more progressive than the State?'

The justification employers use for a pension scheme is to fill the gaps left by the State, and this is one such gap – just like the death benefit, where State provision is so poor.

■ 'We'll wait until the State makes us do it.'

Why? A progressive employer doesn't wait until he's forced by legislation to do something. If he knows it's advantageous, he'll do it anyway.

Section 3: Pensionable earnings

What a scheme must have

A **contracted in** scheme can define pensionable earnings in almost any way. A scheme could, for instance, not take account of earnings over £4000 a year.

If it is **contracted out**, then the restrictions are tighter. A scheme **can** limit pensionable earnings to basic pay only. It *may* also make a deduction 'to take account of the State pension', but this may not be more than $1\frac{1}{2}$ times the lower earnings limit. The Occupational Pensions Board must be satisfied that the formula relates to *real* earnings, and will not be so restrictive that the GMP overriding formula (see page 17) has to be used often. It is one of the items they study closely before issuing the contracting out certificate.

What the Inland Revenue allows

For someone paying tax under PAYE, the Inland Revenue permits *all* earnings, which they call 'remuneration' to be taken into account, although they may say that the 'fluctuating' elements have to be averaged over 3 years. This will apply particularly to people such as sales representatives, who are paid partly on commission. 'Remuneration' can sometimes include, for tax purposes, an amount added on by the Inland Revenue to take account of the fact that you have a company car, or a private health insurance scheme, for instance (see *Non-Wage Benefits* by Michael Cunningham, Pluto 1981) and this can therefore be included also when the pension is calculated. Where, in the final year before retirement or death, your earnings are artificially low, because of sickness for instance, they will allow a 'notional' figure to be used – that is, a calculation of what you would have earned if things had been normal.

There is nothing to stop a scheme using a different earnings formula for the pension and the life assurance, provided that neither benefit goes over the limits.

Typical arrangements and possible improvements

What parts of your pay packet are used to calculate your pension? Earnings, for most manual workers and some white collar workers, are made up of a number of different items:
- Basic wage
- Bonus
- Overtime
- Shiftwork premium

and so on. Some people don't have a basic wage at all, but are paid entirely on piecework. And some items, like bonus and overtime, may be regular and/or contractual, or they may be very irregular. You might get the opportunity to do overtime only in the few months before Christmas, for instance. And there may be some items of pay that older people generally don't get – shift premium, for instance, if the shifts are tough going and people coming up to retirement generally go on to daywork.

The problem, therefore, is to find a formula for **pensionable** earnings that relates sensibly to **actual** earnings. How do pension schemes solve this?

Frequently, they don't. They tend to be designed by senior white collar workers, who take traditional white collar pay patterns, where basic pay makes up all or most of the pay packet, as the standard. Formulas that are common include:

■ annual rate of basic pay,

■ annual rate of basic pay, plus bonus and shift premium, but not overtime,

■ basic pay for the last year, plus 'fluctuating emoluments' averaged over the last 3 years,

■ PAYE earnings for the last tax year.

Some schemes have gone into very complicated formulas:

Rank Xerox define salary as 'Basic annual salary (plus, if applicable, on-target commission), except for hourly paid industrial staff for whom salary means
(i) if in grade 9, annual wages at 95-plus performance level, or
(ii) if in a grade below 9, annual wages at 85-plus performance level.

Others use the same calculator as for holiday pay, or gross up earnings averaged over a number of weeks.

Hawker Siddeley, until contracting out in 1978, had this formula:
Contributory earnings are calculated during March every year, based on the average earnings over the 6 months preceding each 1 March. The following details will be ascertained:
(a) Total PAYE earnings for the 26 PAYE weeks before 1 March, overtime premiums and sick pay being deducted.
(d) This total is multiplied by the employee's standard working week and divided by the total number of hours worked in the period, including overtime hours. Holidays are included at standard hours.

These complications are usually unnecessary. It is generally better simply to base the pension and death benefit on PAYE earnings, unless these tend to vary considerably during the working year and during the working life.

Where they do vary, you should seek that the **steady** elements are taken into account, such as

■ **regular** shift work premiums,

■ **contractual** overtime and

■ **guaranteed** bonus.

If there is a change in the earnings formula, it will probably also affect contributions. You're unlikely to get away with basing the pension on PAYE and contributions on basic pay. It would be helpful to work out, for a few typical people, what the difference would be. For instance:

> William Davidson has PAYE earnings of £120 a week, but his basic pay is only £90. His pension contribution is 5%, and his scheme's accrual rate (see section 7, page 88, and also page 32) is 1/60th. So calculating on **basic** pay his contribution would be £4.50 a week and his pension after 40 years would be £60 a week (assuming no inflation). Calculating on PAYE, his contribution would be £6, an extra £1.50, and his pension would be £80 a week, an extra £20.

Don't be afraid of going for different definitions for different groups of people. Even if you want to move towards a single scheme for staff and works, it may still be more suitable for the staff to have basic pay and the works PAYE. It's quite straightforward for a booklet to include several definitions.

You also need a formula to provide a 'notional' rate where somebody has been off sick for some time. If there is a grade rate that relates fairly well to what people actually get, or an average for the work group, you could use that.

If you find an earnings formula that is out of the ordinary, the Inland Revenue will need convincing that it is fair.

Note: Integration. **Many schemes also deduct something from the 'pensionable earnings' figure to take account of the State pension. This is called Integration, and there are several ways in which this can be done. See page 33 for a preliminary explanation. For convenience, we're dealing in detail with all the different types of integration at once, in section 7.3, page 95. Refer to that section if you feel you need to know more about integration at this stage.**

In any scheme, there will be a point at which your 'pensionable earnings' are fixed for the purpose of deciding what your pension is, or your death benefit. It can be the date at which you retire or die, but often it is the end of the tax year, and is based on your P60. This has the advantage that you will know exactly what you will get, but it has the bigger **disadvantage** (certainly at this time of high inflation) that the figure gets steadily out of date over the next 12 months. So if for instance the earnings figure is fixed in April, anyone with a birthday in March has lost 11 months' worth of inflation.

It is best to have a certain flexibility, and for the scheme to relate the pensionable earnings figure as closely as possible to the last 12 months' earnings. If it is necessary to have a single fixed figure for the whole year (as it may be for the smaller insured scheme) then try to get it fixed shortly *after* the annual pay settlement, to make sure it includes that. Even when you have achieved this, you may be able to get an alternative formula of 'actual earnings over the last 12 months if higher' included for calculating the death benefit.

Possible arguments and responses

Having decided before going into negotiations what formula is most realistic for you, your argument would simply be that you want a scheme that is *genuinely* related to what you earn, and that anything else is misleading. If you have worked out your examples, you can show him those.

The employer's argument, once again, will be cost. If you increase the amount of money which is counted as pensionable, you increase *his* contribution, as well as your own. Make him pin himself down to a figure on this. On page 77 we've looked at some of the arguments you can use to persuade him.

Other arguments may be:

■ Administrative problems. It may be said that the computer could not cope with a change. But computer programmes can always be rewritten. All it takes is money and time.

■ It may be difficult to convince the people who actually administer the pension scheme that there really is a problem, because they have nothing to do with the wage bargaining progress and do not understand the pay systems in operation in the company. After you have gone into it with them, the pensions manager may well be willing to sit down round a table and work something out.

Multi plant companies can have a problem, where the wage payment system is different in different plants. In that case, although you should still try, you may find it impossible to reach a formula that works equally well in each plant, so you may need to leave it to local agreement within some broad guidelines. It would be wise to agree to review the position regularly in this case, to ensure that local management is administering the scheme properly.

On fixing the earnings figure, the argument is that you want a scheme that is *genuinely* related to your normal earnings. Often, when you raise the question of the way inflation tends to distort these schemes, the pension experts will say, 'But we don't expect inflation to go on for ever, and pensions are supposed to be long term.'

They have been using this argument for the last 10 years, since inflation started to be a serious postwar problem. It is *not* a real argument, because a rule change that gives flexibility to cope with inflation does not do any harm when (if) inflation ceases. It simply becomes irrelevant.

Cost, as usual, may be the real reason. The more expensive a change is said to be, the more inadequate the scheme must be at the moment, and therefore the greater the *justification* for an improvement.

Section 4: Final pensionable earnings

What you must have

Only in a **final earnings** scheme will you have a definition of 'final pensionable earnings'. Most **contracted out** schemes are of this type, but not all. To get a contracting out certificate, a final earnings scheme must use one of the following definitions:

■ average annual earnings of the best 3 consecutive years in the last 10 or 13 years of service.

■ average annual earnings of the last 3 years;

■ earnings in the last year;

■ earnings in the best year of the last 3 years.

'Earnings' here means 'pensionable earnings/salary' as defined by one of the descriptions mentioned in section 3 above (pages 63–68).

What the Inland Revenue permits

Whether you're contracted **in** or **out**, the Inland Revenue say (in **Occupational Pension Schemes**, IR12, para 6.12):

Scheme rules may provide for 'final remuneration' [which is what they call final pensionable earnings] to be calculated on any basis which falls within the following:
(a) remuneration for any one of the 5 years preceding the normal retirement date. For this purpose, 'remuneration' means basic pay, e.g. wage or salary, for the year in question, plus the average over a suitable period (usually 3 or more years) ending on the last day of the basic pay year, of any fluctuating emoluments such as commission or bonus . . .

(b) the average of the total emoluments for any period of 3 or more **consecutive** years ending not earlier than 10 years before the normal retirement date.

This means that, if your 'pensionable earnings' are calculated on basic pay, or on basic plus other elements that you can convince the Inland Revenue do not fluctuate very much, you may use *just* the last year's earnings to calculate the pension.

In fact, they will also allow you to use the full PAYE earnings, if they agree with you that they don't fluctuate enough to matter. (There's a lot of discretion allowed, but it depends on the particular inspector.) However, they *may* insist that you either use the PAYE earnings averaged over several years, or that the 'fluctuating emoluments' (which would normally mean things like bonus and overtime) must be averaged, while the basic wage could be calculated for the most recent year.

The reason they worry about this is that tax people have suspicious minds, and believe that 64 year olds are going to work large amounts of overtime in their last year and increase their pension. Presumably averaging over 3 years, they feel that anyone who can keep it up for that long deserves a better pension.

What about the effects of inflation? These *can* be coped with, under another special clause from the Inland Revenue. Practice Note 6.14 (same place as above) says:

> Whenever 'final remuneration' is that of a year other than the 12 months ending with normal retirement date, or is an average of 3 or more years' remuneration, each year's remuneration *may* be increased in proportion to the increase in the cost of living for the period from the end of the year, up to normal retirement date. 'Final remuneration', so increased, is known as 'dynamised final remuneration'.

This means that, before calculating the final pensionable earnings, you may increase each year's earnings to take account of the increase in prices. The Inland Revenue have said that this rule has only been used to any great extent by company directors and senior management.

Typical arrangements and possible improvements

This is yet another area full of pitfalls for the unwary, where the only sensible advice is 'Watch the small print.' In times of inflation, the precise method of calculation can make a world of difference.

The simplest pension scheme will take just the last year's earnings, and base the pension on them:

> George Elliot has earnings of £6000 in his last year before he retires. He has built up a full 2/3rds pension, so his calculation is £6000 × ⅔ = £4000.

But most schemes are not that simple. More commonly, a scheme will take

■ the annual average of the last 3 years' earnings, or

■ the annual average of the best 3 consecutive years in the last 10 (or 13) years.

The second one usually comes out the same as the first, with current inflation, unless someone has had a very bad final year's earnings. What effect do these formulas have?

> George's earnings for his last 3 years' work were
> 1978 £4000
> 1979 £5000
> 1980 £6000
> These 3 figures averaged together give a final earnings figure of £5000. 2/3rds of that is £3333.

Some schemes have their own variations on this:

> S & W Berisford has a male retirement age of 62, and 'final pensionable salary' is defined as 'pensionable salary determined at 31 March immediately preceding your 60th birthday, if male, or your 58th birthday, if female'.

So if George were in that scheme, his final pensionable salary would be his earnings two years back, in 1978, which were £4000. So his pension would be £2666.

What difference would it make if George's earnings were 'dynamised' in the way the Inland Revenue allows, in Practice Note 6.14?

> Assume that in the 3 years before George retired, inflation was running at 10% per year. So his earnings are 'dynamised' by making them into:
> £4000 + 20% = £4800
> £5000 + 10% = £5500
> £6000 + nil = £6000
> So his 'average' then becomes £5433, and his 2/3rds pension is £3622, a big increase.

Very few schemes go in for this, although many allow in their rules for it to be done, at the administrator's discretion. According to the NAPF survey quoted earlier, 36% go for average earnings over the best 3 consecutive years ending in the last 10, while the next most common formula, with 19% of schemes, was the average earnings over the last 12 months. If you can't achieve dynamisation, then you could try for the 'last 12 months' formula to be added as an alternative to the current one, and this could make a considerable difference.

> The Dorchester Hotel booklet, for instance, says:
> 'Your final pensionable salary will be the greater of
> (a) your last pensionable salary prior to normal retirement date, or
> (b) the average of your 3 highest consecutive pensionable salaries during the last 10 years before retirement.'

Allowing the better of the two alternatives can be surprisingly expensive, for what looks like a small change – one company calculated that it would cost an extra 1% of payroll each year – but that shows how much you may be losing with the present formula.

Again, it is important to make sure that the person whose earnings **do** fall in the last year because of illness, is protected, by putting in a clause which allows a 'notional' earnings figure to be calculated in these cases. That is, a figure for what the person would have earned in that year had s/he not been ill.

> Pedigree Petfoods allows, as one of several formulas:
> '. . . your actual annual pay in the year up to your retirement. If you have been absent because of sickness within the year, the resulting loss in your scheduled pay will be ignored.'

Some schemes say that where someone's earnings drop in the last year before retirement, s/he may if they wish continue to pay contributions on their previous earnings. This makes the employee pay for the improvement in the scheme, so is not to be encouraged.

Possible arguments and responses

Once you have worked out what you are going for, it will be useful to work out examples to show what difference it would make. You could ask a particular individual coming up to retirement to let you use him or her as an example, or you could use workplace average earnings to illustrate the point you are making. You might also find a recently retired person, to show how much better his/her pension could be.

But the point you will need to hammer away at is that it **isn't** a final earnings scheme, when you were told it was – that the workforce is being misled.

The employer may say:

■ that inflation will soon go down anyway (see page 68 above for the answer to that); or

■ that it will be too complicated to work out (especially on 'dynamised final earnings') – it isn't, because it's relying on figures which have to be collected anyway: it's simply a matter of adding a new detail to the computer programme, or giving a new instruction to the wages clerk; or

■ (the real reason), that it will cost too much – ask the employer to get the figures, and to give them to you; only then can you decide whether you want to give this priority in your 'shopping list'. The more expensive this improvement turns out to be, the more you are losing at the moment.

Section 5: Pensionable service

What you must have

If you are contracted out, and your accrual rate is 1/80th per year or less, the scheme will not get a contracting out certificate unless it has a service maximum of at least 40 years. But a *better* scheme could stop building up pensionable service after a shorter time.

A contracted in scheme can do what it likes, provided it does not go above the Inland Revenue limits.

What the Inland Revenue allows

The Inland Revenue are interested in the *total* pension you get out at the end – the 2/3rds of final earnings. So if you have a scheme that genuinely gives 1/60th of final earnings, you must have a limit of 40 years on the service which can be counted towards that pension, so that if you do 41 or 42 years you won't earn any *more* pension. If you have a higher accrual rate approved by the Inland Revenue, you must have a shorter maximum period of pensionable service, as you might otherwise go above the 2/3rds limit.

The Inland Revenue will let you count in years, months, and even odd days of service, and in some circumstances you can credit in years you have not actually done – *so long as* it would not take you over the 2/3rds limit.

How pensionable service is calculated

The rest of this section is subdivided into:
5.1. incomplete years;
5.2. maximum service; and
5.3. credited years.

The question of **broken service** is dealt with under section 17 on 'Temporary absence', page 165.

5.1. Incomplete years

Typical arrangements and possible improvements

Many schemes give you pension only for the number of complete years in the scheme. This means, of course, that unless you have the foresight to arrange to have your 65th birthday on the scheme's anniversary date, you could be paying in contributions for anything up to 51 weeks for no benefit.

The London Brick scheme refers to 'each full calendar year of continuous service'.

Other schemes, though, allow you to count the years, months, and weeks of service.

The Weir Group staff scheme says:
'Years of pensionable service: for members joining on or after 15 December 1974, each continuous year of membership of the scheme counts for pension. Whole months count as fractions of a year, on a pro rata basis.'
The Renolds Group scheme says:
'In calculating your pension, account is taken of any additional weeks of total pensionable service over and above completed years.'

It is much more convenient for the scheme administrator to cope with reckoning only complete years, and in a small scheme it may be that the insurance company insist on it, as it is more convenient for them. You will be able to change this, or change the insurance company, but there will be an extra cost in doing so. You should aim at least for complete **months** to be added in, even if you accept that extra weeks might be excessively difficult to cope with.

If the scheme does *not* give you full credit for all service right up to retirement, then to balance it you should not have to pay contributions right up to that date.

The Portals Group staff scheme, for instance, says:
'Your contributions will cease on 1 April preceding your normal pension age.'

Possible arguments and responses

The basis of your argument must be the **injustice** that is being done to the person who retires at the wrong time of year. Try to find an example of a specific person whom it will affect badly – someone whose birthday is in March, for instance, if the date s/he was allowed into the scheme was in April.

The employer's argument will be 'administrative problems'. The concession will cost something, but not much, because for each individual the extra pension cannot be more than 1 year's extra pension entitlement. He may say that the insurance company won't let the contract be changed, or that they are insisting on an extra administrative charge which is too high. You'll need to get the insurer to tell you exactly what that extra cost is *and why*, so that you can decide whether it really is worthwhile or not.

5.2. Maximum service

Typical arrangements and possible improvements

Some schemes have a 40 year maximum service rule.

The Ephraim Philips scheme booklet says:
'Your pension on retirement at normal pension age will be equal to 1/80th of your final pensionable pay, multiplied by the number of years of your pensionable service, with a maximum of 40 years (men) or 35 years (women).

Some deliberately provide for a higher accrual rate and a *shorter* service maximum.

The Rank Xerox scheme has a maximum of 33 years, with a 1/50th per year accrual rate.
S & W Berisford has 1/45th accrual, and a 30 year maximum.

Sometimes these limits will be because of the Inland Revenue limitation. More usually, it will be because the scheme has been designed with a particular level of pension in mind as the 'correct' one. It's important to realise that in the majority of schemes, since they do *not* come up to the Inland Revenue limits, the limits are a matter of choice by those setting up the scheme, not of necessity.

These are limitations which affect only a few people – there aren't many of us who can stand working for the same company for 40 years or more. Where there is no Inland Revenue limit, no other limitation should be imposed.

The William Thyne scheme has a **1/47th** accrual rate, on earnings minus $1\frac{1}{2}$ times State pension, and no maximum service.

Possible arguments and responses

Here you can turn to your advantage the argument that employers always use to justify treating so called 'early leavers' unfairly. They will tell you that 'the pension scheme is intended for those who stay, and are loyal to the company, not for those who leave'. Why then should people be penalised for being *too* loyal to the company?

The employer may say:

■ He sees this level of pension as 'correct'. This is illogical, though: many people will get *below* this level because they haven't been with the company long enough. If it is OK for their level of pension not to be correct, why not those who have worked longer than the 'correct' length of time? You could also suggest that if the employer is so concerned about people obtaining too much pension because they've worked too long, he could allow people who've worked the maximum number of years to go before they reach normal retirement age, without reducing the pension at all.

■ He can't afford it. But it won't cost very much, because so few people will qualify. It might well cost less than giving each of them a watch when they retire.

■ He may simply not have thought of it, or he may have misunderstood what the Inland Revenue say. It's surprising how often this happens in pension negotiations. If for some reason there's a *genuine* doubt about how the Inland Revenue would view a change in this rule, or any other, then it is perfectly possible to write and ask for advice, but you must expect to wait a while for an answer.

5.3. Credited years

Typical arrangements and possible improvements

There are a number of ways in which you can get credit in a

pension scheme for more years than you have actually been in it. Some of these are dealt with in other sections:

■ Years with the company before the scheme started, or when there was a different scheme, are counted in. See section 8 on 'Past service', page 105.

■ Years are credited to you because you have transferred pension rights from another scheme. See section 16 on 'Leaving service', page 106.

■ You have bought 'added years' by making special contributions. See section 20 on 'Additional voluntary contributions', page 107.

Another type is where years have been credited to you because you were with the company but not the scheme, because you were too young to be allowed in, or did not have the service qualification, but were given the full 'back service' *once* you joined the scheme.

The justification for this is that the company do not have the trouble of collecting and refunding fairly small amounts of contributions for youngsters who do not stay long, but that people can still accrue a reasonable level of pension. This is a method by which the employer is **evading** the preservation or buying back requirements for short service people. It is preferable, therefore, to bring people fully into the scheme with a minimal qualification period.

Finally, there are years added to keep up the value of your pension, because you are working shorter hours, or your earnings have dropped in real terms. This is very rare, but it is worth knowing about because in the near future many more people are likely to have their hours of work or their overtime earnings reduced.

> At Thorn Electrical Industries, if a member suffers a reduction in earnings, for instance, by losing shift premium, s/he will be given a credit that places him/her in broadly the same position as before. This credit is cancelled if his/her earnings subsequently return to their previous level, but the basic entitlement is not reduced.

Possible arguments and responses

In this section we are not covering the question of backdated credits for those excluded from the scheme. While there may be arguments for it from the employer's point of view, there are not from the member's.

On the question of credits where the hours of work are reduced, assuming that short time working is something you've already agreed to or accepted in other negotiations, you can point out that

■ unless a special arrangement is made, people will have been contributing towards a benefit they will not in fact receive;

■ people are already making a sacrifice in terms of their day to day wages, and they should not be asked to make a further one; and

■ they are possibly also sacrificing some part of their death benefit by reducing their real wages, and that is as far as any limitation should go (though there are ways of getting round that problem too – see section 12 on 'Lump sum death benefits', page 127).

The employer will be arguing **cost** and **complication**.

On cost, it will be a matter of arguing

■ how much it really will cost;

■ whether he can afford it or not;

■ what profit he really made last year, and what it's been spent on;

■ whether he should be saving money on something else (expense-account dinners? large cars for company executives?) and spending it on the pension scheme;

and so on.

On the question of complication, you can suggest that if a group like Thorn Electrical Industries, with very large numbers of sites and different pay systems, can cope with the problem, so can the average employer.

He may say though that, being only average, he hasn't got the sophisticated records systems that a large company like Thorn can afford. But after all, you could reply, now that running a company is a complicated operation, perhaps he *ought* to be keeping more careful records, so he has better control of costs. (You might though not *want* him to obtain too much control over the organisation of overtime, shifts etc, in which case you need to be careful about using this argument.)

Even if there seems to be no likelihood of short time working, it is wise to make a provision for it in the rules of the scheme. Then, if the issue actually arises on a particular site, you can simply activate that clause.

Section 6: Contributions

What you must have

There is no minimum level of contributions that you or the

employer *must* make to the pension scheme. If you are contracted out, you save 2½%, and the employer saves 4½%, on National Insurance contributions. It is assumed that the joint 7% goes towards the contracted out scheme. But in fact it may be less, and for a good scheme it would usually be more.

What the Inland Revenue allows

The Inland Revenue says 3 things about contributions to an **approved** scheme:

■ the employer *must* contribute something to the scheme. He must not set it up and then charge the employees the whole cost;

■ the **employee's** contribution *must* not be more than 15%; and

■ while the employee may sometimes get his/her contributions back, the employer may not, while the scheme is running, because the pension fund is an 'irrevocable trust'.

This last safeguard can in fact be got round by the employer, if he chooses to do so, in 2 ways:

■ the fund may be able to **lend** money to the company (there are a lot of small funds, for directors and senior managers, that do this); or

■ the employer can reduce the amount he pays in at any time (or even stop paying for a short period, so long as he contributes for most of the year).

Members' and employer's contributions

There are two sets of contributions to consider – yours, and the employer's. Finding out what the employer pays can be difficult. So this section is divided into:

6.1. Members' contributions;

6.2. Disclosure of the employer's contributions; and

6.3. Employer's contributions.

It is unwise to get into a negotiation solely about contributions. The discussion should be first and foremost about **benefits**. If you get drawn into an argument about the precise ½% extra contribution, before you have told the employer exactly what benefits you want, you may find the arithmetic being manipulated against you.

There is a lot of guesswork in calculating what pensions will cost, and the employer is more likely than you are to be able to arrange the guesswork favourably to himself.

6.1. Members' contributions

Typical arrangements and possible improvements

People in **most** contracted out schemes are paying between 3% and 5% of their pensionable earnings. This has stayed pretty much the same in the last few years, as the NAPF survey showed in its table 21 on 'Comparative levels of employees' contributions':

Overall average contribution rate	Staff schemes	Works schemes	Combined schemes	All schemes
	%	%	%	%
1979	4.85	3.75	4.65	4.59
1978	5.29	3.79	4.88	4.84
1977	4.73	3.52	4.34	4.44
1976	4.73	3.48	4.45	4.45
1975	4.90	3.60	4.57	4.60

But it doesn't help much to know what the contribution rate is, unless you also know what slice of your earnings you are contributing on. You should never look at the contribution rate by itself. Always look at the pensionable earnings as well.

Very roughly, if you are contracted out and paying more than 5%, or contracted in and paying more than 3%, you should need convincing that your scheme is good value.

If you are paying more than those guidelines, this doesn't necessarily mean you're in a bad scheme – simply that you should want to know what makes your scheme more expensive than average. And you will want to know how much the employer is paying in proportion, too.

If the employer wants to *increase* the members' contributions (or even make the scheme contributory where it was not before), there are several points to watch:

■ first, it should only happen where there is a clear increase in benefits, negotiated with the unions;

■ second, the employer should be putting in *more* of an increase than he is asking the members to do; and

■ third, before you agree an increase in contributions, you need to be sure your members will accept it. This may sound obvious, but it is easy to get carried away in negotiating, especially since it can get very detailed. Take soundings of how the members feel before wasting a lot of time getting the small print right.

On paper, the legal position on obtaining an increase in contributions appears to be that, if the employer suddenly starts deducting extra contributions from your pay packet, especially if they are to pay for extra benefits, then unless you protest very quickly you will be deemed to have accepted it. This puts you in a weak position if the employer wishes to go over the union's head. There haven't been many court cases on this, though, and the legal system in this country means that you don't know *precisely* what the law is until judges have made rulings on it.

Sometimes employers insist on increasing the contributions, and say that the scheme will be discontinued for anyone who refuses to pay. What do you do?

The *problem* is that if the scheme is discontinued for those who do not pay the increase, they will lose their life assurance benefits, as well as having their pensions frozen at a certain year's levels (see section 16.2, 'Treatment of frozen pensions', page 159, for more information on this) and losing future contributions. Obviously, you can argue about bad industrial relations and a breach of good faith. But, unless you are in a position to achieve effective industrial action, it will be better to give in, and to negotiate to ensure that benefits are not frozen, while a two tier system is allowed to remain.

Finally, what about non-contributory schemes? There's really no such thing.

'Non-contributory' means that the *member* makes no *direct* contribution – the employer pays it all. But where would that money be if it were not going into the pension scheme? It would be available to spend on other things, perhaps on wages. So you are still paying. As an unusually frank pensions manager once said, 'It makes no difference to me whether I take the contribution out of your pay packet before you get it, or after. I still get the money.'

Are there disadvantages in a non-contributory scheme? There can be several, and they chiefly come down to the question of *control*. If your scheme is non-contributory,

- you will find it more difficult to get negotiating rights;
- you'll be in a weaker position to get member trustees; and
- the employer will often resist changes strongly.

Of course the argument that pensions are deferred pay is still as strong as ever. But naturally enough the ordinary member is not so interested in something s/he feels s/he is not paying for, and so it will be more difficult to prevent the employer simply riding roughshod over your arguments.

> Company Y, with a very poor non-contributory pension scheme, was approached by the union seeking a number of improvements. Here is part of their reply:
> 'We have considered the various proposals made in your letter . . . and in view of some of these feel it is necessary again to bring to your attention that the scheme is non-contributory.
> It is the company's belief that in view of the above the scheme . . . is very fair and . . . makes overall markedly superior provisions to those of the new State scheme without any demands on the employee's income. Any employee can of course privately contribute through endowment insurances etc to augment the benefits to be obtained on retiral or to the spouse etc on death of the insured and with a non-contributory scheme of our type each employee is free to make his/her own decision on how much of the income will be invested for these purposes . . .
> In view of the scheme being non-contributory and being an invested fund with an insurance company rather than separate investments by the trustees etc, the company do not propose to depart from their present policy regarding appointment of trustees.'

The **exception**, where a non-contributory basis is useful, is where a low level, 'ride on top' scheme has been agreed, giving a death benefit and a lump sum on retirement (an example of this is given in section 7.4, 'Lump sum schemes', page 100).

This may be all the members want, or you may accept that it is all the employer can afford at the moment. This sort of scheme is very cheap, costing between 2% and 4% of pensionable payroll for most companies, so splitting the contributions will produce a very small amount. It may not be worth the members' while to pay it, especially since they will then get enmeshed in complications about refunds etc. It is therefore simplest for all concerned – including the company, because the administrative costs of collecting a small contribution are high – for the scheme to be non-contributory for the member. But it will need to be made clear that this does not alter in any way the principle that the pension is deferred pay.

Occasionally, a company will offer the alternatives of either pension scheme improvements, or making the scheme non-contributory. The second may look very tempting – but think carefully before you accept it; it's not offered out of the goodness of the employer's heart.

Possible arguments and responses

If the employer is trying to impose too high a contribution rate on the members, you will need to argue:

■ People will not feel that the scheme is value for money, and therefore the 'public relations' advantage to the employer is much reduced.

■ The employer will have continuing industrial relations problems making new entrants, especially younger ones, join the scheme, if they see too much money being taken out of their pay packets.

■ The scheme will look bad in comparison with other employers in the area, and in the country as a whole. Give him the NAPF figures, and also try to collect details of other pension schemes run by large employers in the neighbourhood, (try your Trades Council as a 'clearing house').

The employer, on the other hand, will often say:

■ that the members will value the scheme more, the more they pay for it. But the *important* point, you should reply, is the value for money they are getting.

■ or (if you are negotiating a new scheme), that he can only just afford what he is offering to pay anyway, and any further contribution would 'break the camel's back'. It may be worth reminding him that he is getting Corporation Tax relief on his contributions, so it is not costing nearly as much as it first appears. Beyond this, you will simply need to bargain about how much he really can afford, in the same way as you would on wages. (We suggested some of the lines of argument you could use on page 77).

On *increasing* the contributions, he may say:

■ that he can't afford to introduce the improvements suggested without a substantially increased contribution from the members. In this case, you will have to weigh up your views on this, and decide whether the improvements are value for money in themselves.

6.2. Disclosure of the employer's contribution

Typical arrangements and possible improvements

While most scheme booklets will state somewhere what your contribution is, far fewer say exactly what the company is paying.

Some booklets are fairly specific. For instance, Rank Xerox stated in 1978: 'The company contribution has been increased to 4.3 times members' contributions.' Others are much less so. Bass Charrington says; 'The company contributes several times the total amount contributed by members as well as meeting the expenses of administering the plan.'

Often, even though it is not in the booklet, you will be able to find this information out fairly easily. Other times, though, it will be a closely guarded secret. If employers provide a pension scheme to make their employees feel they are good and progressive, you'd expect them to be proud of the amount they are spending on it, but this isn't necessarily the case.

You should start off by making a straightforward request for details of what the company paid into the pension scheme for the last 2 or 3 years. As well as the global figure, you will also need to know

■ whether there are any **special contributions**, because improvements recently made are not yet paid for, or because the company has credited in past service entitlement, or because of transfers to and from other companies, or because of increases in pensions in payment;

■ how much the contribution has varied over the last few years;

■ whether the company is making any extra contribution because the scheme was underfunded in the past and, if so, over how long the liability is being paid off; and

■ when the contribution rate was last reviewed, and whether the employer is paying more, less, or about the same as the actuary recommended.

If this is refused, you should then state that you are exercising your rights, as members of the scheme, to inspect the pension fund accounts. How far these rights extend in law is not altogether clear, but the National Association of Pension Funds, the body which claims to be the 'collective voice' of all the pension funds of any size, issued a Code of Practice in 1980. It is voluntary, but any scheme that belongs to the NAPF is *expected* to comply. This says:

Financial Information
(a) Statutory or SFO requirements
Trust law, not having been designed originally to cover pension schemes, gives little guidance as to how much information must be provided to scheme members. Nevertheless . . . the spirit of trust law is

clearly applicable and as much information as is practicable should be
available to members. It would seem prudent to assume that a member
or beneficiary is entitled to inspect on request (in addition to the trust
deed and rules):

(i) the audited pension fund accounts,

(ii) actuarial valuation reports,

(iii) general information about investments or insurance contracts,

at that date of the latest published trustees' annual report.

(Pension fund accounts, and actuarial valuation reports, are
explained in chapter 8.)

If the management wish to stick to this very minimal
requirement, 'inspection on request' may mean a trip to the
company's head office, in working time. Clearly this is not enough,
and at the very least, provision of the accounts and valuations to all
the members, in a form you can understand, should be requested.

Once you have got a copy of the accounts, you ought to be
able to work out fairly easily what the employer's contribution
is.

Some insurance companies, however, do not issue accounts
for individual schemes which are insured with them, and so you may
still have problems. You could try making use of the Employment
Protection Act 1975. The provision to quote is section 17, applying
to disclosure of information for collective bargaining purposes. The
Arbitration and Conciliation Advisory Service (ACAS) have also
issued a Code of Practice (No 2), on disclosure, which while not
specifically mentioning pensions, does include 'fringe benefits and
non-wage labour costs' in the list of items where information could
be requested under the code, in para. 11 (1).

Many groups of pension fund trustees are in fact set up as
directors of limited companies (this is explained on pages 206–7).
For instance, the Turner and Newall pension scheme for manual
workers is run by Turner and Newall (Hourly Paid) Pension
Trustees Ltd. In this case, it will have a duty to file accounts in
Companies House, under company law. But accounts here are often
out of date.

Don't be surprised, in a small insured scheme, if an employer
genuinely doesn't know what his annual contribution is (but make
sure he finds out). Quite often, employers simply send off the cheque
to the insurance company once a month, without any idea of how
it's made up.

It may also be difficult, if he gives you under the requirements of the Employment Protection Act, a **global** figure for his total contribution in the last year, to know how it divides up between normal and special contributions, and whether he has made a larger or smaller contribution in that year to suit his cash flow. Arguing about exactly how much is put in could be a waste of energy; so long as you are satisfied that it is sufficient for the benefits provided, it may be better to concentrate on improving the **benefits**.

Possible arguments and responses

First, you can press the point of 'what has he got to hide?' *Sometimes*, there will be something – not because of dishonesty (which you probably won't be able to find out about anyway without a very detailed examination of the accounts), but because he is putting in less than he has implied, and/or less than the actuary has recommended. More often, it will simply be managerial secretiveness.

You could point out:

■ That many members will have no idea what the employer is paying in. Indeed, they may well not appreciate that he is paying in anything at all. The member will value the scheme far more if s/he knows that it is not just his/her 5%, or whatever, going in, but also the employer's 10%. S/he will think better of the employer for putting this money in.

■ Now that in general you are not allowed to have refunds of contributions, the member will understand far better the reasons for having to leave the contribution in, if s/he appreciates how much the employer is also leaving in, and therefore there should be fewer complaints about this aspect.

■ It is the member's deferred pay, and s/he has a *right* to know.

■ As we said above, giving this basic information is *recommended*, not just as good practice, but as the member's minimum entitlement within the spirit of trust law by the NAPF.

The employer may argue, if you are talking about starting a new scheme or greatly improving an old one, that he doesn't *know* what his contribution will be. Technically, this is true, but he should have a fair estimate from his advisers. If he *really* has not got an idea, then that's bad management, and he ought to go away and get a costing from professionals, even if it means holding up the negotiations. A pension scheme is a long term commitment, like building a new office block, and no manager who was any good would dream of going in for that investment without figures that were as accurate as he could get.

6.3. Employer's contributions

Typical arrangements and possible improvements

Most trust deeds have a wording something like this:

> The company shall decide with the advice of the actuary the amount of contributions payable by the company to the plan as are necessary in each year, when, other income and receipts of the plan are taken into account, to provide the benefits payable under the plan in respect of the members thereof.

This means that, over and above the member's contribution, the employer has a responsibility to contribute what the actuary tells him is the right amount for the benefits offered (or to close the scheme down). So the employer's contribution is not fixed in the legal documents, as the member's is. But in any 1 year, there should be a figure he has worked out, in percentage of payroll terms, for what his contribution is. (See chapter 8 for an explanation of how his contribution is calculated.)

The NAPF survey showed that in contributory schemes the **average** employer's contribution is now about 2½ times the average employee's contribution (table 24). Compare this with their table of employee's contributions (table 21) on page 79.

Average contri-bution rate for	Staff schemes	Works schemes	Combined schemes	All schemes
	%	%	%	%
1979	13.13	7.79	10.84	11.26
1978	12.34	7.17	11.16	11.00
1977	11.10	5.64	9.97	9.80
1976	10.39	5.82	9.10	9.30
1975	9.50	4.70	9.10	7.70

As you will see from the table, employers tend to pay far more into staff schemes than into works schemes, and the gap has narrowed only slightly since 1975 (and then only as a percentage, not in money terms).

Leaving aside the schemes where the employer's contribution

is very small because the benefits provided are small, there are many schemes where the **benefits** are reasonable, but the employer's contribution, compared to the employee's, is low.

Thorn Electrical Industries' pension scheme had, in 1979, employees' contributions of £6.3m and company contributions of £7.6m – a 6½% rate for the members and an 8% rate for the company.

Other employers however contribute very large amounts. Imperial Foods, for instance, pay 4 times the member's contribution.

The ratio of 2½ times the employee's contribution should be taken as a minimum rule of thumb. Points to watch out for on this are:

■ If the employer's contribution is less than 2½ times the member's, then it should come up to *at least* that level before there is any discussion of increased payments from the members.

■ Any contribution that is being made to pay for **past service** should be treated separately from this, and met wholly by the company. It is a bill *they* should pick up.

■ If there is an actuarial surplus (see pages 226–238), it should go into increased benefits, especially to existing pensioners, *not* into reducing the employer's contributions. It is not necessary to have this written into the rules of the scheme; it could be clearly set out in a letter of intent or a procedure agreement. If the employer won't go this far, at least get him to commit himself to joint discussions on the disposal of any surplus.

■ If you do get to the stage of talking about increased contributions from the members, the employer's extra contribution should be in the same ratio as above, i.e. if an extra 1% is being asked for from the members, then the employer should be paying an extra 2½%.

Possible arguments and responses

It's best to admit from the start that there's no magic about the 2½ times ratio – it could just as easily be 2 times or 3 times. It is simply a rule of thumb based on the average ratio among good schemes, and no doubt when that average improves, the rule of thumb will improve too.

Based on this, the argument will be:

■ That your employer will not want to fall behind comparable employers – if you can find employers in the district who are paying more than $2\frac{1}{2}$ times as much as the employees, so much the better.

■ That the employer is better able to afford the contributions, and in any case they are the members' deferred wages. Take care with this argument, though – you will not want to be led down the road of a direct tradeoff between pensions and wages.

The employer's main response will be on *cost* – that he cannot afford to put more into the pension scheme – and as with wage negotiations, it will be for you to convince him that he must *find* more. (See page 77 for some arguments on this). He is also likely to come up with other statements such as:

■ His *precise* contribution at any one time is irrelevant, as he carries the risk of making up the balance if anything goes wrong. You can say that you know about, and value, the employer's 'fallback' role, but you are sure that both he and you wish it never to be used, and the best safeguard of this is a proper contribution rate throughout the lifetime of the scheme. To say that his annual contribution doesn't matter because of the 'fallback' is a bit like saying that the shareholders should not be interested in the annual accounts because they can always wind up the company, which is not an idea many directors would support.

Finally, though, we would stress again – *don't* let yourselves be drawn into a sterile argument about contributions, or the ratio of employer's to employee's contributions in isolation, if you can possibly help it. Always try to relate the discussion to the benefits.

Section 7: Accrual rate

(We explained on page 32 what this was – turn back to that if you've forgotten.)

What you must have

If your scheme is contracted **in**, there is no minimum accrual rate, but if you are contracted **out**, the Social Security Pensions Act says that your pension must not accrue at less than 1/80th of final pensionable salary per year of service. (This is the 'requisite benefit' – turn back to page 17 for details.)

As the 'final pensionable salary' can be very different from PAYE earnings (it need only be basic salary and can have an offset of up to $1\frac{1}{2}$ times the lower earnings limit), the Occupational Pensions Board have used their discretion to say that they will accept as equivalent a scheme that gives **1/100th**, based on PAYE earnings.

What the Inland Revenue allows

The Inland Revenue will allow you to have a pension of up to 2/3rds of your final pensionable earnings. They are not worried whether you are contracted in or out, so you can have this on top of your full additional pension from the State, if you want (and if someone will pay for it).

They assume that people stay with a company for 40 years, so will accept a 1/60th scheme without question. They will also accept a scheme with a *higher* accrual rate if

■ it is not based on full earnings (e.g. there is a State scheme offset), and/or

■ it has a service maximum of less than 40 years.

The *most* that a company can give is a 2/3rds pension after 10 years. Needless to say this is not offered to manual workers – it's used for senior management staff who change employers late in life.

In calculating the 2/3rds limit, any pension earned with a previous employer, and either frozen, or transferred, has to be included.

The bulk of this section deals with **final salary** and **average salary revalued** schemes, but the last subsection covers the other types of schemes. This section is divided into;

7.1. Contracted out schemes,

7.2. Contracted in schemes,

7.3. Integration,

7.4. Lump sum schemes, and

7.5. Other types of scheme.

7.1. Contracted out schemes

Typical arrangements and possible improvements

The 1979 NAPF survey did not have a table on accrual rates. But the 1978 survey, covering a good sample of all schemes, showed that staff generally did much better than works members on their accrual rates, as you can see from the table:

Pension fraction	Staff schemes	Works schemes	Combined schemes	All schemes
	%	%	%	%
Better than 1/60ths (integrated scheme)	8	4	12	9
Better than 1/60ths (non-integrated scheme)	5	—	3	3
1/60ths integrated	34	24	36	33
1/60ths non-integrated	39	10	27	30
1/80ths + 3/80ths lump sum*	4	5	4	4
1/80th	3	31	8	10
1/100th	2	7	2	3
Other fraction less generous than 1/60th	5	19	7	8
Total	100	100	100	100

*See section 7.4, 'Lump sum schemes', page 100, for an explanation of these.

There are many manual workers in schemes which only just meet the contracting out requirements; often people would in fact be better off in the State scheme, where they had no problem about frozen pensions.

R H Roadstone's *lower* tier scheme gives 1/100th of pensionable earnings (PAYE earnings) for each year of pensionable service after 1978; which is the minimum you are allowed to give and still contract out of the scheme.

On the other hand, some schemes give much *better* rates.

Rank Xerox gives you 2% a year for a maximum of 33 years. S & W Berisford gives you 1/45th a year, for a maximum of 30 years.

Some schemes give a different rate for either the first few years, or the last few years of pensionable service.

Hercules Powder gives 1/60th of final pensionable salary (which involves a deduction to take account of the State pension) for the first 30 years' service, and 1/50th thereafter.

As a broad generalisation, you can say that the average manual workers' scheme is either
- 1/80th non-integrated, or
- 1/60th integrated.

If it's the first, you need to concentrate on improving the **accrual rate**. If the second, reducing the integration factor. If it's worse than this, for instance, 1/80th integrated, then you'll need to try to improve both.

Once you've reached 1/60th, it probably isn't worth trying to build it up further until you have got all the *other* elements in the scheme improved to your satisfaction. However, if you are looking for an earlier **retirement age**, you might well want to get a better accrual rate while doing so, so that people can earn as much pension as before in a shorter time.

Improving the accrual rate is *expensive* – because it will improve everything else, like the early retirement pension and the widow's pension too.

Massey Ferguson costed, in 1979–80, an improvement from 1/80th to 1/60th (both integrated), at £1.6m, or 3.75% of payroll.

You can calculate roughly how much it will cost by working out how much bigger a typical person's pension will be:

* An 80ths scheme will give a $\frac{1}{2}$ pension after 40 years – £45 for a person on £90 a week.
* A 60ths scheme will give a 2/3rds pension after 40 years – £60 for a person on £90 a week.
The second pension is $\frac{1}{3}$ better, so it will add an extra $\frac{1}{3}$ to the cost of the scheme.

However, this rule of thumb does not work *entirely* for schemes which are only just around the minimum level for contracting out. Because of the need to provide guarantees on the GMP, it may cost very *little* to improve the accrual rate, because the GMP will be payable in so many cases anyway. The commonest accrual rates are 1/60th and 1/80th, but it is perfectly possible to have any other. On page 33 we gave a list of common ones.

If you can't get your accrual rate improved all at once, you *might* consider a phased scheme.

The **disadvantages** of this are:

■ it makes it very difficult for the ordinary member to work out his/her pension, as s/he must grapple with a lot of different sums, and

■ if someone retires just the wrong side of the dividing line (at the end of March when the next phase of the improvement comes in April, for instance), s/he will be resentful about the agreement.

On the other hand, you may decide to make a start on a process of phasing in an improvement now, rather than waiting until the company decides it can do it all in one go.

A claim for an improved accrual rate is often the major item in a claim for staff level benefits. There are many schemes where the only important difference between staff and manual workers is that the staff have a higher accrual rate. If so, the company may well wish you also to pay the staff contribution rate.

Possible arguments and responses

The sort of argument you should be using depends on how good your scheme is to start with, and what sort of level you're aiming at. For an average manual workers' scheme, that is, a 1/80th scheme you're trying to improve to 1/60th, the sort of argument you can use is:

■ The final pension for those with less than 40 years' service (the majority) is not enough to live on.

■ The employer has sold the scheme as being *better* than the State scheme but in fact, because of the different ways in which the GMP and the requisite benefits work, it *won't* be for many people. In those cases, the employer will end up paying the GMP rather than scheme benefits, and so the member, who has perhaps paid more into the scheme than s/he would have into the State, ends up no better off (this would certainly be true in many schemes giving 1/80th of basic earnings). This argument will be stronger when the State scheme has been running for a few years, and you have examples you can produce.

If you're basing your arguments for an increase on a claim for parity with the staff, then all the arguments about staff status apply (see page 51).

You can argue from comparison with other schemes too. Who are your company's competitors? What sort of schemes do they have? Why not write and ask their shop stewards, or get your head office to find out? Who are the competitors for *labour* in the area? What are their schemes like? Does the company aim to be at the top, or the middle, of the league table, or do they not care?

Remember that the accrual rate is the *central issue* of the pension scheme (but remember also that you must link it with the pensionable salary definition). Any improvement you get will overlap on to a lot of other things. So the negotiations on this are extremely important.

However the employer ties his response up, his basic objection will be **cost**. It is expensive to change the accrual rate, and you may as well show you are aware of this. Try to get him to provide an actual figure – the rule of thumb about cost will not apply if there are special contributions for particular items going into the fund. Then you're in a straightforward negotiating position – how much can you get from him, and is this single large item your top priority?

For the moment, and for the foreseeable future, he will probably also talk about the poor investment yield obtainable by the fund, the high rate of inflation, etc. All these arguments are valid: pension funds **do** have trouble keeping up with inflation. But they do not alter your members' needs for a decent pension.

If you're going for an improvement in the accrual rate of a scheme which is already at or above the average, you'll need some pretty strong arguments. For instance:

■ you might be able to point to a high level of profit being made by the company (for instance, a bank or an insurance company);

■ you might be looking for parity with a good staff scheme in the same company; or

■ if it is a multinational company, you might want to do some research on the pensions they provide in other countries, especially in the United States.

Your best chance of success will be if the company is making an embarrassingly high level of profits, and looking for somewhere to put them.

7.2. Contracted in schemes

Typical arrangements and possible improvements

Theoretically, the sky's the limit on contracted in schemes. You can have just as high an accrual rate as in a contracted out scheme, and the State additional pension too. There are quite a few 'top hat' schemes which do just that. *But* they cost a lot of money, and it is not very realistic to aim for this. The majority of contracted in schemes are either 'riding on top', with a low accrual rate, or integrated.

Integration is covered in the next section, 7.3, page 95. This one deals with 'ride on top' schemes.

These are intended to top up the State pension scheme, and so the company's intention will be that you look at the two pensions together to give your **target pension**. Provided the 'target' is of a good standard, there's nothing wrong with that.

> The booklet for Preston Farmers Ltd says: 'Pension at normal retirement age . . . will be 1/120th of final pensionable salary up to upper earnings limit . . . for each year of service in the scheme after September 1977. The ceiling . . . will be increased in accordance with changes to the State pension scheme of which the ceiling is at present fixed.'

Thus the accrual rate is extremely low – but if you add it to the 1/80th accrual rate from the State, you get a better picture.

Some schemes give you a low accrual rate up to the upper earnings limit, and then a higher one above it.

> The Unicorn Industries 'higher benefit' scheme gives: '1/90th of your final pensionable earnings up to the upper earnings limit, plus 1/60th of your final pensionable earnings *above* the upper earnings limit'.

The argument here is that the State pension does not cover earnings above the upper earnings limit, so this must be compensated for by a higher company pension. For many schemes of this sort, the contribution is the same on all earnings so the lower paid are in effect subsidising the higher paid, which should be opposed.

In a contracted in scheme, it is a matter of judgement how far you want to improve the accrual rate. You're doing reasonably well if you get it better than the minimum at which the scheme could contract **out** (1/100th on all earnings, or 1/80th integrated). Rather than concentrate on the accrual rate, you may do better to look at other areas of the scheme where the State does particularly badly – widow's pensions, or early retirement, for instance.

The **cost** problems are the same as for a contracted out scheme, except that there is no need to provide the same guarantees. If you haven't already read that section, 7.1 on pages 89–93, you may find it helpful to do so.

Possible arguments and responses

The arguments in section 7.1 above also apply here. The essential negotiation will still be about *money*, as it is with a contracted out scheme. There are further points you can throw in.

■ Point out that the employer has put a large proportion of his pension fund into an inflationproof investment – that is, the

State additional scheme. He is therefore not taking the same risks as those in contracted out schemes, and so is in a better position to give you an improved pension. There will usually have been a leaflet or announcement when the employer originally persuaded you that contracting in was the best course. If you can find it (or make him provide you with another copy), it may well provide you with some useful quotes.

■ You can also say that it was no one's intention that you should lose by contracting in. The pension provided from two sources was supposed to be as good as that which a contracted out scheme can provide from one. So if there is any danger of your falling behind, the employer ought to be willing to catch up, and improve the scheme.

7.3. Integration

Typical arrangements and possible improvements

We explained what integration was, and the different methods of achieveing it, on pages 33–36, so turn back to that if you've forgotten the basic points. As we said there, there are two methods of integration:

■ with pensionable earnings, or
■ with the pension itself.

The first means that an amount is deducted from your earnings before the pension is calculated, to 'take account of the State pension', and the second, that an amount is deducted from your pension *after* it is calculated, for the same reason.

Integration is now a very common feature of pension schemes. If anything, it is becoming more common. It applies to both contracted out and contracted in schemes, but they raise different issues, so we will deal with contracted out schemes first.

The reason employers will give for integration is that the State is already providing a pension on that part of your income, which you are paying for out of your NI contributions, so there is no need for them to make further provision. The unions, however, generally dislike it.

What are the *disadvantages* of integration?

■ It gives you a lower pension than you would otherwise have. *But* it will also mean you are paying **lower contributions**. Abolishing integration will almost certainly mean an increase either in the percentage taken or in the amount of earnings on which contributions are calculated.

■ It bears particularly hard on the lower paid, because they will have a bigger slice of their earnings deducted. If your company has a lot of lower paid people in it, then one of the biggest improvements you could make would be to abolish integration, but if the majority are high paid, then it might be better to concentrate on improving the accrual rate. (The 'cross-over' point comes when you are earning about 4 times the State pension.)

It tends to be the white collar unions who are keenest on abolishing integration, because they are anxious to have nothing to do with the State scheme, but in fact it will often be the lower paid manual worker who gains most.

If you can't get the integration factor abolished in your scheme, or if you think people wouldn't like a sudden jump in their contributions, you could take a first step by freezing the deduction at its current money value, and then as time goes on it can be cut down and finally abolished altogether. That way, no one will pay more in a sudden jump, but the effects of integration will be very much reduced.

> WGI Group froze their deduction at £910 in 1978, and intend, when the fund is sufficiently healthy, to remove it altogether.

How do the two main types of integration compare? It depends on the exact arithmetic of any particular scheme. In general, for a person with 40 years in the scheme, they will give an identical result; but for the shorter service person, integrating with the **pension** gives the worse deal, as the example on pages 33–34 shows.

So if you have 'pension type' integration, if you can't get it abolished altogether it may be worth trying to get it changed to 'earnings type' integration. (Check the arithmetic for your own scheme first though, using the example on pages 33–34 as a guide.)

What if your company wants to 'trade off' introducing integration against a higher accrual rate?

> McCain International announced in 1979:
> 'Due to Social Security benefits and costs increasing rapidly in recent years, it is common practice for private pension schemes to take account of the basic State pension in relation to both pension benefits and contributions. With effect from 1 July 1979, a form of integration between the benefits from the State and the company will be adopted.

> The overall effect is a more attractive package which we feel provides a better overall balance between the immediate problem of contributions, the medium term problem of sickness, and the longer term problem of pensions.'

It therefore went from a 1/80th non-integrated scheme to a 1/60th integrated scheme. The union contested this, but the company were able to show that, because of the reasonably high earnings levels, no-one would be worse off, and so it was accepted.

If you find you have to accept integration:

■ Try to obtain a 'no worse off' formula, so that for people in employment at the time of the change-over, the company does two benefit calculations, and gives the individual the pension derived from the better one.

■ If you can't get this, but can get the old scheme maintained as well as the new, it will be important to be sure that people are getting **proper** advice, on an individual basis, on their course of action, whether from the personnel department or from some outside adviser.

Integration with a **contracted in** scheme raises different issues. You *are* getting an additional benefit out of the State, and you are paying extra money for it, instead of putting that money into the company scheme. So it is illogical to resist integration when contracted in.

As we saw on pages 34–36, contracted in schemes tend to have more complicated integration formulas than contracted out ones. Because the State scheme works so very differently from a private scheme, the private one can only fit in *exactly* with it if you have an arrangement so complicated that most people can't work out their own pension, and probably can't even understand how the formula works.

One way to get exactness is to work on the same formula as the State does, of **revalued average earnings** (see pages 38–39), but very few schemes do this. Many people have come to the conclusion that it is worth sacrificing the *exact* fit for a scheme everyone can understand; this is a decision that must be up to you.

Another point that you need to take care on is that the deduction is not made in circumstances where *no* State additional pension is payable – where someone is retiring early, for instance, but not due to ill health, or when a widower's pension is paid for death in service. Other than that, however, it is probably best not to tinker too much with this aspect, but to concentrate on improving the accrual rate, and other factors.

Possible arguments and responses

You have a difficult argument on your hands. Many companies, particularly multinationals, are very committed to integration because they see themselves otherwise as paying twice for the same benefit – once to the State, once to the pension fund. Some of the arguments you could use are:

■ integration provides a lower pension but with the illusion of a higher one, and is misleading to many people;

■ it discriminates against the lower paid, and against women, who in the past may not have had the chance to contribute for a full State pension;

■ in times when prices are rising faster than wages, the State pension increases will eat up more and more of the private pension entitlement;

■ the State pension is a benefit paid to anyone who has made contributions, as of right. It is unfair for the company to take away, in effect, the rights the State gives.

Below is an example of the sort of argument the Ford unions used in their 1979 pensions claim. You may not want to go into such enormous detail – most small employers would be totally confused by the length and complexity of the Ford claim – but it might give you some ideas.

The illusory fraction

The unwary Ford manual worker might easily get the impression that his company pension will be based on 1/60th of the basic pay rate applicable when he retires. If this is the case he would be rapidly disillusioned. In reality the company's contribution to the pension will be nearer 1/100th than a 1/60th; moreover this fraction is applied to a basic pay rate which is invariably lower than that actually paid immediately prior to retirement. There are two main reasons why this situation occurs:

* firstly, the use of an integration factor;

* secondly, the way in which a base date for calculating pensionable salary is chosen.

The integration factor is the means by which the company's contribution to the total pension is reduced. This is done by deducting an amount equivalent to $1\frac{1}{2}$ times the single person's basic State pension from pensionable pay before calculating the company's pension contribution. The theoretical objective is to ensure that the total pension, State plus company, is equivalent to 1/60th of the relevant basic pay rate for each year of service. However, in practice it ensures that the true company pension contribution is only a proportion of this. Moreover, each time the state pension is increased there will, if no adjustment is made to pensionable salary, be a fall in this already infinitesimal fraction. Another point worth noting is that the current scheme assumes that a worker is entitled to the full State pension. If this is not the case the total pension will be less than 1/60th.

The true value in pounds per week of the company pension is shown in column 1 of table 10 [not included]. From this it can be seen that for a grade B worker with 20 years' service the company proportion of the pension would be only £14.65 a week. This amounts to less than 20% or 1/5th of the current basic rate. In the case of a similar worker with 40 years' service the weekly company pension rises to £29.34 a week, or less than 40% of the current basic rate. Clearly the company pension will not provide more than a partial maintenance of living standards when a Ford worker retires. . . .

Discrimination against the low paid

Another unsatisfactory feature of the current pension scheme for Ford manual workers is that it is heavily biased against the low paid. That is, the lower the level of basic pay the lower the 'true' company fraction. This is a direct consequence of using a flat rate integration factor as a uniform offset regardless of grade. The effect is illustrated in table 2.

Table 2   Pension entitlement per year of service by grade; 6 April
1979–5 April 1980

Grade	Annual payment £	True company fraction
A	33.10	1/101
B	38.13	1/96
C	40.50	1/94
D	42.98	1/92
E	46.97	1/89

Table 2 shows that in the year from 6 April 1979 the true company fraction varies from 1/101 for grade A to 1/89 for grade E. Put another way, whereas in basic pay terms grade E's basic pensionable pay is approximately 25% higher than grade A's, this gap is increased to nearly 42% in terms of the company's contribution to the pension. Thus not only is the true company fraction considerably less than a 1/60th for each grade but it gets progressively smaller the lower the level of basic pay.

If you're in a **contracted in** scheme, again the same arguments will apply. You're unlikely to win on completely abolishing integration – but you could try to reduce the size of the deduction made. You may be able to show that the scheme is getting into administrative difficulties because of the complicated sums that need to be done. How quickly, for instance, are people who leave the company being notified of their entitlement? Then you could argue that simplification would leave everyone, including the administrator, better off. Try to get the pensions manager involved in the negotiations, if you think he'll be on your side on this one. (In chapter 7, section 3, 'Negotiating bodies', pages 213–18, we go into the question of who should be involved in negotiations.)

7.4. Lump sum schemes

Typical arrangements and possible improvements

Most schemes make provision for you to have a cash sum on retirement, but it is usually done by cashing in a part of your pension. This is dealt with under section 9, 'Commutation', pages 113–16. However, there are two types of scheme which give you a lump sum automatically on retirement.

The first are **public sector** schemes (along with some private sector ones that have followed their pattern). For instance, the Local Authorities, the Health Service, and the Civil Service schemes give you a pension of 1/80th per year of service, plus a lump sum of 3/80ths per year of service. The Inland Revenue, and the experts, assume that the 1/80th plus 3/80ths lump sum scheme is of the same *value* as a 1/60 scheme.

There are no particular advantages to this method as opposed to the more usual one; it's simply a pattern that's grown up. If anything, there's the *disadvantage* that inflation proofing applies only to the pension, not the lump sum, and the pension is smaller than it would otherwise be.

The other sort of scheme is the **cash benefit** scheme. These have grown in importance since 1978, and there are now quite a few in existence. The basic principle is that, instead of providing a pension at retirement or early retirement, the scheme gives a lump sum (which is tax free) and then has no more responsibility. This makes it simple to administer, and it can be popular with part time workers, who would not normally build up a worthwhile pension on the basis of their earnings.

A typical scheme of this sort would give:

■ 3/80ths of final earnings for each year of service, on retirement,

■ 3/80ths of final earnings for each year of actual and prospective service (the years you could have done up to 60 or 65)

for anyone who has to retire early because of ill health bad enough to prevent him/her from doing another job, and

■ a death benefit of $1\frac{1}{2}$ times final earnings.

The *disadvantage* of this sort of scheme is that, because of the Inland Revenue restrictions on how much you can take as a lump sum on retirement ($1\frac{1}{2}$ times final earnings), it can be pitched only at a fairly low level. In the example above, you could improve the death benefit, and/or you could get the full amount of cash benefit paid after 20 rather than 40 years ('acceleration'), but that is all. It is however, quite possible to start on this sort of scheme, and then build a full pension scheme on top.

> Pilkington's began wih a scheme of this type, then *added* a pension of 1/80th of revalued average earnings per year of service, and contracted out two years later.

A 'cash benefit' scheme of this sort ought to be non-contributory, despite the disadvantages outlined on pages 81–82. It will only cost 3% or 4% of payroll, and if the company is collecting very small contributions from the members it will cost a lot in administration, and also involve the need to make some very small refunds. If the company insist that it **must** be contributory, as some do, then you'll have to decide whether the attractions outweigh the annoyances.

As well as these two main types, there are also some 'hybrid' schemes, where the remains of an old 'lump sum' scheme, on a flat rate basis, has been added to a final earnings scheme.

> Lead Industries Group gives a pension plus a cash sum of £10 for each year of service.

There are also schemes that give you **only** a flat rate lump sum, unrelated to earnings.

> Christian Salvesen gives a lump sum of £50 per year of service.

If you are in a scheme of this type, then your first negotiating aim must be to get the lump sum linked to actual earnings, so that however much value it has lost since it was introduced, it will not now lose any more. It may be that it will need to be at a rate that gives most people no immediate increase in benefit, to get the employer to agree to it at all. In the example given above, for instance, of Christian Salvesen, you might seek ½ **a week's** earnings, or £50 if greater, for each year of service. If you can't get this, you'll have to ensure that you go in and renegotiate an increase to keep up with the cost of living, every year.

Possible arguments and responses

Arguments you can use for 'accelerating' the lump sum are:

■ Very few people stay with a company longer than 20 years, and the reason you have this sort of scheme, rather than a full pension scheme, is presumably because the company recognises that there is a fairly high staff turnover.

■ If there are a lot of married women workers (which is often the case with companies which have schemes of this sort) they will often have come back to paid work when their children are grown up, and so 20 years or so will be a fairly standard working lifetime.

■ For those who **do** stay longer, the benefit will still be increasing as it is linked to the increase in wages, so this group will not lose.

The employer will probably talk about the need to reward long service and loyalty – in which case, ask him to put his money where his mouth is by introducing a *full* pension scheme. His real objection will be cost. The scheme will cost more because he'll be paying out full benefit to more people – so you will be arguing straightforwardly about how much he can *really* afford.

If your scheme gives **less** than the Inland Revenue maximum, then again it's straightforward – you're asking for a bigger lump sum because you feel your members deserve a bigger lump sum. You could add that:

■ it's tax effective, both for the employer and the employees, and

■ it's a good advertisement for the firm.

7.5. Other types of scheme

Typical arrangements and possible improvements

If your scheme is not a final earnings or revalued average earnings type, trying to get an improvement in the accrual rate as the scheme stands is very much a fallback position. First of all, you should be trying to get the whole basis of the scheme changed. If you're stuck with your scheme, and the company won't budge, the following points are worth remembering:

■ In a **money purchase** scheme, there is an arithmetical relationship between the amount that goes in and the amount that comes out as pension. There may well be 'bonuses' declared by the insurance company, as well as the guaranteed pension, but it will not be possible to negotiate with them to get a better deal, although when interest rates are high they may be doing very nicely. So if you want to improve the pension, either the company or you – and preferably the company – must put in a higher contribution.

■ In a **career average earnings** scheme, there is an accrual rate, and improving it will improve the pension, as it does in a final earnings scheme; going from 1/80th to 1/60th will give a one-third better pension. But it still won't be good, because inflation will eat away at it so quickly.

■ In a **flat rate** scheme, if you can't get it improved drastically, the next best thing is to get the sum payable per year of service linked to earnings or the Retail Prices Index, so that it increases automatically. If you can't get that, you'll have to go in each year and negotiate for an increase in line with inflation.

■ If you've got a really small amount coming to you for each year of service out of a flat rate scheme, it might well be worth 'trading in' for a tax free lump sum on retirement (see section 7.4 above, pages 100–2). Even if your employer won't put a penny extra into the scheme the cash sum will be worth a lot more at the point of retirement than a trivial pension going on for years will be. For every £1 of pension per year you give up, you should expect to get at least £9 lump sum for men, and £11 for women (the difference is because women retire earlier and live longer, so they are expected to draw their pension for longer).

Uniroyal converted their old flat rate pension into a lump sum on retirement, and gave £54 to a man, £66 to a woman, on retirement, for each year's service, in return for giving up a £6 a year pension.

Possible arguments and responses

For money purchase schemes, the argument will be simply about the adequacy of the benefit provided, especially for the older, shorter service employee. Then it will come down to negotiating about cost. How much is the employer prepared to provide to make the scheme better?

For the other types, career average earnings and flat rate schemes, your strongest argument is that the fund, being largely unaffected by inflation, will be doing very nicely out of the high interest rates that tend to go with inflation. Many of these schemes are pretty ancient, and will have been devised in very different conditions, so the members' contributions that are being paid in will be far more generous than are needed in current conditions. What's happening, therefore, to the surplus? Is it piling up in the fund, or is it effectively benefiting the employer, because his contribution is being reduced? It *ought* to be used to make improvements in the scheme. There is no point in keeping it in the fund because the fund is not taking a risk, being unaffected by inflation.

> Ransome Hoffman Pollard, with a career average earnings scheme, had a surplus of £790,000 on the actuarial valuation in 1980. [See pages 226–38 for an explanation of this.] They used up 10% of it to pay for an increase in the pensions actually payable, and the unions then argued that they should use all the rest to improve benefits.

Your other strong argument is that while on wages the employer accepts that they should be increased broadly in line with the cost of living, pay policies etc allowing, on pensions he is actually *reducing* your expectations, in real terms, by not increasing the pension or changing the pension scheme. If he accepts that pensions are deferred pay, then he must agree that this is an intolerable position.

The employer will argue that there is no guarantee that high interest rates will continue for long, and therefore they ought not to use the 'windfall' as a reason for changing the pension scheme. This is rather like the argument that inflation is only temporary, which we looked at on page 68. For the last 10 years interest rates have been at levels which are astronomically high by prewar standards – long enough for a 'temporary' windfall to become permanent.

What *may* be behind the employer's resistance to improving a scheme of this sort is a dislike of the whole concept of pensions, and therefore a hope that, if the scheme deteriorates steadily because of inflation, the members will lose interest in it and allow it to be wound up without too much of a fuss. If you suspect this is what's happening, make sure you carry on putting in claims year after year, so the employer knows you're still interested, even if you get nowhere.

In the end, if you're trapped in a *really* bad scheme, it may be worth allowing yourselves to be bought out – on good terms. But try all the arguments first.

Section 8: Past service

What you must have

The Social Security Pensions Act does not say anything about providing past service entitlement. The only limit it does impose is that you can't be contracted out retrospectively. So if a company is introducing a contracted out pension scheme and wants to credit you with previous years, it will have to accept the fact that from 1978 to the date you're contracted out, you'll already have a State additional pension due to you.

What the Inland Revenue allows

As before, the Inland Revenue's only interest is in seeing that you don't exceed the 2/3rds limit overall. Any frozen pension, and any credit from a previous scheme, counts fully towards those limits. If a scheme that reached the Inland Revenue limits gave full past service entitlement, therefore, the very long serving employees might need to have their benefits restricted, but otherwise there is unlikely to be any effect.

The granting of full past service where there wasn't a scheme before is very rare. The better, larger schemes do tend to pick up and give credit for service in **previous schemes** when they introduce a new scheme or take over a new company.

The question of mergers and takeovers is complicated, so we have put it in chapter 10, separately, so that all aspects can be covered in the same place.

If the past service you are negotiating about arises from service in a *previous* company, turn to that chapter.

This section is divided into:

8.1. Credited years where there was **no** previous scheme, and

8.2. Benefits under a discontinued scheme.

8.1. Credited years with no previous scheme

Typical arrangements and possible improvements

What do we mean by this? Let us assume that Rich Idiots & Co are persuaded to be good employers at last, and introduce a pension scheme, in 1981. With a sudden fit of social conscience, Rich Idiots decide to atone for past neglect and give all their 50 employees, none of whom has less than 20 years' service, 20 years' credit at the full rate, in the scheme when it begins.

> Wat Tyler is 55 and has worked for Rich Idiots for 20 years by 1981.
> When he retires in 1991, he will have 30 years' worth of pension – 10
> years in the scheme, and 20 credits for past service.

That's the theory, anyway. In practice, it is far more usual for
a new scheme either to give no credit, or to give credit at a much
reduced rate.

> Jenks & Cattell (a real company) give a lump sum of 1¼ weeks' pay for
> every year of service after 1980, and ¾ week's pay for each year before,
> to a maximum of 30 years.

Frequently, a company that is introducing a new scheme will
say that it feels it is taking on a big enough financial commitment for
the moment, and that it would prefer to 'wait and see how things go'
before giving entitlement for past service. If you accept this, you'll
need to ensure that you return to the question in later years.

Giving past service entitlement is expensive, because the
money must be paid in at current values, not at the value it would
have been at if the scheme had been running a few years ago. The
scheme contribution *should* come entirely from the company, and
the money will not have so long to earn interest, so that *more* will
have to be paid in for each £ of pension it is expected to get out.

The company can, quite legitimately, spread the cost by
what's called 'controlled funding', a sort of hire purchase system,
which means it decides what total amount it has to pay, and then
divides the bill up over 10 or 20 years. So the burden is not as
enormous as the company may make out.

Past service credits benefit most those who have been with the
company longest. If the company or plant is fairly new, you may not
need to give them much priority; equally, in that case they would
not cost the company much to provide. On the other hand, if you
have a large group of long serving members who are going out of the
door with pitiful amounts, then you may feel it is very important –
to the extent of younger members giving up for the moment a claim
for an increase in the overall pension.

The *best* standard is to get full past service entitlement –
1/60th in a 1/60ths scheme, and so on. Though you might wish to
claim this as a negotiating point, it would not be realistic to expect
agreement on it. More possible would be a **half** accrual rate –
1/120th in a 1/60th scheme, 1/160th in a 1/80th scheme, and so on.

Don't forget, if you're increasing the **current** service accrual rate at any time, to ask for the past service rate to be increased also.

If this level is not achievable, even a smaller fraction is better than nothing. If the company refuses even that, you *could* try a phased approach. For instance, you could say that anyone retiring in the next 10 years, with 10 years' service or more, should have credits given to make up their pension to the 10 years' level. Thus:

■ anyone retiring now would get 10 years' credit;

■ next year, they would get 1 year's actual pension and 9 years' credit;

■ the year after, they'd get 2 years' pension and 8 years' credit; and so on.

This would very much reduce the cost, and also mean that management could see an end to their commitment.

Some companies have reduced the cost by limiting the rights of those who leave in the *first* few years of the scheme.

Thus, Steetley Chemical Company's booklet says:

If you retire at normal pension date, your pension will be calculated like this:

number of years ÷ 80 × final pensionable earnings

plus, for men aged up to 55 and women up to 50 who join the scheme at 6 April 1978,

years of past service ÷ 160 × final pensionable earnings.

Past service pensions for members who leave the service of the company: members who leave service after 5 April 1979 will receive an extra pension of

special factor × years of past service ÷ 160 × final pensionable earnings.

Special factor depends on date of leaving:

Year of leaving 6 April to 5 April	Special factor
1979/80	0.1
1980/81	0.2
1981/82	0.3
1982/83	0.4
1983/84	0.5
1984/85	0.6
1985/86	0.7
1986/87	0.8
1987/88	0.9

Members leaving service after 5 April 1988 will receive a full past service pension.

Members who leave service before 6 April 1979 will receive no past service pension.

This is not a good arrangement, as it gives least to those who need it most, and it should only be accepted if you can get nothing better.

One *important* point always is to get the credits expressed in terms of final salary, so that they keep up with wage increases. Otherwise, they will be eroded by inflation in a very short time.

Possible arguments and responses

The essence of your argument would be that it is unfair for the company to make provision for the future, without being prepared to do something for those who have already given their lives to the company. Some points you can use to develop your argument are:

■ Younger people have time ahead of them anyway to build up a pension. People coming up to retirement age, however, will get little or nothing out of a new pension scheme for future service only, however good it is.

■ If the company are prepared to put a substantial sum of money into a pension scheme, they ought not to discriminate between their employees by giving the vast bulk of the value of it to younger people.

■ The pension scheme will get off to a very bad start if people who have been promised big pensions in 40 years' time see the first people to retire under the new scheme go out with miserable pittances. They will be very cynical about the scheme, and all the goodwill the company was hoping to generate by introducing it will be dissipated.

■ The company obviously agree that there is a need for the pension scheme, and that the State scheme isn't adequate, or they wouldn't be putting in a scheme at all. Surely therefore they must acknowledge that the case for a benefit for the people nearest retirement is strongest of all, because they don't *even* have much in the State scheme to fall back on.

The company may say:

■ 'It costs too much.' As we said above, it must be acknowledged that past service *is* expensive. But do they appreciate the priority you're giving this point?

■ 'We've got to start somewhere – we can't do everything at once.' But people near retirement can't wait until you've got everything else right, and then get around to dealing with them.

■ 'They can't expect to get a benefit now which they haven't paid for over the years.' The company has made bigger profits over the years because it hasn't had to siphon off some of the money into a pension fund. Isn't it time they gave some of the cash back to those who made the profits for them?

8.2. Benefits under a discontinued scheme

Typical arrangements and possible improvements

Perhaps more usual than a scheme starting off with a completely clean slate, is for the company to decide to clear up its old schemes and put everyone into a new, better one. The general tendency in the past has been to freeze the old benefits, and you will find this sort of phrase in the booklet:

(taken from Clancy Ltd's booklet)
'. . . if you were a member of the pension and life assurance plan (1973) you will receive in addition the pension that has accrued to you under the existing plan in respect of your membership up to 30 September 1977.'

It's often not clear from the pension scheme booklet just what has happened to the old scheme benefits, and the only way to find out may be to ask the scheme administrator.

If the benefits are frozen, this means that your entitlement is worked out, on the day when the changeover comes, **as if you were leaving the company**, so that your pension is preserved for you when you retire, at the level it is then.

Brian Heatley retires in 1988 after 20 years with the same company. Ten years ago, in 1978, the pension scheme was changed from 1/120th to 1/60th, and generally improved because of contracting out. His old scheme benefits were frozen. So when he comes to retire, he has 10 years' pension at 1/60th, based on his earnings in 1988, and 10 years' pension at 1/120th, based on his earnings in *1978*.

With the current rate of inflation, a frozen pension loses its value very quickly. The unions have only recently got wise to this. Like so many others, it's a problem that matters much more during inflationary times than otherwise.

Ideally, when a new scheme is started, you should see that the old ones are 'brought in' and full past service credits given in return. This will mean that each member must sign a form giving up his/her rights to the benefits under the old scheme, and these are paid over to the new fund to help finance the credits. Assuming you've got a good deal, you'll probably need to make a pretty strong recommendation to the members, *and* make sure the company gives a clear explanation, to overcome people's understandable suspicion of signing away anything on the company's say-so.

If you have missed the opportunity when the new scheme came in, it's something you can pick up at any time, although your bargaining position will not be strong.

> BOC, for instance, decided in 1980 to increase, in line with the rise in their wage levels, the pensions frozen in 1975.

If the old scheme (or one of the old schemes, because you will often be dealing with clearing up several), was much worse than the new one, then the employer will usually resist giving *full* credit. A reasonable fallback position would be to look at how much the pension accrued so far per year is worth, on average, in money terms, and then turn that into the new scheme's final salary terms.

> Mike Jupp has worked 10 years for the company, and has accrued **old** scheme pension of £200. Under the new scheme he would have had £600 for the same length of time. So you can then turn his service into credits at 1/3rd the rate being provided in the new scheme.

This would mean a 1/240th rate in a 1/80th scheme, for example. *But* this should be the point at which you *settle*, not where you start negotiating.

In any settlement, you always need a 'no worse off' clause. Someone who retires in the next few years and whose salary has dropped sharply *might* be better off under the old scheme than under the new one, so the company ought to do the two calculations at least for a few years, and pay the better.

> When SKF brought in a new works scheme, instead of their old arrangement, they said:
> 'If you joined the plan on 6 April 1978, your pension entitlement for prior continuous service will be based on 1/3rd of such service, or the following table, whichever is the better:
>
> | Years of works service prior to 6 April 1978 | Minimum pension per annum |
> |---|---|
> | 10–19 | 176 |
> | 20–29 | 264 |
> | 30–34 | 352 |
> | 35 or more | 440 |

Where the pension scheme previously was **voluntary**, you'll find it difficult to get agreement that the people who did not volunteer should be included, and your own members might well resent it if they were. *But* if you believe that people were not genuinely given the chance to join – if, for instance, the scheme was theoretically open to both staff and works, but at a lot of sites manual workers were heavily discouraged from joining, whereas it was taken for granted that staff would – then you should press for everyone to be included.

If a particular group was specifically **excluded** from the old scheme, which will often be the case where women were kept out of the scheme, then they should be brought in on the same terms as those who were in, and this should be regarded as the remedying of past injustice and therefore should not involve any extra cost to the members.

If your old scheme was **very** poor, the company may say that the credits given in the new scheme would be so small it would not be worthwhile. This might apply, for instance, if it was an old £6 a year scheme. In that case, the *least* they should do is agree to increase the frozen pension by x% per year compound, from the date the scheme was frozen until the date a person retires, and including deferred pension for those who leave. Given current levels of interest rates, this should not be less than a 10% increase, and preferably more.

> Joanna Smith has a frozen pension in the old scheme which was discontinued three years ago, worth £100 a year. The company agree to increase it by 10% compound, backdated for the three years. So it is now worth £133.10. Five years later, when she retires, it is worth £214.36.

Finally, if the old scheme pensions are invested with an insurance company, there may be problems.

■ They may take a very long time to give information, let alone to get a settlement. While the policy is still with them, it still counts as business.

■ When a settlement is reached, the insurance company may give the new pension fund a very bad deal on the 'surrender terms' just as they do if you give up a private insurance policy before the time is up. The company may well try to argue that they can't afford to give you a better credit for past service because of this, but there's no reason why you should suffer because of the insurance company's commercial practices. You could always embarrass them by asking them along to explain themselves.

Possible arguments and responses

The arguments given in the previous section, 8.1, on pages 105–9 apply here too, because again it will be the older people, with long service in the old scheme, who will suffer most if they find their benefits frozen. In addition, some other arguments you could use are:

▪ The unforeseen effects of inflation. Perhaps in the past it did not look unreasonable to do this, and people felt they would get value for money. But the situation *has changed*, because of continuing inflation, and changes in the treatment of old scheme benefits are also urgent.

▪ The destruction of people's expectations. People worked for the company, under the old scheme, on the assumption that they were going to get a particular pension benefit out of it. Maybe they paid a particular level of contribution, maybe they accepted a particular level of wages because of this. Now, without their taking any action, they find that the benefits have changed (and worsened). If they had left that job, to go and better themselves, that might have been fair enough – but they stuck it out, and therefore ought to be reasonably treated.

The answers you will get from the company will once again be basically about cost, but they may be wrapped up in other ways:

▪ 'It's not company policy to do this.' That is, the board have decided it will cost too much. If you've been negotiating at local level and you come up against this brick wall, try to get the opportunity to put your case to the board (see pages 214–15 for the need for central negotiations.) If possible, contact people in other plants with a similar problem, and get them to make a joint approach with you.

▪ 'We can't make a special case of this plant.' You should make clear that (unless there are genuinely special circumstances) they're not being asked to – what is being sought is a better deal for everyone in discontinued schemes, even though that raises the cost

▪ (Where you're picking up something that happened a few years ago). 'No one complained at the time.' This may well be true, firstly because unions were not as interested in pensions as they should have been and employers would not generally talk to them about it anyway, and secondly because inflation was not such a problem then. But it cannot be regarded as a closed issue, because the frozen pensions are *continuing* to lose value.

If you can get beyond all these excuses and talk about cost, then perhaps you can get a serious dialogue going, and even if you can't obtain all you want, you may be able to achieve something. Once the company have decided they want to give *some* credit for benefits under the discontinued scheme, then the argument is straightforwardly about how much they can afford to do.

You may also need to talk about *comparative* value for money. If they're buying out several schemes, are they giving each group the right terms? If not, those who are being badly done by should have better terms, but without of course worsening the position of those coming off better.

Section 9: Commutation

What you must have

Commutation means the chance to **convert** some of your pension, when you retire, into a lump sum.

If you're contracted out, you *must not* commute any of the guaranteed minimum pension, or the widow's GMP. They must always be kept as pension. The only exception to this is if either of them are *trivial* – which means under £52 a year, or £1 a week.

Your scheme rules *may* allow you to commute any equivalent pension benefit left over from the old graduated scheme (see appendix II).

Under the Social Security Act (No 2) (1980), you are not entitled to supplementary benefit if you have more than £2000 capital, and this would include cash from a commuted pension. But any cash you get from commutation is **tax free**.

What the Inland Revenue allows

The Inland Revenue restrictions have already been partly dealt with under section 7 (pages 100–2). It is a firm rule that you may not take more than $1\frac{1}{2}$ times your final earnings as a lump sum, whether it comes automatically (as in the case of the Civil Service scheme) or you have to give up some of your pension to get it. You can have that $1\frac{1}{2}$ times salary after 20 years – if your service is shorter, the maximum allowed is less. There are 2 exceptions to this, which are dealt with later (page 114). Any other cash benefit provided by the scheme (or any other scheme with the same employer) must be counted against the total.

The Inland Revenue also control the **commutation factors** – that is, what lump sum you get for each pound of pension you give up. Practice Note 8.14 of the Inland Revenue notes (IR12) sets out the standard commutation factors which are £9 lump sum for each £1 of pension given up by a man, £11 for each £1 given up by a woman.

Alternatively, a scheme may allow for the commutation factors to be calculated by a qualified actuary in every case. These will tend at the moment to give you less cash than the standard rates, but this may change if interest rates go down. The 'actuarially correct' commutation rate would be about £7 for each £1 of pension, for a man of 65. Some schemes have special factors, which will have been agreed with the Inland Revenue. If a scheme has a different retirement age from the normal, it would have a different commutation factor from the usual one too. And if someone is retiring **early**, s/he would expect to get a different lump sum per £1 of pension also.

What are the exceptions to the $1\frac{1}{2}$ times rule?

■ First, trivial pensions. Where the pension would be less than £52 per year, this can be fully commuted regardless of the amount of lump sum that will be payable as a result.

■ Second, serious ill health. This description is intended, say the Inland Revenue, to be interpreted narrowly, and it applies essentially to people 'where the expectation of life is unquestionably very short, by comparison with the average for the same age and sex'. Practice Note 8.11 says: 'Whether a particular individual is in this position is a matter for decision by the administrator, but the inclusion of a rule on these lines in an approved scheme is accepted on condition that it will be interpreted invariably in this sense, and that adequate medical evidence will always be obtained.'

Both these exceptions, of course, are only what is *permitted*. Whether it actually happens in any particular scheme depends on what is in that scheme's rules.

Typical arrangements and possible improvements

The previous 'Old Code' followed by the Inland Revenue until the 1970 Finance Act came into force had a different formula for the maximum commutation: you were not allowed to convert more than $\frac{1}{4}$ of your **pension** into a lump sum. This formula, which is usually more restrictive, still occurs in some schemes which haven't bothered to change it.

Most schemes have now gone over to the 'New Code' formula, and allow you to commute, on the 'standard' factors, up to $1\frac{1}{2}$ times your final salary. The maximum is frequently only allowed after 40 years' service, rather than the 20 years the Inland Revenue allows. It will usually be based on a straight calculation of 3/80ths of earnings per year of service which gives you 120/80ths after 40 years.

Some scheme booklets don't give you details of the commutation factor.

> The McKechnie Group booklet says: 'When you reach retirement you may, before your pension becomes payable, normally commute part of your pension for a tax free cash sum. The amount of pension you may cash, and the rate at which pension may be cashed, cannot be specified in advance, but you will be given full details when you retire.'

In other cases it may be different from the standard rate.

Very few schemes say in their booklets that they allow full commutation for triviality or ill health, but in fact many of them do have these clauses in their rules.

Occasionally, a scheme booklet says that you must have the employer's or trustees' consent before you commute any pension. This is distinctly paternalistic, and needs to be discouraged.

If your scheme has less than the Inland Revenue maximum, you should look for the maximum on this – 1½ times earnings available as a lump sum after 20 years, subject to the GMP, of course, in a contracted out scheme having to remain as pension.

■ If the pension is automatically increased to take account of inflation, it's worth more in lump sum terms. You could try to get the commutation factors increased because of this – but very few schemes do.

■ The amount you commute should have no effect on the anmount of pension the widow/er gets – that should be 50%, or 2/3rds or whatever, of the member's pension *before* commutation.

■ Are people being correctly informed about their option to commute when they retire, and are they being given sufficient time for this? One of the advantages of commutation is that, with current interest rates, you can go out and buy yourself an annuity that is higher than the pension you have given up (and is more favourably treated for tax purposes). *But* it will not be increased, whereas the pension may be. Are people advised of this, and given an idea of how to go about getting an annuity?

Possible arguments and responses

This is an area where the **cost** factor doesn't matter much. The Inland Revenue standard formula is more generous than the strict actuarial rates, but not by much. A change in the commutation factors would not usually be regarded as significant enough to alter the costing of the scheme. What other objections can employers have to commutation?

■ Paternalism. 'The workers won't know what's best for them, and will go out and spend it on the Derby favourite, and then come to us and say they don't have money to live on.' You should point out that you are talking about 65 year olds, not 6 year olds, and if the employer thinks his workers are so stupid, why has he been employing them all these years?

■ Inertia. The pension scheme administrator does not want to go through all the bother of changing the rules. It's true that rule changes can be a nuisance, and if this is the only rule needing changes the administrator might have a point. But unless you're in a perfect pension scheme, it won't be the only change you want, so you might as well put a batch through at once.

Section 10: Early retirement

What you must have

The Social Security Pensions Act does not lay down any minimum rules for early retirement, for contracted out schemes. If you retire early because of ill health, and are entitled to an invalidity pension, then you will always be treated as if your scheme does not give a pension under those conditions. You'll therefore be given by the State an earnings related addition to your invalidity benefit. If on top of that you get the benefit from your private scheme, the State does not want to know.

If you retire early due to any other reason, the State is not interested either, and does not pay you any benefit because of it. Apart from the Job Release scheme, there is no State provision for flexible retirement. If you leave your job before 65 for a man, 60 for a woman, you will be treated as unemployed, and get National Insurance benefit for a year, *provided* that your pension is less than £35 a week, and you are regarded as available for work. Following that, if your income isn't adequate for you to live on, you'll have to rely on Supplementary Benefit, paid at the short term rate.

What a contracted out scheme *does* have to do, though, is guarantee that, when someone retires early, s/he is paid the GMP s/he was due on the date s/he left, plus $8\frac{1}{2}\%$ compound per year, or 5% plus the limited revaluation premium, when s/he reaches normal retirement date. In other words, they must be treated just the same as anyone else leaving the company, for any reason. (See pages 21–22 for an explanation of this.) A scheme can do this by:

■ paying only, as early retirement pension, the amount over and above what is needed to pay the GMP at 60 or 65. So if there was £150 pension accrued for that person, and £100 of it was needed to preserve the GMP, the early retirement pension would be only £50; or

■ restricting the circumstances in which an early retirement pension is paid, so that, if there is only enough in the scheme to cover the escalated GMP, or not even enough, then the person can get no early retirement pension at all; or

■ the scheme can pay the pension the person is entitled to at the date of early retirement, and guarantee to increase it when s/he reaches 60 or 65.

The 3rd method is the best for the member, but the 1st and 2nd have slipped unnoticed into a lot of schemes. The liability for widow's GMP applies in the same way.

What the Inland Revenue allows

The Inland Revenue sees 3 different circumstances in which early retirement might happen:

■ through ill health,
■ through redundancy, and
■ 'at the member's own request'.

For **ill health**, which the Inland Revenue call 'incapacity', they are quite generous, provided you stick to the rules. Practice Note 10.6 defines incapacity as 'physical or mental deterioration which is bad enough to prevent an individual from following his normal employment, or which seriously impairs his earning capacity. It does not mean simply a decline in energy or ability.'

For anyone who fits into this definition, the scheme may give a pension based on his/her pensionable earnings at the date when s/he retires, and on all his/her **actual plus potential service**. Someone retiring because of incapacity is also entitled to calculate their maximum lump sum (whether automatic or through commutation) on their actual plus prospective service. S/he is also entitled to continue the life assurance up to the normal retirement date, but not beyond it.

Sheona York is 55, and has been in the pension scheme 15 years. When she has a heart attack and has to retire, she **may**, under the Inland

Revenue rules, get a pension based on 15 years' actual service plus the 5 years she could have done up to retirement date, that is, 20 altogether. She can also calculate her lump sum on the basis of 20 years' service.

For **redundancy**, or as it's sometimes called 'retirement in the interests of company efficiency', the Inland Revenue will *in practice* allow the same rules to be followed. However, they will not include it in their Practice Notes, presumably in case people start taking advantage of it, and so if a company wants to put these provisions in its scheme rules, it will have to apply separately to the Superannuation Funds Office for permission. But this would not normally be refused.

Any payment made under a pension scheme need not be set against payments made under a redundancy scheme, for tax or other purposes. It may, however, affect your rights to unemployment benefit or supplementary benefit.

For retirement **'at the member's own request'**, the limits are much tighter. The scheme may give a pension based on *actual* service only. It need not, however, reduce it further because it's being paid early. The Inland Revenue will not let anyone retire early for this reason below the age of 50 (or 45 for women if their scheme retirement age is 55 or less).

The lump sum that can be taken is also restricted, in a rather complicated way, and in general the maximum will be considerably less than the $1\frac{1}{2}$ times formula.

Alternative schemes

This section is divided into:

10.1. Ill health, and

10.2. 'At the member's own request'

It should be pointed out that there is an **alternative** method of coping with ill health, called **permanent health insurance**. In effect, this is long term sick pay. Where it exists, it is a separate scheme from the pensions, so we have a separate chapter on this (chapter 5). If this is an area where you want to make improvements, you should read that chapter after you've read section 10.1 below.

Redundancy retirement is also dealt with separately, in chapter 10.

10.1. Ill health

Typical arrangements and possible improvements

The NAPF 1979 survey showed that 16% of staff, and a mere

8% of works members were given the Inland Revenue maximum allowed for retirement on health grounds. But whereas a certain number of staff were covered by permanent health insurance instead, very few works people were. There are many hourly paid members who, however ill they are, are treated by the scheme in exactly the same way as if they were retiring early of their own free will.

There are some schemes with good benefits around.

Rank Xerox say:
'If you are retiring early because of serious ill health your pension will be calculated in the normal way but will not be reduced for early payment and will include full credit for your remaining service to normal retirement date. What constitutes serious ill health will be decided by the trustees of the scheme, having regard to medical advice.'

Some schemes give half, rather than full, prospective service – Tube Investments and BOC do this. Others give this only if you fulfil a service qualification. ICI for instance has a 10 years' service qualification, and Dickinson Robinson Group 5 years.

The public sector has a pattern of its own.

The Civil Service, local government, NHS, teachers and the Post Office, all give a partially increased pension for members who have completed 5 years' service, calculated as follows:
* service between 5 and 10 years is doubled;
* service between 10 and $13\frac{1}{3}$ years is made up to 20;
* over $13\frac{1}{3}$ years, $6\frac{2}{3}$ years are added.
In each case, the addition must not increase service to more than 40 years or beyond age 65.

There are some schemes with a two tier definition of incapacity, giving an increased pension for the really bad cases, but merely not reducing the actual pension for less bad cases.

The Delta Staff Scheme says:
'What happens if I cannot work because of ill health or disablement?
'If in the opinion of the trustees there is adequate medical evidence that you cannot follow your normal employment and no suitable alternative employment is available, then irrespective of age you could be paid an immediate pension which would be calculated on a more favourable basis than that [for ordinary early retirement].
'What happens if I become totally incapacitated?
'If you are over age 50 and have completed at least 10 years' service in the group then subject to adequate medical evidence you could be paid your full pension immediately.'

This is not satisfactory, as it creates too many borderline cases.

Other schemes give only what they would give in any other early retirement.

> The Francis Sumner Group says: 'subject to the consent of the trustees and your employing company, you may retire and immediately receive a reduced pension, at any time after attaining age 50, or at any time on account of serious ill health'.

There is *usually* a clause in the rules saying that the pension can be 'augmented' (that is, increased), in cases of particularly bad health. If you press for an improvement in the general provision, you may be told it's not necessary as the trustees always look sympathetically at difficult cases. If this is really true, it would cost no more to put it fully into the rules.

However carefully the rules are drawn up, however, this is an area where the trustees will always have some discretion. They will have to decide whether a particular case does or does not fulfil the definitions.

Improving this provision is not very expensive, unless your company has a particularly bad health record. For the average company it would cost less than $\frac{1}{2}\%$. Smaller companies may be wary of it, because the potential cost of a young person struck down by a serious disease can be huge. But this can be dealt with by insuring against that risk. The negotiating aim should be a pension based on all actual plus prospective service, without a service qualification. If you can't get that, the first concession would be to allow a service qualification to creep in. This would affect comparatively few people, as it's mainly older people, who will often have been with the company quite a while, who need to retire early because of ill health.

The service clause tends to be included because of the pension administrators' usual fear of being taken advantage of. It is a myth that seriously ill people are in a position to shop around and choose a company that has a good pension benefit that they can collect the day after they've started.

Other points to watch are:

■ The company may insist on a definition of incapacity more rigorous than the Inland Revenue's. They may, for instance, say that you can't have a pension if you are fit to do *any* job, regardless of whether or not there's a job to do. The more restrictive the wording, the fewer people will be eligible, and the less it will cost.

■ It is quite possible to arrange things so that someone who can only take **part time** employment, because of disability, can get a part pension, and this can be helpful. You do need to make sure that this is being properly administered, and not abused.

■ Any increases in pensions in payment, whether funded in advance or not, should also be payable to early retirees.

■ In general, the administration of this item needs to be carefully monitored, by the trustees if they include shop floor members of the scheme, by the shop stewards if not. It is not unknown for senior managers to be retired early 'due to ill health' when the company has really decided it just doesn't want them in the job. If they don't in fact qualify, then it's an abuse of the scheme, and will cost the pension fund money which could be used for other members. If the company want to retire someone and make a *special* payment into the fund, then it's open to them to do so.

■ At the other end of the scale, are the ordinary members who *might* qualify getting proper information? Are workers who have taken a lot of time off due to sickness being pressured to leave, rather than retire early? Do local management, who will be the first 'official' point of enquiry, know the conditions?

■ The company may say that anyone seeking early retirement due to ill health must have a doctor's examination in addition to any evidence from their GP. This is fair enough, as GPs' diagnoses do vary a great deal in quality, but the doctor doing the examination should be someone you can trust, and should be responsible to the **trustees**, not the company. There ought to be clearly laid down procedures in cases of dispute.

■ The life assurance should continue. Someone who's had to retire sick will find it virtually impossible to get private life assurance at all, let alone at a price s/he can afford.

Possible arguments and responses

The general arguments here are:

■ First, that the whole idea of a pension scheme is to protect you and your dependants against the time when you cannot work – whether because you are too old, which is a foreseeable event, or because of an unforeseeable event like death in service. Serious ill health is a similar unforeseeable event, and ought to be treated as such within the pension scheme, by making provision for reasonably generous benefits to be paid out.

■ Second, **equity**. It is not in anyone's interest to put a premium on death. But unless you have a decent ill health benefit, the family of the person who just *doesn't* die in a car crash, but is an invalid for the rest of his/her life, will be much worse off than the family of the person who does die, who will at least have the death benefit and probably a widow/er's pension. This is a cruel and illogical situation.

Other points you can make are:

■ Without a proper early retirement provision, the company will be in an inefficient, and in the long run more expensive, position in which 'hard cases' are kept on the payroll out of sympathy, but are unable to do their jobs well. Keeping someone on the payroll incurs higher overheads than paying a decent early retirement pension, and may also mean that it blocks someone else from taking up that job. (This is *not* an argument, though, for forcing out people who want to continue to work even though their health is not really up to it. The partial pension suggested above should provide sufficient flexibility for them.)

■ One of the justifications for having a private pension scheme is to fill in the gaps in the State scheme. Although the State scheme does give some recognition of long term invalidity, it is not satisfactory – especially since the Tory government cut invalidity benefit in real terms in the Social Security (No 2) Act in 1980.

The employer's response will essentially be:

■ Cost. As we said above, this is not a very expensive benefit, and there are offsetting savings, in terms of efficiency, although these may not be very easily quantifiable. So you should view with suspicion any claim that it would be too expensive.

■ Fear of abuse. Especially if there has been what he regards as bad experience with the sick pay scheme, the employer may well suggest that 'too many people will take advantage of it'. If you are willing to agree to the safeguard of a genuinely independent medical examination, this should be enough. If the company is afraid that the trustees will not do a proper job, and will be a 'soft touch', then they should say so, and be forced to provide evidence.

■ 'Other companies in our field don't do this – we can't afford to be more generous than they are.' It's true that these benefits still apply to only a limited number of manual workers. But they are spreading. In the 1978 NAPF survey, only 11% of works schemes gave full actual **and** prospective service, compared to 16% in 1979.

It's a logical extension of the fact that sick pay schemes are also becoming much more widespread.

Management may also have a feeling about differentials. One of the long established traditions of British industry is that if anything drastic happens to managerial staff, they are looked after, whereas for manual workers and, for that matter, lower grade clerical staff, it's just too bad. Hence the habit, still to be found, of sacking manual workers who are off sick for long. Management may therefore not want to erode the difference in status. If you think this is behind their reluctance to improve in this area, bring it out into the open and ask them direct to justify it. The union view would be that *any* differential should be kept inside the job, and not extended to conditions of employment like this.

10.2. Retirement 'at the member's own request'

Typical arrangements and possible improvements

Many schemes provide only the minimum on this, which is to say that you must take a pension based on the service you have actually done, **minus** an amount for early payment. The justification for this is that:

■ the pension will be paid for longer, so the same amount of money must be spread over a larger number of payments; and

■ since the pension is being paid earlier, it will have less time to accumulate interest, so *more* money will have to be used up to provide the same level of pension.

There are 2 ways of calculating the amounts (also called 'factors') by which the pension is reduced.

■ A 'straight line' method may be used in which the pension is reduced by the same percentage per month or year of early retirement. The 'no cost' level is about $\frac{1}{2}$% per month (6% per year), so someone retiring 10 years early would have his/her pension reduced by 60%. Some schemes use this method but reduce by less than this; BOC, for instance, reduce by only 2% per year.

■ Or an actuarial scale may be used, showing the precise amount per year by which the pension must be reduced, to give the same actuarial value.

The Ofrex Group reduces the pension to:
* for retiring 1 year early   91%
* for retiring 2 years early   82%
* for retiring 3 years early   73%
* for retiring 4 years early   67%

The result is a very heavy reduction at the top end, as you can see, and is generally worse at all ages.

Some schemes make no actuarial reduction if you retire above a certain age, although often they include a service qualification. The public sector schemes, as usual, follow a particular pattern.

> The Local Government scheme, for instance, allows people to retire between 60 and 65, without a reduction in their pension, if they have over 25 years' service.

In the private sector, there are a few reasonably generous schemes.

> Ferranti make no reduction if a member retires within 2 years of normal retirement date. BOC and Volkswagen allow you to go up to 5 years before normal retirement date without reducing your pension.

Better than standard terms for early retirement are one way of moving towards shorter working time, as they allow people with long service with the company to go early without being penalised. It is expensive, however.

Many actuaries will assume that it will cost the same as giving a reduced age for normal retirement, because they believe that everyone who has the chance will take it. In fact this is not the case, because people with small pensions will not be able to *afford* to retire even if they want to. So you should argue with the company if they produce too high a costing for this. A reasonable level of cost would be around the 2% mark (but remember this is only a guideline). On page 233 there is an example of how an actuary treats this point, and you may find it useful to refer to this.

As management are likely to be in closer touch with the workforce than the actuary is, they may well agree with you. Even if they feel they have to be cautious to start with, and accept the costings given by the actuary, you can argue that experience will show these to be generous, and they will then be able to reduce the cost, or better still, use the extra to improve something else.

It is not realistic to ask for the Inland Revenue maximum here. A more limited claim might be:

■ that men retiring between the ages of 60 and 65 should have no actuarial reduction made; and

■ that where an actuarial reduction is made, it should be less than the 'no cost' level, e.g. 4%, or $\frac{1}{3}$% per month; or

■ at least, where a reduction is made, that it should be taken on the age at the next, rather than the last birthday; and in any case,

■ if you are in an **integrated** scheme (see pages 95–100), try to make sure that there is no deduction to take account of the State pension until it is actually paid.

If you want to go for a substantial improvement in this area, it may well be necessary to phase it in.

It will also be important to ensure that it isn't *misused* by local management, pressurising people coming up to 55 or 60 to take early retirement, rather than going through the more difficult operation of a redundancy programme. You should also check that 'borderline cases' are not being unreasonably pushed into early retirement 'at their own request' when it should really be due to ill health.

The option of earlier retirement is one of several methods of obtaining a shorter working life, as sought by the TUC, and this is how it should be presented. Management may, however, ask why you are looking for this rather than for reducing retirement age overall. The point to make here is that this is a more flexible method of achieving the same end. There is no point in saying that everyone *must* go at 60, if it means that substantial numbers of people will be pushed into poverty because their pensions are not big enough. If you say people *may* retire at 60, then those with pensions big enough to live on will do so, but others will stay on. If you wish, in a few years' time you may be able to reduce the retirement age generally, when the scheme has had longer to build up.

The company may say:

■ They shouldn't favour one group above others by providing a bigger pension than is actuarially sound for those who **choose** to go early. This is a phoney argument, because any item in a pension scheme favours the group that happens to fit in with it above other groups. If you die in service, you're more 'favourably treated', so far as the death benefits are concerned, than if you don't. The company are not being asked to *cut back* other benefits, they are being asked to put more money in.

■ They are not sure that people really want this, as opposed to having it dictated by the TUC. You'll need to do your own homework in order to counter this argument. But you can also suggest that, if *they* are right, the improvement is not going to cost very much because people won't take advantage of it, so they might as well do it anyway.

Section 11: Late retirement

What you must have

If you wish to work on beyond 65 (men) or 60 (women), you are allowed to **defer** your ordinary National Insurance pension for up to 5 years, and it increases by 1/7th% for each week it is deferred. You don't pay National Insurance contributions once you're over normal retirement age, but nor do you get any further credit.

The same applies to your State additional pension. You stop building up 80ths, but what you've got increases by 1/7th% for each week you defer. Your pension will be based when you retire on your earnings *then*, not on your earnings when you are 65/60.

A contracted out scheme must do the same. Its pension therefore must also increase by at least 1/7th% for each week it is deferred.

What the Inland Revenue allows

The Inland Revenue will let you go on accruing benefit after retirement age, up to a maximum of 5 years. Someone who worked until 70 (or 65 for a woman) could therefore get 45/60ths. The lump sum commutation can also be worked out in the same way.

Alternatively, the scheme can freeze the pension at normal retirement date and increase it either by an **actuarial factor**, or by the increase in the cost of living, whichever is the greater.

If someone dies in service after normal retirement date, s/he can have *either* the benefits given for death in service (see section 12 below, page 127, or s/he can be treated as if having retired the day before their death. It is also technically possible to 'retire' and draw your pension but carry on working.

Typical arrangements

Schemes will generally follow the Social Security Pensions Act minimum; sometimes they are more generous so far as the death benefit is concerned.

Late retirement is something trade unions would not normally wish to negotiate on. If an *individual* wishes to work beyond retirement age, for a particular reason, his/her union representative might want to support him/her, but negotiation of a late retirement scheme as such would be very rare. It goes against TUC policy, which is to reduce, not increase, working life.

We are therefore not covering this question further in this book, as it seems unlikely to be useful to readers.

Section 12: Lump sum death benefits (death in service)

What you must have

The Social Security Pensions Act does not say you must have any lump sum death benefits, and all the State itself provides is a meagre £30 death grant.

What the Act does say is that, in a contracted out scheme, you must have a widow's pension. Companies are allowed to eat into the lump sum death benefit to provide this.

What the Inland Revenue allows

The Inland Revenue permits a **maximum** death benefit of 4 times earnings (or £5000, if that is greater). It will allow a scheme to provide this on the basis of full PAYE earnings, even if the **pensionable** earnings figure is less than this. They will also allow you to use a 'notional' figure, by updating the last full year's PAYE figure by an amount to take account of inflation. This would apply if someone has been ill, for instance, for a while before dying, so that their final P60 is a very low figure.

The cash sum is **tax free**, provided you fulfil the conditions laid down. The essential condition is that the benefit is payable at the discretion of the trustees. This means that, so far as the taxmen are concerned, when you die *you* don't own the money; the trustees do. It's therefore not counted into your estate. Because of this, you cannot *direct* who receives the benefit; the final decision must be with the trustees.

There is a general legal rule that money left unclaimed after death, if it is still outstanding when sufficient time has been left for the settlement of a person's affairs, goes to the Crown. For this reason most pension scheme trust deeds have a clause saying that the ultimate beneficiary once the trustees have taken all reasonable steps to find a relative of the dead person, or a dependant, is the pension fund itself which means that the money is **not** unclaimed and therefore the Crown doesn't get it. This does not often arise, but you do occasionally find a person who appears to have **no** relatives or dependants at all. The maximum amount of time a fund is allowed to hang on to the money, without deciding what to do with it, is 2 years.

A scheme may also refund all the member's contributions on death, with the addition of interest. The Inland Revenue does not specify what it regards as the correct rate, but in general it will be much lower than actual rates of interest. As the refund is of the member's own money, the question of avoiding Capital Transfer Tax does not apply, and frequently it is paid to the member's 'legal personal representatives' without any scope for discretion on the part of the trustees.

The beneficiary for a lump sum on death *must* be an individual. It can be a relative, or a person who was financially dependent on the member (a cohabitee, or an elderly parent the member was supporting, for instance) or another nominated person such as the friend s/he shared a house with. But it may not be a society, club or organisation.

Typical arrangements and possible improvements

The 1979 NAPF survey showed the following picture (table 38):

	Staff schemes	Works schemes	Combined schemes	All schemes
Lump sum benefit as a multiple of salary	%	%	%	%
Married males				
Less than 1½ years' salary	11	29	15	15
1½ but less than 2 years' salary	5	12	5	6
2 but less than 2½ years' salary	27	29	35	31
2½ but less than 3 years' salary	4	2	1	2
3 but less than 4 years' salary	20	6	17	17
4 years' salary	27	4	13	17
Greater than 4 years' salary	—	—	—	—
A fixed monetary amount	—	11	1	2
Varies	7	6	13	10
Total	101	99	100	100

Single males

Less than 1½ years' salary	8	25	14	14
1½ but less than 2 years' salary	4	13	6	6
2 but less than 2½ years' salary	27	29	32	30
2½ but less than 3 years' salary	4	2	1	3
3 but less than 4 years' salary	21	6	20	18
4 years' salary	28	5	13	18
Greater than 4 years' salary	—	—	—	—
A fixed monetary amount	—	11	—	2
Varies	8	8	13	10
Total	**100**	**99**	**99**	**101**

Females

Less than 1½ years' salary	9	25	15	14
1½ but less than 2 years' salary	4	13	6	6
2 but less than 2½ years' salary	28	31	32	30
2½ but less than 3 years' salary	4	2	1	2
3 but less than 4 years' salary	20	6	19	17
4 years' salary	26	3	12	16
Greater than 4 years' salary	—	—	—	—
A fixed monetary amount	—	11	1	2
Varies	9	9	14	11
Total	**100**	**100**	**100**	**98**

As usual, staff come off considerably better than manual workers in this. Far more staff than works schemes provide 4 times salary. There are a great many works schemes, in fact, which provide very small lump sums.

Unicorn Industries' 'standard benefit scheme' provides 4 times the single person's State pension – which at current rates gives about £5000.

London Brick gives a *maximum* of £3000, or less depending on length of service.

Kitson's Insulation gives £1000.

A number of schemes vary the amount by length of service, and/or whether or not you have children.

McKechnie Group's grade A scheme gives:
for death after less than 10 years' membership: $1\frac{1}{2}$ times pensionable remuneration
for death after more than 10 years' membership: 2 times pensionable remuneration
   plus
where the member is a married man: 1 times pensionable remuneration
   plus
where the member is financially responsible for children (for each child, to maximum of 2): $\frac{1}{2}$ times pensionable remuneration.

A good many schemes discriminate between men and women, or between **married men**, and **single men and all women**.

Steetley Chemical Co gives $2\frac{1}{4}$ times earnings for married men, and $1\frac{1}{2}$ times for all others, plus a refund of contributions.

This is based on the idea that the husband is always the 'breadwinner'. It is legal, because the Sex Discrimination Act does not cover occupational pension schemes. This sort of discrimination is not good. A single person may have just as high a level of financial commitments as a married person, and it is not for the company to make a judgement on what people should do.

Some schemes also discriminate between grades of employees in the same scheme, and paying the same contribution.

The Ofrex Group has a system explained in this table:

	Number of times annual earnings			
Job category	Less than 5 years' service	Less than 10 years' service	Less than 20 years' service	In 21st year and thereafter
1. Shop floor operatives and all clerical grades	2	2	2	2
2. First level supervisory grades (shop floor and office) and salesman	2	2	2	3
3. First level management	2	2	3	4
4. Subsidiary company directors and senior executives	2	4	4	4
5. Main board directors and subsidiary company managing directors	2	4	4	4

Occasionally, this will be the result of an old 'red circling', that is, special provision to ensure that a group with better conditions in one particular respect do not lose in that respect when the conditions are changed overall. For instance, if a scheme was changed from giving a death benefit of 4 times earnings, to giving 2 times earnings *plus* a widow's pension, those who already had 4 times earnings might be allowed to retain it and have a right to the widow's pension, whereas new entrants would have to start on the new terms.

More usually, it is simply a matter of giving management better value for money in the pension scheme, and thus the manual workers subsidising them.

A few schemes have a death benefit and then an extra 'accidental death benefit' either for everyone, or for a particular group of people. If this is included in the pensions booklet, the chances are again that it is a result of an old 'red circling', in that the scheme had a much higher life assurance than the Inland Revenue now allows, and so part of the benefit has been hived off into a technically separate scheme, so as not to jeopardise approval.

> Rank Xerox Ltd pay a lump sum of 4 times salary, plus a refund of contributions plus interest; and in the event of death by accident, a further 2 times salary.

A number of schemes deduct from the lump sum the cost of providing the minimum widow's pension required by the Social Security Pensions Act for a contracted out scheme. (See section 13, pages 135–45, for an explanation of the widow's pension.) At the moment, the widow's pension required is very small, because it's only had a short time to build up, and so the deduction is small too, but in due course it will become much bigger, and swallow up a substantial chunk of the lump sum. In effect the widow is being asked to pay for her own pension. This should be *opposed*.

The lump sum and widow/er's pension should be looked at together. If there is a good widow/er's pension there will be less reason to seek a large lump sum as well. So a contracted **in** scheme that does not provide a widow/er's pension should give a bigger lump sum than one that does.

An average level of lump sum for a contracted out scheme is

about 2 times salary for a works scheme, rather more for a staff or joint scheme. If your scheme does not give this much, you should probably make death benefit a priority. If it does, you might well think about leaving this alone for the moment and concentrating on other things.

A *very rough* rule of thumb for cost is that a death benefit equal to 1 year's earnings will cost about ¾% of payroll, 2 times earnings 1½%, and so on. This does depend *a lot* on the ages of people covered, and on the proportion of men and women. Because of their lower mortality rate, women are cheaper to cover for death benefit than men.

As so often in pension schemes, the small print here is important. Points to check up on are:

■ The definition of salary. Even if the rest of the scheme is calculated on basic earnings only, or has a deduction for State pension, for the death benefit the definition should be *either* PAYE earnings for the last 12 months, or the last week's (or month's) earnings multiplied by 52 (or 12). If people's earnings fluctuate at different times of the year, the first method is better, because otherwise someone dying at the 'wrong' time of year is penalised. If earnings are fairly steady, the second is a better safeguard against inflation.

■ If someone has been sick for (say) 4 weeks or more in the final year before his/her death, then a 'notional' PAYE figure should be created. If there's an easily calculated group average rate, then you can use this. Alternatively, you can use the average for the weeks the person *has* worked, and multiply this by 52. You can't use this, though, for anyone who has not worked at all because of illness in the last year, and so another alternative is PAYE earnings for the last full year worked, uprated by the increase in prices since that date.

■ You should look for some interest being added to the refund of contributions. Some of the contributions will have been paid in when the general level of interest was much lower than it is now, so it is not reasonable to ask for anything approaching current market rates, nor would the Inland Revenue allow it. A 4% or 5% rate would be reasonable.

■ Those who are excluded from the pension because they are too young, or too old, or have not worked for the company long enough, should be included for at least some death benefit.

■ Part timers ought also to be covered, however few hours

they work. The loss of their income, even if fairly small, is bound to create financial difficulties for the family.

If you have a fixed lump sum in your scheme, for instance, £500 or £1000, try to change it to an earnings related one, even if at a level which gives no immediate improvement. In the long run this will mean that it keeps up with inflation. Otherwise, you will need to renegotiate the level of death benefit every year if it is to keep its value.

Death benefit is one of the simpler things in a pension scheme to change. Even in a fairly large scheme it is usually insured, to safeguard the scheme if a busload of people went over a cliff. So improving it is just a matter of raising the premium, and this can be done very easily. If you're negotiating on a scheme, and the discussions have dragged on so that it is too late to implement most changes this year, you should at least be able to get the improved death benefit brought in *and backdated*, so that the dependants of anyone who dies between the anniversary date and the date you finally settle get an increased payment from the company in due course. Make sure you dot the 'i's and cross the 't's on this before you finalise the agreement.

Whatever level of death benefit you have negotiated, you need to keep an eye on how it is actually being administered as well. The sort of questions you will need to ask, via the member trustees if they exist, or via the shop stewards' committee if they don't, are:

■ How long is it taking for benefit to be paid out?

■ Is it simple for members to make their own wishes clear as to where the benefit goes? Is a form to fill in for this included in the scheme booklet?

■ Just as important, is it simple for the member to change the form if it gets out of date?

■ Is it genuinely kept confidential? Or, if someone has family circumstances which are not all they seem, is s/he going to find gossip spreading after s/he fills in the nomination form?

The procedure followed by a number of schemes, which others might adopt, is to send, once a year, a new nomination form to each member, and an envelope with the individual's name and the date on. If the member wishes to change the nomination form, s/he fills it in, and puts it in the envelope, which is then sealed up. The pensions administrator then throws away the previous envelope, without looking at the form inside, and puts the new one in its place.

Only if the member dies, is the envelope unsealed and read. The *disadvantage* of this, though, is that when the letter is read, if it has been incorrectly or unclearly filled in, there is nothing that can be done.

Possible arguments and responses

The arguments for a bigger death benefit are:

■ First, that it's cost effective. It takes only a comparatively small increase in premium to give a much better level of life assurance.

■ Second, that *not* to have a good death benefit puts the employer in an extraordinarily bad light. People naturally feel very strongly if someone they have worked with a long time dies and they see the company treating his/her dependants shabbily. It may well give the company a bad name, and undo all the goodwill a progressive policy elsewhere may have created.

■ Once again, this is a glaring gap in the State scheme, that the private scheme *ought* properly to fill.

■ Finally, that this is an area where the economies of scale are enormous. It is much cheaper for the company to take out or increase group life assurance than for the member to do so as an individual, certainly so far as the older person and anyone not in the best of health is concerned.

The company's objection to any improvement will primarily be *money* – that, even though the benefit is cost-effective, they can't afford it. As always, it will be a matter of what priority you give this item in your overall claim, and how much cash is really available. It's easy to be flexible in negotiating on this point, without damaging or over-complicating the structure of the scheme as a whole.

The company may also say:

■ It doesn't feel people will be able to handle a large sum of money, and so this may be wasted. This is a paternalist argument – and sexist as well, since the implication is often that *wives* cannot cope with money. In response, you can say that there is no objection to the company ensuring that proper financial advice is available to the dependant – indeed, it should be welcomed. But *advice* is as far as it should go. There should be no question of the company making a judgement on that person's abilities.

■ It doesn't see the *need* for a large death benefit. Funerals are expensive, but they cost hundreds rather than thousands of pounds, and you can't *know* that any member has large financial commitments. In response, you can point out that people frequently *do* have substantial debts, whether the company appreciates it or not. They will have organised their lives, one assumes, to take account of this, but unexpected death will create considerable problems. Even a young person, not yet married or with a family, may have piled up debts for consumer goods.

The company may suggest that, as there is only a limited amount of money to go round, it would be better spent on improving the widow/er's pension. (On the other hand some companies will say the opposite; see page 148.) What your reaction to this is will depend on the size of the widow/er's pension because, as we said above, a balance needs to be struck between the immediate lump sum, and the longer term widow/er's pension. A benefit of 2 times salary, plus a spouse's pension of ½ the member's prospective pension, would be a reasonable balance.

Section 13: Death in service pension – spouses and dependants

What you must have

A scheme that is contracted **out** under the Social Security Pensions Act *must* provide a widow's pension, but of a limited amount. The scheme must calculate this by two methods, and pay the better one:

■ First, the widow's requisite benefit. This must not be less than 1/160th of the member's final pensionable salary (calculated in any of the ways allowed under the Social Security Pensions Act), for each year of accrued service since contracting out.

■ Second, the widow's guaranteed minimum pension (WGMP), which is half the member's own GMP.

The requirements are for only *half* the member's own pension, whereas if you are contracted **in**, the State scheme pays the member's *full* accrued pension to the widow. In order to keep the promise that no one contracting out will be worse off, the State picks up the bill for the other half, and it will pay to a widow 50% of the member's GMP, regardless of how much she is actually getting from the company's scheme.

This applies, though, only in cases where a widow is entitled to a State **basic** pension – that is, if she is over 40 or, if under 40, has dependent children. If there is no entitlement, the company scheme need not provide in its rules for the pension to be paid.

Although the State scheme pays a pension in some circumstances to a dependent widower, a private scheme need not. Again, the State picks up the bill. Nor is there any obligation to pay a pension to any other dependant. If a legal widow exists, the WGMP *must* be paid to her, even if she is not living with the member.

If the scheme is contracted **in**, there is no obligation to pay any dependant's pension.

What the Inland Revenue allows

The Inland Revenue will permit a pension scheme to provide a benefit for widow, widower, or dependant, of not more than 2/3rds of the member's pension, calculated on his/her earnings at the date of death, and his/her *potential* service up to normal retirement date.

As with the lump sum benefit, the 'earnings' definition can be different from that used for the member's own pension. This means that even if the member's own pension is **integrated** (see section 7.3, pages 95–100), the widow's need not be.

If there is a widow/er and a dependant, or more than one dependant, then more than one pension can be paid, provided that the **total** does not come to more than the member's own prospective pension. 'Dependant' is defined (in a footnote to Practice Note 11.5) as 'a person who is financially dependent on the employee, or was so dependent at the time of the employee's death . . . A relative who is not or was not supported by the employee is not a dependant. But a child of the employee may always be regarded as a dependant until s/he reaches the age of 18 or ceases to receive full time educational or vocational training, if later.'

A scheme is allowed to reduce the pension if the dependant is younger than the member, and it can suspend it, or remove it altogether, if the person remarries.

Typical arrangements and possible improvements

You'll see from the sections above on 'What you must have' and 'What the Inland Revenue allows' that there is a very big difference between the minimum and the maximum here. The minimum allowed by the Act is extremely low, while the maximum is generous.

The NAPF 1979 survey (table 40) showed what fraction of a member's pension or salary existing schemes actually provided.

Fraction	Staff schemes	Works schemes	Combined schemes	All schemes
	%	%	%	%
⅔	7	3	7	6
Other levels more generous than ½	2	1	2	2
½	76	83	77	78
⅜	—	1	1	1
⅓	6	2	2	4
Other levels less generous than ½	5	4	5	5
Varies	4	6	6	5
Total	100	100	100	101

As you can see from this, the majority of schemes provide a widow's pension of ½ the member's pension. Just over 50% of the schemes in the survey also provided a widow*er*'s pension where he was a dependant, and 22% of all schemes now give a widower's pension automatically.

The cost of providing a widower's pension as well as a widow's pension will depend a lot on the proportion of men to women within the scheme. In practice it will not vary very much between a **dependant's** and an **automatic** pension, because the actuary will assume everyone will claim to be dependent. Either way, it should be small, because the chances of a woman dying in service are small.

The **basis** on which the widow's pension is calculated also makes a big difference, especially to the younger person. The NAPF survey (table 39) also gives figures on this.

Method of calculation	Staff schemes	Works schemes	Combined schemes	All schemes
	%	%	%	%
Based on the member's accrued pension	14	22	15	15
Based on the member's prospective pension	59	48	61	58
Based on the member's salary at date of death	16	10	11	13
Other basis	11	20	13	13
Total	100	100	100	99

There are many variations in the amount and type of pension given. The meanest schemes give only the minimum required by the State, and deduct it from the lump sum benefit.

> Bryant and May's scheme (which is otherwise quite good) states: 'Part of the life assurance payable on death before retirement must be used to buy the widow's guaranteed minimum pension . . . or if greater a widow's pension of 5/8ths of 1% of pensionable earnings for each year of membership after 6 April 1978.'

More common, but still pretty mean, is to give only that minimum, but not to deduct it from the lump sum. Some schemes which are otherwise fairly generous do this.

> The GKN works scheme, with an accrual rate of 1/60th, gives as a widows' pension 1/160th of . . . final pensionable earnings for each year of pensionable service completed since 6 April 1978'.

This is based on a reasoning which is the opposite of that used by other companies for reducing the death benefit – that the widow ought to have as much control over the money she receives as possible, and therefore as *little* as possible ought to be tied up in pension. *Neither* argument is right. The lump sum is needed to help the widow/er meet immediate commitments, and to adjust his/her way of life, and the pension is needed for long term living costs. So there needs to be a balance between them. There are some schemes which give pretty well the full amount allowed by the Inland Revenue.

> Albright and Wilson give a pension of 2/3rds of the member's pension, and say: 'Where a widow's pension is not payable a dependant's pension up to the amount of the widow's pension may be paid at the trustees' discretion to any person whom they consider to have been substantially dependent on the member at the date of death.'

For most schemes, though, you would find the employer would reject this target out of hand. It may be more realistic to look for a ½ pension based on all actual plus prospective service. 'Service' should include any years when the pension scheme was in existence, *before* there was a widow's pension, and any years for which back service entitlement has been given for the member's own pension. Any pension should be payable equally to the widow or widower, or to any other dependant where no widow/er exists.

Some schemes, rather than paying a proportion of the member's pension, pay a proportion of salary.

Ferranti Ltd pay 30% of salary regardless of how long the member has been with the company.

This is a good idea, because no one's likely to lose by it, but the gainers will be the shorter service, older, people. Those who have the chance to do 40 years' service may resent it, though, so check their views before making a claim for this.

Any improvement in the widow's benefit is a moderately, rather than very, expensive item. Extending the pension to any other group – widowers or dependants – is also not expensive. So a claim on this may as well be for an extension to *everyone* eligible.

The next table shows the position on children's pensions, according to the NAPF survey (table 35).

	Staff schemes	Works schemes	Combined schemes	All schemes
	%	%	%	%
Children's benefits as of right in addition to a widow's pension	41	34	51	44
As of right only if the child is an orphan	23	16	15	18
Children's benefits on a discretionary basis in addition to a widow's pension	2	1	2	2
Children's benefits to orphans on a discretionary basis	5	4	4	5
Some other basis	3	4	4	3
No provision	27	41	23	28
Total	101	100	99	100

As you can see, rather than provide an automatic additional **children's pension**, there are a lot of schemes that say that, if the widow dies while the children are dependent, so that they become orphans, then the widow's pension is carried on for their benefit. This is cheaper than paying a children's pension in every case, because only a small proportion of the widows will die.

A number of schemes, while providing a widow's pension which is *below* the Inland Revenue limit, add on to it reasonable children's pensions which bring the package as a whole up to the limit.

> The Vauxhall Motors booklet says:
> 'Your widow will receive a pension equal to $\frac{1}{2}$ of your pension entitlement calculated on your final pensionable pay at death and your actual and projected pensionable service right through to age 65 . . .
> If you die in service and have dependent children a pension will be payable to them in addition to the other death benefits payable. The pension will be paid to any child up to age 16 or 18 where s/he is in full time education.
> 'The maximum total children's pensions payable will be $\frac{1}{2}$ of your pension entitlement calculated on your final pensionable pay and your actual and projected service right through to normal retirement age.'

In this case, you could only improve the widow's pension by **cutting back** on the children's pensions. This would often in fact be a reasonable thing to do, as the children will also receive the benefit of the widow having a higher pension, and it will also help the widow *without* children. It will therefore cost money to do this, because far more widows' pensions are payable than children's pensions.

Where there is a children's pension payable, it is fairly usual to give better treatment to children **both** of whose parents have died. It is also very cheap, because the risk of a child becoming an orphan is statistically very small.

> Volkswagen Ltd pay 10% pension for each child up to the age of 18, but double it if there is no spouse's pension payable.

Some schemes extend the same special benefits to children whose parents, when they died, were single for other reasons (divorced, or never married). This is sensible, since for them the death of the parent will be as drastic as the death of two parents in other situations. This tends though to be only for the children of **male** members, not female. Many schemes still take the pension away if the widow remarries, as the NAPF survey (table 41) shows:

Period of payment	Staff schemes	Works schemes	Combined schemes	All schemes
	%	%	%	%
Continue payment for life	65	66	57	62
Discontinue payment on remarriage	27	26	32	29
Review pension on remarriage	9	8	10	10
Total	101	100	99	101

There are mixed views among scheme members about this. It's often justified as a way to save money: 'We don't want to give benefit to someone who doesn't need it.' But apart from the discrimination implied in the suggestion that any woman needs a man to support her, it has very little value in saving the scheme money, because of the cost of enforcing. This will be quite high especially if it includes a bar on cohabitation as well as on marriage. The argument that a pension *should* be paid for life is that it is given as a right, and has been paid for by the member's contributions on that basis. (The State pension *does* stop on either remarriage or cohabitation.)

Another limitation that is often imposed is to reduce the pension if the widow is more than a certain number of years younger than the member.

> The Pegler Hattersley works scheme says: 'If a widow is more than 10 years younger than the member, the pension will be reduced by an amount to be determined by the actuary.'
> The Associated Cement works scheme reduces the pension by $1\frac{1}{2}\%$ for each year, over 10 years, by which the widow is younger than her husband.

The logic of this is that, if a widow is much younger than her husband, the pension is likely to be paid for longer. But to pursue the logic fully, the pension ought to be **increased** if she is older than her husband, and this is never done. It is a penny pinching device not affecting many people, since most husbands and wives are quite close in age, but very annoying for those it does affect.

Whatever limits are put on, the pension can never be reduced to below the WGMP. Nor can the WGMP be paid to anyone **except** the widow. It is possible, and desirable, for the rules of the scheme to include discretion for the trustees to divide the benefit where necessary. If a member has a legal widow, but has lived with someone else for the last 20 years, then the trustees could divide the benefit so that the legal widow got the WGMP and the other person got the rest.

In a contracted **in** scheme with a low accrual rate, a spouse's pension for death in service tends to be rather a waste of time, as it will be very small and may only stop the spouse from getting means tested benefits. If no spouse's pension exists, therefore, you should do your best to maximise the lump sum death benefits instead. On the other hand, if it exists already it would be unwise to try to abolish it. In that case you would have to try and make it as large as possible.

Possible arguments and responses

What you need to impress on the employer is the need for a 'balancing out' between pension and lump sum. The lump sum is to cover the dependant's immediate needs, to pay off whatever financial commitments have been accrued by the member, and to allow the dependant to settle into a new way of life. The pension, on the other hand, is to go some way at least to replacing the income lost by the death of the member. It may need to do this for a very long time, as the spouse, especially of a younger person, may survive for many years. Providing a large lump sum is not enough – some continuing income is also needed. But too small a pension will not do any good either, because it will simply deprive the dependant of the ability to claim means tested benefits. So since in a contracted out scheme the company *must* pay some widow's pension, it ought to pay a good one.

The company may respond by suggesting that the tax position is better if a widow takes a lump sum, and spends it on an annuity, than if she receives it as pension – Associated Engineering, for instance, have used this as their justification.

The flaw in this argument is that, if the company gives any sort of increase in dependants' pensions, whether automatically or at their discretion, s/he will get it only on the small amount of pension not on the lump sum. All the arguments that have been used elsewhere, about comparability with competitors' schemes, good industrial relations, and so on, also apply. The company will probably not disagree to any great extent with your arguments – they will just say they can't afford it. It *may* be possible to phase it in – for instance, by giving a pension on accrued service only for a few years, and then later extending it to prospective service, but it's not very satisfactory, because it will mean a lot of people living on very small pensions for quite a while.

It is on the question of widow*ers*' and dependants' pensions that emotions tend to get stirred up. For some reason, although they may well have noticed that not all the widows to whom they are paying pensions were financially dependent on their husbands, since they had paid jobs of their own, management tend to get quite shocked at the idea of a husband in comparable circumstances receiving a pension. If anything, consultants and insurance company representatives are even worse. The company may feel it is able to pay a pension to **dependent** widowers, but no more than that – even though, as explained above, the cost difference is very small.

The most important argument for providing a widower's pension as well as a widow's pension is that the scheme should not discriminate between men and women. (But don't accuse the company of breaking the law: the Sex Discrimination Act doesn't cover pension schemes.) Very often, the women members of the pension scheme will feel pretty strongly about it. If this is so, you should make sure management knows this. There is a tendency to assume that women don't care one way or the other about pensions, and this is partly how pension schemes have got away with so much discrimination in the past. The scheme administrator may be genuinely surprised to discover women **do** care a lot about this.

One argument the company may use is that of value for money. The actuaries' view is that the pension of a man retiring at 65, *plus* a contingent widow's pension (that is, payable only if the man dies first and therefore not in the case of every member) is about equal in value to the pension of a woman retiring at 60, taking into account her longer life expectancy. This may well be so, but that's not the whole picture.

■ First, it doesn't override the arguments about discrimination. There are a lot of other areas where companies have been forced to make equal provision even though it is more expensive for one sex than for the other. For example, it's often claimed that women tend to take more time off sick than men, but a company is not allowed to provide different sick pay schemes.

■ Second, a pension scheme is not a piggy bank. No one individual should expect to get precise 'value for money' out of it. All the members cross subsidise one another – that's the point of having a group pension scheme and not a set of individual ones – but only in the case of cross subsidies between men and women is this seen as a reason for giving unequal benefits. The gap between mortality rates for men in the top and bottom social classes is at least as big as the gap between men's and women's mortality rates, but this is not normally used as an argument for giving different benefits to those groups.

The company may also say, 'The man is the breadwinner – women only work for pin money.' You do get these arguments still produced at times, from prehistoric (male) managers. Restraining the natural inclination to thump them, you can respond that, if it ever was true (which is pretty doubtful), it certainly isn't any more. Most families need two incomes on which to survive, and the loss of *either* income is going to create financial problems, because the family's standard of living has been built on the expectation of that income continuing. The majority of women today do paid work for a large part of their lives, and surveys show that many more would do so if they could make satisfactory arrangements for looking after their children.

You could also point out that the surviving parent of a family is going to be in considerable difficulty looking after the children, whichever parent dies, and in fact it will be more difficult if it is the wife who dies, because of the way the State scheme works. A **widow** receives the State widow's pension, which is not means tested, for as long as she has dependent children, but a **widower** who was not a dependant of his wife has to rely on supplementary benefit, which is means tested and is anyway at a lower rate. Private schemes are intended to fill in the gaps in the State scheme, and this is one of them.

Arguments about cost will of course be brought up, but the cost will only be substantial if there is a high proportion of women in the workforce, and in this case the company has so far been getting its pension scheme on the cheap. The cost of a widower's pension is *less* than the cost of the equivalent widow's pension, because fewer women die in service. Make sure that the company has obtained a costing before you start arguing, as there may be some very incorrect notions on this.

On children's pensions, there is usually fairly general agreement that they are a Good Thing, and the argument is therefore straightforwardly about cost, and the priority to give them.

A pension for adult dependants, however, can be controversial. Management frequently jumps to the conclusion that you are talking *only* about common law wives and husbands. They would be covered by this, certainly – and why not? If someone has chosen not to bother with a wedding ceremony, is it any of the pension manager's business? But also covered would be the member's elderly parent, or a sister who has kept house for a bachelor brother, or the invalid relative who has been supported by the member. Management may consider that these at least are 'deserving cases'.

You could point out that there seem to be double standards operating as between the lump sum and the pension. The company has no objection to the lump sum going to the widower, or any other adult dependant – indeed, they will often claim 'flexibility' as one of the main advantages of it – so how is the pension different? If they're honest, they'll say 'Because it costs more', so that you will at least be able to strip away the less genuine arguments and start talking about money.

Section 14: Death after retirement

What you must have

A contracted out scheme *must* provide a widow's pension of $\frac{1}{2}$ the member's GMP, or 1/160th for each year of service since contracting out, where the member dies in retirement. The State pays the rest, and also picks up any increases that have been made since the member retired. (In any case the State takes responsibility for paying the increases on the GMP after the member has retired.) If the member has married *after* retirement, and dies within 6 months, then even if a scheme is normally more generous it need pay only the WGMP in this case.

Although the State additional scheme does provide widowers' pensions for death after retirement, there is no duty on a private scheme to do this. The State will always provide the additional widower's pension in this case. If the private scheme also gives one, the widower will be better off than a comparable widow, who will only get $\frac{1}{2}$ the additional pension from the State. (But for the next few years at least, the widow/er's pension from the State will be so small that it is hardly noticeable.)

What the Inland Revenue allows

The Inland Revenue limit on pension for death in retirement follows the same pattern as for death in service – up to 2/3rds the member's pension. This pension can be calculated before any amount that is to be commuted is deducted, so that taking part of the member's own pension as cash need not affect the widow.

They are, however, for some reason much more rigorous on the **death benefit** after retirement. They will allow:

■ a 'funeral benefit' of up to £500 (which hasn't been changed recently, and must once have been quite generous, but still buys a decent funeral),

■ and a guarantee that the pension will be paid for a minimum length of time, even if the member dies in the meantime. If the guarantee is for 5 years or less, the balance may be taken as a lump sum. If it is for longer, it must be a continuing pension.

The Inland Revenue will allow the member to **surrender** some of his/her own benefit to increase the size of the widow/er's pension, or to give a pension to any other dependant. However, this must not mean that the widow/er's pension will be *bigger* than the member's own. A scheme can also provide a pension for any other dependant, including a children's pension, without the member needing to surrender, but it must not bring the *total* package above the maximum.

Typical arrangements and possible improvements

Even before the Social Security Pensions Act, the majority of schemes had widows' pensions for death after retirement, in one way or another. Now that a contracted out scheme *must* do so, about 96% of all schemes provide one, and about ⅓ of these also allow for an extra pension to be payable if the member surrenders part of his own. (This has to be done at, or shortly before, retirement.)

The NAPF survey (table 43) shows that the majority of schemes paid a widow's/dependant's pension of half the member's own.

Fraction	Staff schemes	Works schemes	Combined schemes	All schemes
	%	%	%	%
⅔	7	2	7	6
Other levels more generous than ½	1	1	3	2
½	88	94	85	88
⅜	—	—	1	—
⅓	1	—	1	1
Other levels less generous than ½	1	2	2	1
Varies	1	2	2	2
Total	99	101	101	100

Not many schemes pay a widow's pension of the maximum 2/3rds. One that does is British Airways.

It's therefore not worth pushing for a better pension than 50%

until the scheme is well above average in all other areas. If you decide to go for an increase, try to get the improvement reflected in the amounts of widows' pensions already being paid.

What you can look for, though, is an extension of the benefit to widowers, and other adult dependants, in the same way as for the death in service pension (see pages 137, 139 and 140), and for improvements in the small print. You could look particularly at

- remarriage rules;
- deathbed marriages;
- provision of, or improvement of, a guarantee; and
- provision of a funeral benefit.

As we said in the previous section 13 (page 144), widowers' pensions are cheaper to provide than widows' pensions as there are far fewer widowers, since the majority of wives outlive their husbands. Children's pensions for death after retirement are even cheaper, as very few pensioners have dependent children, but those that do can leave their family in a difficult position.

In negotiation, it will be worth bringing discussion on these aspects together with similar discussion on the death in service benefit. If you achieve a breakthrough on one, it may well be conceded on the other anyway. Don't rely on this, though. Some companies are much more generous to the widows of retired members than they are to the widows of those who die in service. This can be seen, for instance, in the treatment of death after retirement pensions on remarriage; compare the next table (table 44 from the NAPF survey), which shows the period for which widows are paid after a member's retirement, with the one on page 140 showing death **in service** pensions.

Period of payment	Staff schemes	Works schemes	Combined schemes	All schemes
	%	%	%	%
Continue payment for life	71	77	67	70
Discontinue payment on remarriage	21	17	25	23
Review pension on remarriage	7	6	8	7
Total	99	100	100	100

If your scheme has a remarriage rule, it ought to be dropped. Whatever justification there is for imposing it on a young widow (though it's already been argued that there is none), it really is distasteful that it should be imposed on a person over 60.

Equally so is the quite common rule that, where a member has married or remarried *after* retirement, and then dies within 6 months, only the WGMP, not the full pension, is paid. This is because of pension fund managers' fears of 'deathbed marriages' but there are not likely to be many of these, and there are better ways of making one's fortune than by marrying an elderly occupational pensioner. It's another small penny pinching device that ought to be abolished.

On the **guarantee**, there are many variations. The best clause is one that says that the fund undertakes to pay the pension for at least 5 years and that, if the pensioner dies before that time, the **balance** will be paid to the spouse or any other dependant in a lump sum. Many schemes 'discount' the lump sum; that is, reduce it to take account of the fact that it's being paid early; but this should not be accepted. Other schemes say that the guaranteed lump sum will only apply if there is no widow/er. This considerably reduces the cost, but also the usefulness, as the majority of people who die within 5 years of retirement will be married.

Massey-Ferguson costed the guarantee for pensioners with no surviving spouse at 0.05% of payroll, and a fuller guarantee for all pensioners at 0.25% – not a large sum in either case.

The NAPF survey (table 45) showed the time for which payments were guaranteed.

	Staff schemes	Works schemes	Combined schemes	All schemes
	%	%	%	%
Not guaranteed	16	19	22	19
Guaranteed for 5 years	67	65	61	64
Some other guarantee	8	7	9	8
Only if no dependant's pension payable	9	9	9	9
Total	100	100	101	100

People sometimes get the impression from obscure scheme booklets that the guarantee means that the pension is paid for *only* 5 years. This is not the case and, if you feel your scheme booklet is misleading on this, ask for it to be changed.

The funeral benefit allowed by the Inland Revenue is rarely given in practice. One example where it does exist is Inco Ltd, whose booklet says:

> Disability, early and normal pensioners are covered for a lump sum death benefit of £200 . . . This is paid to the person you nominate. You do this on a nomination form . . . This benefit is assessable to estate duty if your estate is also assessable.

It's not clear why this benefit is so rare, unless because it would be a nuisance for administrators to keep track of any pay out. Although it is only a small sum it would be worth obtaining. As this is an obscure area, it will be worth quoting the Inland Revenue Practice Note in any claim – it is No 12.18.

Possible arguments and responses

If you are looking for an increase in the level of widow/ers' pensions, it will be helpful to do some research. Try to obtain figures which you can present to management on:

■ the typical level of a widow/er's pension for death after retirement, for a fairly recent pensioner from your firm; and

■ the level of costs s/he has to face, especially housing costs (have council rents gone up recently? Or have the council put up the charges for social services such as home helps?); and

■ the proportion of widow/ers being paid from the company scheme who are having to claim supplementary benefit, or who are only just above the poverty line because of their pension, and are therefore only marginally better off.

If you're in a small company, with only one site, you'll probably find a number of pensioners living locally anyway. In a large company, you'll probably have to take a sample of a couple of sites, perhaps those that run pensioners' clubs. With luck, you might be able to get a few active pensioners to find out the information for you (especially if your claim includes an improvement in pension for them). Then you can present the information to management, and ask them if they really think it is right for their pensioners, or their pensioners' dependants. Their reaction will probably be that they agree with you, but it costs too much, and so then you will need to argue about how much they can really afford. On page 77 we gave some ideas for arguments you could use.

On the question of extending the pension to widowers and dependants, turn back to 'Death in service' (section 13, pages 142–45) and read that section, because the same arguments apply here. The question of **remarriage** is also dealt with in that section.

The next issue is the 'deathbed marriage'. Usually, if you make sufficient fuss about this, the company will decide it's not worth defending. If they decide to stick to it, though, you could ask them to provide some facts. For instance:

■ How many cases of this sort have there been in the last 10 years?

■ How much of the administrator's time was spent in finding out the facts, discussing the problem with the trustees, etc?

■ How much money, taking administrative time into account, did they save?

Even if the figures show that it is not cost effective, the company may say that they *must* retain the clause 'to save the fund from the possibility of abuse'. In that case it might be possible to compromise on having the pension reviewed, at the discretion of the trustees, rather than removed altogether.

On the guarantee period and the funeral benefit, the issue will primarily be financial, although neither improvement costs much in itself. But you can also make the point that the guarantee provides a very visible safeguard ensuring that people are getting value for money. People will often say that they don't feel they're going to live long in retirement anyway, and the guarantee at least means that they can know their dependants won't lose. The most generous form of guarantee gives the biggest safeguard, and the difference in cost between the least and most generous is very small for the company.

On the £500 funeral benefit, pensioners' anxieties about the cost of their funeral are well known. The next of kin of a pensioner will often be a pensioner him/herself, and if they get to hear of difficulties a good company would probably make an ex gratia payment anyway, to cover a debt incurred because of a funeral. In that case it would be less humiliating, simpler and, in the long run (taking account of the administrative time spent dealing with each case as a one-off), probably cost no more, to have an automatic payment at the level the Inland Revenue allows.

Section 15: Escalation (pension increases)

What you must have

Under the Social Security Pensions Act, a scheme has *no* obligation to provide increases in pensions in payment. The State takes on the responsibility for increasing the GMP in line with the Secretary of State's estimate of the increase in prices (a formula which allows political manipulation) but the private scheme's duty is only to continue paying the pension at the same level as when it originally started.

In the case of the widow's pension, the State provides half of the original pension (see sections 13 and 14, pages 135–50), but *all* of the increases. Again, the private scheme has no obligation on this.

What the Inland Revenue allows

The Inland Revenue allows any scheme to increase pensions by any amount up to the increase in the cost of living, *provided* that the scheme rules allow them to do so (as most do). A scheme need not give the same increases to all categories of pensioners. Some schemes leave the widow's death in service pension out. Also, schemes need not use the same formula to increase deferred pensions (see section 16, page 156), as they do for other pensions.

Typical arrangements and possible improvements

Only one group of schemes has automatic inflation proofing, and there is a lot of argument about it. This consists of the various public sector schemes – the Civil Service, the National Health Service etc – several of which are not funded, but 'pay as you go'. We can't go into great detail on this issue, but broadly in the **funded** scheme *your* contributions are invested to pay for *your* pension in x years' time, and so must be big enough to cover the cost of the promises made to you, including any increases in pension after you have retired. In the 'pay as you go' scheme, your contributions are going to pay the pension of an existing pensioner, and so only need to cover the cost of that.

If there were no inflation, the cost of funding would be well below the cost of 'pay as you go'. But inflation makes things difficult for funded schemes, and especially in the area of increases. It is easier for a 'pay as you go' scheme to pay pension increases to compensate for the inflation that is happening here and now than it is for the funded scheme to save up the money to cover future inflation. The Civil Service has therefore been able to go on doing so, resulting in loud complaints of 'featherbedding' by jealous people.

There *are* funded schemes which have kept up with inflation, such as the nationalised industries, and it's been argued that it is quite possible for any scheme to do so, if it gives it enough priority in its investment policy. In fact very few private sector schemes fund in advance for inflation. The NAPF survey (table 44) shows that a substantial number, especially of works schemes, give no increases at all, and that many of the increases that are given are very small.

	Staff schemes	Works schemes	Combined schemes	All schemes
	%	%	%	%
Automatic increases	43	32	40	40
Non-automatic increases	44	43	50	47
No increases given	13	25	10	13
Total	100	100	100	100

Table 52 of the survey shows the level of automatic escalation in private sector schemes.

	Staff schemes		Works schemes		Combined schemes		All schemes	
	%		%		%		%	
No automatic escalation	59	(n/a)*	70	(n/a)*	66	(n/a)*	64	(n/a)*
Automatic escalation of								
Under 2% p.a.	—	(—)	—	(—)	—	(1)	—	(—)
2%	—	(—)	—	(—)	—	(1)	—	(—)
Over 2% but under 3%	4	(11)	2	(7)	3	(9)	3	(9)
3% but under 4%	25	(60)	25	(83)	22	(67)	24	(66)
4% but under 5%	2	(5)	1	(2)	3	(8)	2	(6)
5% and over	8	(19)	2	(7)	4	(13)	5	(15)
Matches RPI	2	(5)	1	(2)	1	(2)	1	(4)
Total	100	(100)	101	(101)	99	(101)	99	(100)

Information was not collected by the NAPF for these items.

Many schemes that do give automatic increases give them only on the pension above GMP, the part not increased by the State. According to the NAPF 49% of schemes do this. A few also take account of the increases in the basic State pension.

A scheme that is funded in advance for some level of inflation can still make a further 'ex gratia' increase if it can afford it and some companies do this.

> BOC guarantee increases of 3% per year. It has topped these up, in the last few years, with:
> 1978 an extra $4\frac{1}{2}$%
> 1979 an extra $4\frac{1}{2}$%
> 1980 an extra 8%

Guaranteeing to pay pension increases in advance is expensive, though not as much as some pensions specialists say. As a rough rule of thumb, 3% increases on the whole pension will add about $\frac{1}{4}$ to the cost of a pension scheme. At the moment, this is a fairly standard cost across schemes, but in the future, as the GMP becomes larger, it will be less so. Schemes increasing a minimal amount of extra pension above the GMP will find it fairly cheap, compared to schemes increasing the whole of a more generous pension. What sort of priority it is for you will depend, therefore, on how much pension there is over and above the GMP.

There is some justification for a company saying that it prefers to pay increases in pension out of current revenue, rather than fund them. In the short term it is cheaper, so the company can afford to give a higher increase, and it does not tie up money in the pension scheme which could be used for something else. *But*

■ if increases are paid only at the company's say-so, and on an ex gratia basis, then if the company is taken over, the new owners may feel no obligation to continue the practice;

■ if the profits slump, or the company gets into financial trouble, then the increases to pensioners may be expendable; and

■ pensioners have no bargaining power. They can't go on strike against the company, so it is *entirely* goodwill they are relying on. In the USA the unions bargain for increases in payments to the company's pensioners at the same time as they do so for wage increases for themselves, but that only means that the goodwill of the unions is also invoked.

How much weight you give to these points is up to you. In practice, the sort of company where in theory you could be unwise to rely on ad hoc increases is very unlikely to concede funding for pension increases anyway, so you will not often have a choice.

If you look for funded increases, it is unrealistic to ask for more than 5% per year (compound), and you may well have to agree on only $2\frac{1}{2}$% or 3%. Increases in the State basic pension should *not* be taken into account, whether the scheme is integrated or not, but if the scheme is contracted **out**, it's reasonable for the fund to increase the pension only in excess of GMP. Having got a guaranteed level of increases, you can still ask for extra payments to the pensioners when the company is doing well, or when inflation is high and the pensioners are suffering.

If the increases are being paid at the discretion of the company, you will need to monitor the situation every year, and find out:

■ what increases have been paid;

■ whether anything else has been offset against them (for example an increase in the State pension);

■ whether different groups have had different increases – have staff and works pensioners both got the same percentage? And what about very senior staff in 'top hat' schemes? – but also

■ whether there is a group that *deserves* special treatment: are the very oldest pensioners getting pitiful pensions, and therefore even more pitiful increases; should you press for a one-off large increase, to anyone who's been retired 15 years or more, to help them catch up; or,

■ if you can't get this, are the very small increases being paid in the right way? Social Security penalises very small increases in **income**, but would generally ignore the same amount turned into an annual Christmas present – say, £1 a week or £52 a year.

Any increase should apply to all pensioners, including widow/ers, dependants, and early retirees. Ideally, it should also apply to deferred pensions (see next section), but in practice very few schemes do this.

The *cost* of making ad hoc increases to pensions in payment varies very much, depending on how many pensioners there are. Some quite large schemes have very few pensioners because they are very new, but older ones may have as many pensioners as current members.

Possible arguments and responses

The strongest argument is the level of inflation, which has meant that even people who retired quite recently are finding their standard of living substantially reduced. Particular points you can make on this are:

■ The scheme promised security in retirement. In fact, due to the rate of inflation, there's no such security. Even after 1 or 2 years, people have to worry about how they can cut their spending to survive.

■ Produce examples of how company pensioners are *actually* coping. In section 14 on page 149, concerning widowers' pensions, we suggested ways in which you could collect information on how they were actually managing on what the company provided. You could do the same here, taking a sample of all pensioners from the oldest to the youngest.

■ If your procedures allow it, you could consider bringing along one of the pensioners – perhaps a retired shop steward – to put the case to the company. Clearly s/he wouldn't be a representative, and if you've taken pension increases into the collective bargaining arena it must be *existing* stewards who decide whether anything is to be accepted or rejected, but it might mean both sides are in touch with reality while discussing the increases.

Management will probably start by expressing sympathy, explaining how much a pension increase will cost (try to get them to put a precise figure on it), but add:

■ 'It's not company policy to increase pension', or

■ 'We feel that with the generous level of pension on which a person retires from this firm, there is less need for increases than there might be in other schemes', or

■ 'We have done our best by the pensioners in the past, but this year the level of profit has been just too low' (or alternatively, 'the level of wage increases . . . too high'.)

Responses on the first 2 points are pretty obvious. On the last, you might point out that the pensioners cannot be blamed for the profit level. Why then should they suffer for it?

Management may then ask how far you are willing to trade off an increase to pensioners against an increase in wages. Put that way, it is unlikely that the majority of the workforce will be willing to forgo any increase in wages – indeed, why should they? You may find it acceptable to postpone an improvement in the pension scheme – but if you do, *make sure* the pensioners get the full value of it. But *don't allow* management to divide workers and pensioners in this way. The workers will be pensioners one day.

If you have decided to ask for funding in advance, the company will argue against it on the basis that:

■ any security it provides is illusory, because if the company went bust the majority of people would have deferred rather than actual pensions, and these would not be covered; and that

■ funding in advance is not only expensive, but also wasteful during a time of high inflation, and they can put the money to better use in the pension scheme.

They may also say that they are generous with ad hoc increases, and could not afford to be if it was insisted that they should pay into the scheme for future increases – so existing pensioners will lose out. Presumably if you have decided to seek funding in advance it is because they have *not* been generous in the past, or because you do not trust their intentions in the future, so this is what you would tell them.

The other point to make is that funding in advance is good pensions practice, recommended by actuaries and other experts. This is useful if they've argued about 'good practice' on some other issue. The idea of funding is that you pay for your promises at the time when you make them, rather than offering jam tomorrow for which you make no commitment to pay. If there is an actuary, or a pensions specialist, on the company's side of the table, s/he will probably agree in principle, but plead necessity as a reason for not doing it.

Section 16: Leaving service

What you must have

The requirements under the Social Security Pensions Act, and the other overlapping pieces of legislation that affect this item, are dealt with on pages 19–23, and so they are not repeated here. Turn back to those pages for the information.

What the Inland Revenue allows

The Inland Revenue rules in this area are very complicated, and what follows is a broad outline of them.

Leaving aside the option of taking a refund of contributions, there are 3 other options that the scheme rules can allow:

■ a preserved pension and/or lump sum, kept within the scheme:

■ a preserved annuity and/or lump sum, bought from an insurance company;

■ a transfer value to the scheme of your new employer.

('Preserved' and 'deferred' mean the same thing in this context, so they are used interchangeably in this section).

The first two methods are much the same in effect – it is simply a matter of mechanics.

In preserving a pension the scheme *must* value it on the basis of the member's actual earnings, times the number of years of actual pensionable service, divided by the accrual rate. No prospective service can be included.

In a contributory scheme that does not give automatic increases in preserved pensions of at least 3%, then, if it would be greater, the pension secured by the member's own contributions must be preserved instead. That is, if on the actuary's calculations of rates of interest, etc, the contributions the member has put in will provide a bigger pension than one based on his/her service and earnings, s/he must be paid that.

A scheme can increase a deferred pension by any amount up to the increase in the Retail Prices Index, and it can be a completely different level of increase from that given to existing pensions. If the scheme allows for earlier payment of current pensions, then it must also allow, on the same conditions, earlier payment of deferred pensions. Any commutation (see section 9, pages 113–16), that is allowed on ordinary pensions must also be allowed on deferred pensions. The scheme can also give the deferred pensioner a widow/er's pension and a children's pension, and a lump sum death benefit which can be any amount up to the normal Inland Revenue limit of 4 times earnings, but it must be calculated on the basis of the earnings at the time when the member left.

If someone **drops out** of a pension scheme, but stays in the employment of the company, they *must not* have a refund; the pension must be treated as deferred. There are two exceptions to this – a woman who gets married, and a woman who becomes pregnant. They may take a refund of their contributions paid up to 6 April 1975, if as a consequence they leave the scheme but not the company (para 13.28 of the Practice Notes). If they wish to rejoin the scheme, they must either repay the refund, or have it treated as a lump sum benefit when it comes to calculating the maximum benefits.

If someone takes a **transfer**, rather than a refund or a preserved pension, (see pages 160–62 below for difficulties that can arise) then the amount that is brought **into** the new scheme is counted in with the benefits under it, when the maximum allowed is calculated. This applies both for the pension and for the lump sum.

> Jay Lambert brings a transfer value into his new scheme, and is given 5/60ths 'added years' as a result. When he retires, he must not therefore have more than an extra 35/60ths out of his new scheme, or he will go over the 2/3rds limit.

There are a number of other complications in the Inland Revenue rules, which do not affect the majority of people. The scheme administrator ought to be able to tell you whether there are any other limitations in your scheme's case.

Typical arrangements and special problems

There is only one group of schemes where the arrangements for leaving service are largely satisfactory. These are the public sector schemes, which have done two things:

- they have formed what is called the 'transfer club', and
- they have decided to do the actuarial calculations for leaving service using the same assumptions, so that pensions in identical or closely similar schemes will be valued at the same amount. There is a table from which they can work out how much a pension in one scheme is worth in another. Thus, for example, it is accepted that a pension in the British Steel manual workers' scheme is worth 75% of a pension in the British Steel staff scheme.

They also, unlike private schemes, revalue deferred pensions in line with inflation, so that the deferred pension keeps its real value.

This means that someone moving from, say, local government to the health service is able either to transfer his/her pension over to the new pension scheme, and buy in all the years s/he has already done in the old one, or to decide to freeze his/her pension with the old employer, secure against inflation. If s/he is moving from a worse scheme to a better one – if, for instance, s/he is promoted from manual to staff in the steel industry, then s/he would get added years that were 75% of the years actually done.

In the **private** sector, things are very different, because there is no transfer club, and no agreement on a common set of assumptions. So anybody who changes jobs is liable to lose, unless the new employer wants that person to work for him so much that he is prepared to make special arrangements. As so often, this applies to senior managers, for whom large sums are frequently paid into the pension fund to improve their pensions when they change jobs, not to manual workers.

Various problems arise, and these are dealt with in separate sections below as follows:
   16.1. The 'value for money' requirement
   16.2. Treatment of frozen pensions
   16.3. Treatment of revalued GMP
   16.4. Transfer values

16.1. The 'value for money' requirement

As we said above, a scheme must, if it gives a better result, provide the actuarial value of the member's own contributions, rather than a pension based on the accrual rate and pensionable salary. For a younger person, in a scheme with a reasonable contribution rate, this 'value for money' clause might well give the better result, given today's high interest rates. **But** many actuaries and scheme administrators calculate on the basis of much lower interest rates than they know they could actually get so that this guarantee doesn't come into effect. (They can also take into account the fact that you've had the benefit of life assurance for the years you've been with the company, and deduct the cost of that before calculating).

It would be reasonable at the moment to use anything up to a 10% or 12% compound interest rate to calculate the value of contributions. You can often get a much higher rate on fixed interest Government stocks, but when you come to reinvest the income, rates may have fallen, so this seems a fair guess at an **average** rate. But actuaries often use an interest rate as low as 5% or 7% in their calculations, and this makes an enormous difference.

> Ahmed Choudry is 30 and has been in the scheme 10 years. His total contributions paid in during that time are £1500.
> On an interest rate of 5%, over 35 years this will increase to £8274.
> On an interest rate of 7%, over 35 years it will increase to £16,015.
> On an interest rate of 10%, over 35 years it will increase to £42,154!

16.2. Treatment of frozen pensions

Once the pension is frozen, very few schemes increase it. The NAPF survey did not cover this point, so there are no statistics that can be quoted. Some schemes do give the same guaranteed increases to deferred pensions as to others, though.

Bryant and May, and the other Wilkinson Match schemes, increase the whole deferred pension by 5% compound, and pay the limited revaluation premium (see page 21) to the State also.

Very few schemes, either, preserve the full death benefit from the scheme (though they may make special arrangements for you to take out a policy on your own account: see page 176). Sometimes, they give you a death benefit based on the value of your preserved pension, or of your contributions.

The Pegler Hattersley works scheme says: 'If a former member entitled to a deferred pension dies before normal pension age, a lump sum will be payable, equal in amount to his own contributions plus interest at $2\frac{1}{2}\%$ per annum, calculated from 6 April 1978 to the date of his death'.

Some of the schemes that used to have such a provision, however, dropped it when the Social Security Pensions Act required them to preserve a widow's GMP.

16.3. Treatment of revalued GMP

Again, there are no figures, but it is clear that a good many contracted out schemes are taking some advantage of the loophole given by the Social Security Pensions Act. Many schemes use up **all** the extra pension over and above the GMP to 'frank' (that is, pay for) the revaluation of the GMP. This can result in the benefit earned years ago, before the Social Security Pensions Act was even thought of, being swallowed up. Other schemes use only the extra accrued since April 1978 for this, and leave the pre-1978 money separate. This is much less harmful, but still bad.

The result is that the majority of people, when they retire, will find that for some of their periods of employment they will have no more pension than they would have had if they had been in the State additional scheme all along.

16.4. Transfer values

A transfer is *not* by any means always the best option on leaving your job. There are three reasons for this:

■ First, actuarial assumptions. As we explain in chapter 8, the people who calculate the value of the pension fund, and of the individual pensions within it, the actuaries, are in fact basing a lot of their arithmetic on guesswork – assumptions about inflation, interest rates, and so on. Companies don't like seeing money going out of their funds, so they instruct the actuary – who is in effect their paid servant – to calculate a transfer value outwards on optimistic assumptions; that is, to give away the smallest amount of money he thinks he can get away with as buying the pension that has been promised to the person leaving. On the other hand, the receiving company will want to give as little return in terms of pensions as their actuary thinks he can get away with, so **he** calculates on pessimistic assumptions, which means that the lump sum buys much less than the first actuary assumed it would.

> George Smith leaves Wetherley and Co after 5 years. The company's actuary, calculating on a 2% rate of return on investments (after taking account of inflation) says that he will need £1000 to secure his 5/60ths pension, so his transfer value is £1000. George takes this to Plumtree and Co, his new employer, expecting to be able to buy 5 years' pension with it. 'Oh no,' says his new boss, 'Our actuary calculates that he can only get a $\frac{1}{2}$% rate of return on the pension fund, after allowing for inflation, so your £1000 will only get you $1\frac{1}{2}$ years' service in our scheme.'

Alternatively, the scheme administrators may be unwilling to give added years at all. They may only be willing to agree a money value as pension, for when the member comes to retire, which means it is very little different from keeping a frozen pension in the old scheme.

■ The second problem is with the GMP, and is only a problem because of the general framework of mean behaviour to early leavers. A scheme which keeps a GMP preserved need only revalue it by $8\frac{1}{2}$% a year compound. A scheme which takes on a **transferred** GMP has to revalue it in line with the Government's index of national average earnings. But the scheme that the GMP is transferring *out of* will not hand over sufficient money to the new scheme to pay for this, as it would have to spend less money to keep it in its own scheme. The new scheme will not do the revaluing unless it is given sufficient money, so it refuses to take on the GMP. The net result of this is that the GMP gets stuck. A great many schemes now refuse to allow transfers **out**, unless the GMP goes too (but they will not pay for it), and also refuse to allow transfers in unless the GMP is retained by the old scheme.

■ Third, often the transfer is calculated on the basis only of the employee's contribution, with all the limits we mentioned in the first point above, rather than on the scale of benefits laid down in the scheme, so that the transfer formula is even more mean than the preservation formula. It is almost never spelt out that this is done: you have to ask the specific question of the actuary.

Transfers were always fairly difficult to arrange, but since 1978 they have become impossible in many cases and far fewer are taking place than used to. In at least one case people working for two subsidiaries of the same parent company, if they have different pension schemes, can't transfer their pension rights between them. In 10 or 15 years' time there are going to be vast numbers of deferred pensions around, steadily declining in real value, waiting to be claimed when (or if) people retiring can get together all their bits of paper and find out who to write to.

Why can't the situation be sorted out? It can, if two things happen:

- actuaries give up their independence, and
- more money is put in.

(It's not certain which is the bigger difficulty!) If actuaries would agree on a standard set of assumptions and values, as the public sector 'transfer club' has done, it would mean whatever value was put on a pension in scheme A would also be put on it in scheme B. But that agreement would mean taking away a lot of actuaries' work, and also a lot of their special mystique involved in 'exercising judgement' about what's going to happen in the future.

Also, without substantial extra contributions from somewhere, the uniform values set would be very low. This is because 'early leavers' (that is, anyone who doesn't stay his/her whole life in the same pension scheme) are subsidising the rest of the pension scheme. If they were to get a better deal, then the subsidy would be taken away, and the money would have to come from somewhere else instead, if the benefits were maintained. At the moment no one is willing to pay the extra cost.

The problem of early leavers and transferability is being studied by the Occupational Pensions Board, and they are due to report in March 1981. Any government which manages to produce legislation on this will have to weave its way through some very heavy vested interests to get anything done. So the current state of affairs, or something very close to it, is likely to remain for some time.

What is the best one can look for in the average private sector scheme, then? There are a good many variations, but the following points could be sought:

■ The company should explain *and justify* how it works out its 'value for money' guarantee. If it's based on an unrealistically low interest rate, then they should be asked to *increase* that rate and recalculate frozen pensions. They may say that they don't know how it's calculated – it's left to the actuaries. So you'll need to insist on either bringing the actuary into the discussion, or getting a letter from him setting out the details.

■ A deferred pensioner should receive the benefit of any increase given to pensions in payment (you're more likely to achieve it if the increases are guaranteed in the rules).

■ The extra pension above GMP should be preserved separately from GMP (both the pre- and post-1978 pension). You'll probably have to explain to the employer what you're on about on this, as they tend not to have understood the point when it was brought in.

■ Transfers out, including those of excess pension above GMP only, should be available.

■ Special terms should be applied to transfers to and from other schemes in the same group – whether between different subsidiaries, or between works and staff schemes. It is not unknown for a pension in a works scheme to be frozen when someone transfers to staff service.

■ Deferred pensioners should be allowed to take early retirement pensions as soon as they reach the appropriate age.

If you cannot obtain this for everyone, you could try at least to get it for those who have been made redundant (see chapter 9, section 3, pages 255–59).

There are two other points on deferred pensions:

■ Some schemes preserve the pension after *shorter* periods of service than they have to under the Act. There are some that insist on preserving it even if you leave after 1 or 2 months, which means you will have a very small pension stuck there. This did not look such a bad idea a few years ago, when inflation appeared to be coming down, but it is now. If your scheme is preserving pensions after shorter lengths of time than they have to, ask them to change it.

■ If someone leaves within 5 years, some schemes offer only the minimum terms for preservation if someone leaves 'of his own free will or due to fraud or misconduct' and better ones if s/he goes for any other reason. This sort of punitive attitude should be stopped.

Possible arguments and responses

The argument about the rights of leavers has been going on for a long time, and follows fairly well-worn tracks. The arguments for a better deal are:

■ The *majority* of people are 'early leavers'. Those who stay are in the minority. It is unfair that the majority should be penalised to subsidise the minority.

■ People leave their jobs for all sorts of reasons, not just to 'better themselves'. They may indeed be forced to leave by the actions of the employer, in making them redundant. Why then should they lose so heavily?

■ The effect of inflation is that frozen pensions are swiftly declining in value. It's not the *intention* of the pension scheme that this should happen. If there was no inflation, frozen pensions would work fairly well. Since inflation appears to be with us to stay, should not the scheme be taking account of it, and adapting the rules to match? (This is an argument we've used on other items.)

The employer's response will be:

■ There's only a limited amount of money to go round, and they prefer to spend it on those who stay, rather than on those who go. At times this gets expressed in an almost feudal attitude of 'looking after those who are loyal to the company'. It reveals part of what pension schemes, like other 'fringe' benefits, are about – tying people into the company so that they do not have a free choice of jobs.

■ Or they will throw up their hands in horror and say that it's a very complicated area, they can't swim against the tide, only the Government can sort out the problems. It's true that a *full* solution won't come without legislation, but this is very unlikely in the near future; meanwhile they could do something to mitigate the problem.

You could ask them whether they intend to stay with the company for the rest of their lives. If not, how do they wish their current pensions to be treated? A recent survey by the British Institute of Management showed that only 10% of managers spend all their working lives with one employer. *Two-thirds* of managers are likely to retire with pensions which are only about half the entitlement they expect (reported in *The Times*, 11 March 1980).

On the question of the 'franking' (offsetting) of the GMP, you're on strong ground. The essence of it is misrepresentation – that people thought they had been promised a pension better than the State would provide, and now they find they will get only what they could have got from the State. There are a number of actuaries and consultants who condemn this practice, for that reason. The company may try to argue, if the member's contribution rate is low, that it doesn't matter because they have not lost any money by being in the company scheme rather than in the State scheme, but this is *not relevant*. The company will still have made statements about how good it's being providing a 'better scheme', how much money it's putting in as it's own contribution, and so on.

Another standard response is that the other members of the scheme, 'those who do intend to stay', won't like money being spent on those who leave. This may have been true in the past, when it was chiefly long serving white collar staff who had a pension scheme. But now that schemes have been extended to so many manual workers, who are highly conscious of the problems of redundancies and closures, it's a myth, and the employer needs to be told so.

The employer's other response will as usual be that it costs too much. If you can get him to go at least halfway, with no offsetting pre-1978 service, that will be a start, and you can return to the attack later.

Section 17: Temporary absence

This means periods when you are away from your job – through sickness, or pregnancy, or if you're away studying, or if you've been laid off for a period, but are still definitely an employee.

What you must have

Under the Social Security Pensions Act, if you're a member of a contracted out scheme, then you are a **contracted out employee** while you have a contract of service, and are in a job that is covered by the contracting out certificate. So however long you are away, if you still have a contract with the company you *need* not be treated as having left the scheme.

If you are getting no money from the company for a time, it will reduce your annual earnings figure on which your GMP is calculated, and therefore the GMP you finally get.

A woman who is away due to pregnancy, even if she has technically left work while away, can still be treated as a contracted out employee for that gap, **if** she exercises her right to return to work. (If she doesn't, she must be treated as having left service on the date her contract ended).

What the Inland Revenue allows

The Inland Revenue says that, except in cases of sickness, a person may be treated as temporarily absent for up to 3 years for any reason, or for longer if absence is due to 'secondment to a United Kingdom Government Department, or work of national importance of a like nature', so long as there is a definite expectation of a return to work, and s/he doesn't become a member of another pension scheme.

If s/he is sick, s/he can be retained in the pension scheme indefinitely, even if s/he is not expected to return to work. If wages are being paid (for instance under a sick pay scheme), the company may deduct the pension scheme contribution, but if there are no wages the company may, in effect, pay both its and the member's contribution for as long as necessary.

Typical arrangements and possible improvements

In general, schemes do not treat temporary absence, even when it is due to sickness, very well. The wording below, taken from the Toyworks scheme, is fairly typical:

> If your absence is due to injury or illness, your membership will be maintained up to your normal retirement date so long as you are treated as remaining in employment. If you are absent for any other reason your membership will be maintained for up to 6 months.
> Cover for death benefits will continue during a period of temporary absence.
> Your contributions to the scheme will continue to be payable whilst you are receiving an income from the company.
> If you receive no income from the company, your pension entitlement will be reduced for any period of non-payment of contributions. Upon return to work you may, by agreement with the company, pay the arrears of contribution so as to maintain your full pension entitlement.

Some schemes will allow you to retain your membership for longer if you are sick than for any other reason. Others will pay your contributions if you are sick without sick pay, at least for a limited period.

> Ferranti Ltd says: 'A member will continue to contribute if he is in receipt of earnings during absence. Those employees who do not receive earnings during medically certified sickness will have their contributions paid by the company for a maximum of 13 weeks in any one period of absence.'

Death benefit is *usually* maintained during periods of temporary absence, but some companies stop it after a while.

Not many companies have amended their booklets to take account specifically of maternity leave (and they have not even heard of **paternity leave**). Those which have, mainly where the scheme is insured and the insurance company have given the advice, usually have a standard clause saying something like this (again from the Toyworks scheme):

> If you are a female member leaving as a result of pregnancy or confinement and exercise your right under the Employment Protection (Consolidation) Act 1978 to return to work, you will be treated as temporarily absent while you are away, but the period of absence will not rank for pension.

If the temporary absence clause in your booklet is very brief, as they often are, or non-existent, the point is almost bound to be covered in the rules at greater length, and in this case you will have to look at them to find out the position.

Layoff is hardly ever specifically mentioned in scheme booklets, although pension schemes are now quite widespread in industries which are prone to layoff, like engineering and the motor industry. Often it is left to local procedure. One example where it **is** mentioned is Vauxhall, whose booklet says:

> In deciding whether service has been continuous, absence due to the following circumstances will not count as a break in service:
> (a) absence not exceeding 12 consecutive months because of sickness or accident;
> (b) layoff not exceeding 6 consecutive months because of lack of work.

What should be looked for in a temporary absence clause? The following items should be covered:

■ When someone is absent through sickness, but is retained on the payroll, then s/he should be kept in the pension scheme indefinitely.

■ If someone is being paid wages by the company, then contributions can be deducted from them. But if no wages are being paid, then the company should make up the contributions. Ideally, this should be indefinitely in cases of sickness, pregnancy and layoffs due to the company's decision, and for a specific period for any other reason. The company may refuse to countenance any indefinite commitment, in which case you will need to decide what is a reasonable period.

■ Death benefit should always be maintained where a member is accepted as temporarily absent.

■ When a member is finally taken off the payroll and treated as having left service, his/her service should be ended at the date when s/he is taken off the payroll, not at the date when s/he first became absent.

■ Where it is a member's responsibility to make up the contributions on his/her return, s/he should have the option of paying by a lump sum *or* in instalments over a long period.

■ Whenever you are negotiating an agreement which means people will be temporarily absent (for example, for study leave), remember to check on the pension rules, and, ensure that these people will not be adversely affected. See the companion volume in this series, Michael Cunningham, *Non-Wage Benefits*, 1981. In order to keep the pension booklet simple, it is probably best to give general guidelines there, and expand any special points in the specific agreement.

Chapter 5 deals with permanent health insurance, which covers long term disability. Arrangements need to be made within this for paying the pension scheme contributions – but see this chapter (page 182), for details.

Reasonable treatment of temporary absence is not expensive. Just how much it will cost depends on the arrangements for sick pay, special leave, and so on. The fairly mean treatment of this in the past has probably resulted from the general assumption that most people in pension schemes are white collar, are fully covered by sick pay schemes, and will be paid by the company during any other periods of temporary absence that happen with their approval; so that cases in which people have to fall back on their provisions are rare. The reality, now that pension schemes have been extended to the hourly paid, is different, and so these clauses need to be brought up to date.

Possible arguments and responses

The detailed arguments on this will depend on what type of absence you are talking about. The general principle, however, will be the same. People should not suffer in retirement by having a reduced pension because there have been short periods when they have not been at work, perhaps many years earlier.

This argument is much stronger where the absence has not

been the employee's fault – where it is due to sickness, for instance, or where it is sanctioned by another agreement with the employer. Study leave might be an example of this. It would contradict such an agreement if the pension scheme was then to penalise people.

For absence which the company permits, but is not paying for – an extended holiday without pay, for instance – you need to ask for better arrangements for the payment of the member's own contributions. You could argue that the company, having permitted the absence, should not then make it more difficult or inconvenient for the member to fit back in than need be. Paying contributions all in a lump sum may cause hardship, especially if a person has been without pay for some time, and it is only common sense to make it smoother by allowing arrears to be paid off bit by bit.

The company will probably reply that better arrangements for temporary absence are too expensive, both in terms of pension and administration. Ask them to tell you what the actual cost will be, because it probably *won't* be much, and if necessary suggest that they work out how many cases it would have applied to in the recent past. On your side, try to find actual examples where there has been an obvious inconsistency of treatment between the industrial relations and pensions departments, and of where there has been hardship because of inflexible treatment.

Section 18: Alteration, amendment and termination

18.1. Alteration or amendment

What you must have

If
■ a contracted in scheme is amended to contract out, or
■ a contracted out one to contract in, or
■ a contracted out one is amended in a way that affects, or might affect, the terms of contracting out,
then the company must give **3 months' notice** to all the members, and **consult** the independent recognised trade unions. It need not accept their views; 'consult' means only that. The Occupational Pensions Board must then give its **consent**. The unions have a right to complain to the OPB if they believe they have not been properly consulted, but no certificate has ever been refused for that reason.

If the OPB feels the change being made is technical or unimportant, it may agree to the notice period being shortened to only 1 month.

If the scheme is being amended so that it is no longer contracted out, then the fund must either preserve the GMPs, or buy them back into the State scheme through paying what is known as the 'accrued rights premium'. This fully reinstates you in the State scheme, as if you had never left it.

What the Inland Revenue allows

The Inland Revenue will allow the alteration of schemes, but insists on approving the alteration. Making an alteration without their blessing may jeopardise the status of the whole scheme.

Getting final definitive legal documents for the trust deed and rules is a long, slow process, partly because of the detailed technical work that has to be done, partly because lawyers are anyway very slow. While the documents are being prepared, the scheme will run on 'interim' deeds and rules – this is accepted by the Inland Revenue, and everyone else, as alright, and as binding as the real thing. An additional amendment will create another interim deed or, until even that has been prepared, will be contained in the announcement of the change, which will be regarded as definitive.

Exactly how the rules of any particular scheme are changed will depend on the provisions of the original trust deed. Deeds may say

■ that the members must be given a specified period of notice before any alteration can become effective, or

■ that the approval of a majority of the members must be obtained (this is rare), or

■ that only amendments that do not prejudice the accrued rights of existing members will be permitted.

If the scheme's powers are too cumbersome and restrictive, it is possible for the Occupational Pensions Board to override the terms of the scheme, under section 64 of the 1973 Act, but this is not often done. Where an alteration is made to any of the main benefits of the scheme, the members who are affected must be informed before the Inland Revenue will approve the change. The information can be given either by sending it in writing to each member, or by drawing each member's attention in writing (by, for instance, a slip in the pay packet) to a notice on the main notice board or something similar.

Most schemes have a clause like this, somewhere in the booklet:

> The board has every intention of maintaining the scheme, but it will be understood that future conditions cannot be foreseen; the right must therefore be reserved to amend or terminate it at any time.

This is there to protect the company. It has the effect of ensuring that you do not have the rights you would otherwise have under your contract of employment.

Typical arrangements and possible improvements

We would of course seek that any changes in a scheme are **negotiated** with the unions; this point is dealt with more fully in chapter 6. If a scheme is going from contracted out to contracted in, or the other way, so that formal consultation has to take place, the union should be brought in at the earliest stage, if possible before the notice of intention has even been issued.

Negotiators need to look also at the **communication** of changes. The general practice of schemes in the past has been to follow the Inland Revenue rules, and no more. Changes would be made in the scheme by the board of directors, without the involvement of the unions, and the employees told, as if a revelation had come from on high, in an announcement issued to all employees. Very often, the announcement letter made no concessions to simplicity, but used the same obscure language as for the Inland Revenue. The scheme **booklet** was often not changed for a long time after the actual change was made in the rules, and so anyone who wanted to check what his/her rights were had to find out by wading through the booklet plus various other odd bits of paper.

During the contracting out process, many schemes went through extensive programmes of consultation, giving all the members a chance to attend meetings to discuss the changes being made. Although this was welcomed by many pension scheme administrators as a very worthwhile exercise, since then the practice has often not been followed when other major changes have happened.

It would be worthwhile having a 'briefing' on the scheme every few years anyway, because people forget the information quite quickly. You should seek also that:

■ any change, however minor and technical it looks to the

administrator, should be discussed with the appropriate negotiating body **and agreed**, before being announced;

■ not only the content, but also the wording, of any announcement should be discussed with the negotiating body, or a subgroup, to ensure that it can be understood by ordinary people;

■ where a major change is being made, details of it should be given to members via meetings, in **working time**, either of the members or of their representatives (depending on the size and structure of the membership), at which people can ask questions and clarify issues as much as they need;

■ that any amendment, even a minor one, is issued as soon as possible in a form that means it can easily be added to the ordinary pension booklet – by slips of paper that can be gummed in, or by a leaflet that can be slipped inside;

■ and that, after changes are made, the booklet itself should be reprinted as soon as reasonably possible, incorporating all the changes made, and should be kept up to date.

Possible arguments and responses

In general, bad communication about changes in the scheme will not be deliberate, but because the administrator feels that,

■ since the members don't seem very interested in the scheme, there's no point in taking a great deal of care about how they are informed of changes – 'They won't read it anyway' –

■ and that s/he must be very careful to keep the small print legally correct, because s/he is worried about the possibility of claims from people which will have to be allowed although not strictly legitimate, because of loose wording.

On the first point, you could suggest that there is to some extent a 'chicken and egg' problem. If people can't understand their pension scheme, or the changes that have been made in it, then naturally they will not be very interested in it. Worse than that, they are quite likely to be suspicious of changes announced in obscure language, and thus regard the pension scheme as a management ploy for getting their wages back off them.

On the second point, *clear* wording need not mean loose wording. Professional communicators, on television or in the newspapers, can get over complicated ideas in simple words. The DHSS is another example. Their leaflets about State benefits used to be very obscure, but they have improved their recent ones greatly, mainly through efforts made by people who knew what they were doing. At the insistence of the civil servants, there is still tucked away in every leaflet a sentence saying that 'This leaflet is for general guidance only and is not a statement of law.' Many pension booklets also contain this sort of statement, and if the rest of the booklet is clear, it is quite adequate as a safeguard against ill-informed claims.

Note: accrued benefits

What we've said above applies to amendments to the **future** benefits of the scheme. In *most* (but not all) schemes the rules do not allow amendments which would reduce the **accrued** benefits (those you have already built up through being a member of the scheme), without the specific consent of each individual concerned.

It is very rare for a reduction in the accrued benefits to be proposed. In cases where it is (for instance, where it is claimed there is not enough money in the fund), then the need for individual consent gives a powerful bargaining counter to the unions. However, this shouldn't be overestimated. The company still has the ultimate weapon of closing the scheme down altogether, which will freeze the accrued benefits (see section 18.2).

Sometimes a set of alterations will be proposed, and the members asked to consent, on the basis that though it may reduce some accrued benefit for some people, the overall effect is beneficial. This should be resisted: in any changeover the aim should be that no one individual should be worse off (see page 110). It should be agreed that anyone who is potentially going to suffer will have benefit calculated in the two alternative ways, and the better paid.

Again, the company may threaten that if signatures are not forthcoming, it will discontinue the whole scheme and start again. If the proposed improvements have been discussed in detail, this is unlikely. It might well, in any case, cost them more in administrative trouble than the extra calculations involved. As a compromise, you could agree to limiting the length of time during which the scheme had to do the alternative calculations to, say, 5 years.

18.2. Termination

This section deals with winding up a scheme where the company remains in existence. Winding up because of a closure or bankruptcy is dealt with in detail in chapter 9, section 2, 'Closures', page 252. Winding up because a new scheme is being introduced is dealt with in section 8.2 of this chapter, page 109.

What you must have

If a contracted out scheme is being wound up altogether, there is a duty to **inform** the members, by giving them a **notice of intention**, and to **consult** the recognised independent trade unions. The notice of intention will normally run for 3 months, but this period may occasionally be shortened with the sanction of the Occupational Pensions Board. When the time given on the notice runs out, the scheme will surrender its contracting out certificate (after the OPB has agreed that proper consultation has taken place) and the members will revert to paying contributions at the contracted **in** rate. The company must make a payment to the State, of the **accrued rights premium**, which reinstates you in the State scheme.

The duty to inform and consult can be (and sometimes is) evaded if the company simply stops paying its contributions to the contracted out scheme. In that case, sooner or later the OPB will **cancel** its certificate, with immediate effect.

What the Inland Revenue allows

A scheme that is **discontinued** — which is the word the Inland Revenue always use – can be either **frozen** or **wound up**. If it is **frozen**, the Practice Notes say: 'All contributions cease, but the assets of the scheme continue to be held by or on behalf of the administrator, and are applied to provide benefits according to the rules when existing members retire, or die, or withdraw from service.'

In a **winding up**, how the benefits are dealt with, and the order of priority if there is not enough money to go round, will be covered by the rules of the scheme (see below for this).

Employees still in employment cannot usually have a return of contributions when the scheme is wound up. The employer *can*, which seems very unfair. The Inland Revenue's reasoning is based, as usual, on the view that pension schemes are a tax fiddle for the higher paid, and that, if people can get their contributions back, company directors who can decide for themselves whether to run a pension scheme or not will keep on opening new ones and closing others just to get a tax benefit.

What happens to your rights

The trust deed and rules of a scheme will invariably have a

section specifying what is to be done on discontinuance. Usually this will include a list of priorities – that is, who has first call on the funds available. A scheme that has been properly funded for discontinuance ought to have enough money to pay all the outstanding claims. Often, though, this is not the case, and then the money is divided up in the order given in the deed and rules.

Pensions in payment will have the first priority; then, in a contracted out scheme the GMPs, and any leftover benefits from the old graduated scheme get priority along with the members' benefits in general. The money will be divided up, if there is not enough to go round, so that everyone has the same proportion of his/her full entitlement.

If a scheme is wound up and there *is* enough money to pay the accrued benefits the trust deed usually says that any extra goes back to the company. It is quite possible, though, for a deed to be amended (while the company is not in financial difficulties) to say that any extra is used to increase the pensions of people who have retired and also the deferred pensions. Very few schemes have a rule of this sort, but it is a point worth pursuing, especially since it costs the company nothing.

It is very rare for a company to wind up its pension scheme when it's not going into liquidation, but because it feels it can't afford it. If it happens, it should be resisted, just as any reduction in your wages and conditions (which is what it is) should be resisted. Even if you *accept* that the company is genuinely in financial difficulties, winding up the pension scheme is unlikely to be the answer, for several reasons:

■ The legal and administrative problems of doing so are considerable, and grappling with them would distract management from their proper job.

■ In the short term, the costs of buying you back into the State scheme will be considerable, and there will also be substantial legal fees, payments to consultants etc.

■ How much are they paying in anyway, above the amount they would pay into the State scheme if you were contracted in? As a last resort, you might allow them to **cut back** future benefits – never benefits already earned – so that it was costing no more than contracting in. It would be easier to improve benefits back to their original level than to start again if a scheme has been dismantled, if the company's fortunes improve. But you should be *extremely reluctant* even to contemplate this.

Section 19: Miscellaneous clauses

As well as all the main sections of a pension scheme, there are usually a number of miscellaneous clauses tucked away somewhere in the booklet. We are dealing with them all here, for convenience.

19.1. Life assurance continuation

In many booklets, especially where the scheme is **insured**, you will find a section that says something like this:

> Death benefit cover ceases on leaving, but if you leave before your 60th birthday you will normally have the option, without having to produce any evidence of good health, to take out a new and individual whole life or endowment assurance policy with the ABC Insurance Company to replace any death benefit cover which has ceased.

This is really there to give the insurance company a bit of extra business, but it can be useful to the older, less healthy, member who would have to pay a lot more for life assurance if s/he had to have a medical examination.

19.2. Assignment

Most booklets have a clause saying something like:

> The benefits provided by the scheme are strictly personal and must not be assigned, mortgaged or alienated in any way.

This means that you *must not*, for example, use your expectation of a lump sum when you retire in a few months' time as security for the mortgage for a new house, nor can you as a pensioner agree to sign over the pension cheques as they come in to your landlady. If you do, you'll usually find that the benefits are forfeited altogether (that is, no one will get them).

This is because the scheme is designed to provide money for you and your dependants to live on, not for some finance house. It is intended as a safeguard both for the fund, which does not want to be in a position of paying out large sums of money to Loan Sharks & Co Ltd, and to some extent for the pensioner, to protect him/her from pressure by unscrupulous people. The clause is an Inland Revenue requirement, and where it is not actually in the booklet it will be in the rules.

19.3. Evidence of health

Some booklets have a clause saying: 'Evidence of health may be required before you are permitted to join. If this is the case you will be notified.'

This is generally because of an insurance company practice called the 'free limit'. They will have said that they will insure anyone for up to, say £40,000 without a medical examination, but if the liability goes over that limit, they reserve the right to ask for one. The limit is usually pretty high, so it won't affect most manual workers. If it *is* affecting a substantial number of people, it's because the contract is very restrictive – so that it is cheap to the employer – and it needs to be renegotiated.

Some companies insist on *all* employees taking a medical examination before they can join the scheme. There's nothing wrong with this, provided that:

■ the results of the examination are not used to *exclude* anyone from the scheme;

■ the company pays any costs; and

■ the results are retained strictly for use in the pension scheme, and are not released to anyone else without the member's permission.

A related clause that you will find in many schemes is that employees who are away sick on the day the scheme starts, or on the day they become eligible, will not be allowed into the scheme until they have completed 2 months' continuous employment.

This is, as usual, because of cost. It is a crude way of weeding out some of those in poor health. If the employer and/or the insurance company cannot be persuaded to drop this condition altogether, then *at least* life assurance should be provided for everyone, whether sick or not.

Section 20: Additional voluntary contributions

What you must have

There is *no* compulsion on any scheme to provide for additional voluntary contributions (AVCs), that is, for individuals to pay in extra to the scheme to get extra benefits. If the rules do allow it, then the scheme must be equally open to men and women.

What the Inland Revenue allows

The Inland Revenue will allow the member to contribute up to 15% of earnings to a pension scheme; and this can be *either* a basic contribution *or* an ordinary rate plus the facility of making extra contributions. The *employer* can contribute any amount. You are entitled to tax relief on these contributions, just as on the ordinary ones.

But the Inland Revenue imposes heavy restrictions on what can happen to your contributions:

■ They come under the same **preservation** rules as the ordinary contributions. If you have to take a frozen pension on your basic contributions, you must do so on your extra ones as well.

■ However much you've paid, you *must not* have a pension bigger than the Inland Revenue maximum. So if the amount of pension you've earned on your voluntary contributions would take you above that limit, you will not receive any benefit from it. The money will stay in the fund.

■ Once you have started contributing, you *must not* stop paying, unless you can show financial hardship.

Typical arrangements

Many schemes have provision for extra contributions to be paid. There do not seem to be any figures on it, but this is definitely a growth area.

How does the ordinary AVCs scheme work? In most of them, the company is not putting in money. It will administer the scheme, but not add anything to the contributions, and usually they are channelled into a separate account. Even in a self administered scheme, this account is generally with an outside body. **Building societies** and **insurance companies** are involved in running these schemes.

Both are offering specialised savings schemes which take advantage of the tax relief allowed in pension schemes. A number of building societies are keen to offer them at the moment, because they have the great advantage of giving a regular flow of savings (since once you're in, you can't usually stop), whereas building society income in general goes up and down very much.

Outside the public sector, these savings schemes are usually based on money purchase principles (see pages 39–40) with the disadvantages of that type. At the end of this section, we explain some of the different sorts, briefly.

The public sector schemes, however, work in a different way. They offer **added years** for extra contributions. If you fulfil a number of detailed conditions (too many to go into here), you can buy extra 'years' of pension so that where before you had perhaps 10/80ths you now have 15/80ths. This means that the extra benefits you've bought are treated in the same way as the ordinary benefits. This means they're inflation-proofed, both before and after retirement; since they're about the only investment that is, they're well worth having.

A few private sector schemes also work on the 'added years' basis; Bryant and May is one example of this.

This will usually mean that, in order to guarantee the benefits, the **company** is putting in something as well as the members, so it is an above average scheme. The benefits of the usual sort of private sector AVC scheme are more dubious. Because of the tax position, you do usually get a better return on your investment than you would in a private savings scheme. So it is useful *if you were going to save the money anyway*.

But

■ if you leave the company, the money will generally be trapped there;

■ you can't get the cash out except at retirement (or on death – there's usually a life assurance provision attached); and

■ once you start contributing, you've got to go on.

This means that it's really only a sensible option for those coming up to retirement in the near future, who are fairly sure they will stay with the company until they retire. People with more than 10 or 15 years to go before retirement should not be encouraged to join. They might find it useful to join an additional **life assurance** scheme though.

For negotiators, there are additional problems:

■ If at some point you succeed in improving parts of your scheme to somewhere near the Inland Revenue limits, the people making the additional contributions will not be able to get the full benefit from them – which will not please them.

■ Because of this, and because the most pension minded of your members will be paying in to the AVCs scheme to get a bigger pension, there will be even less steam than before behind attempts to get the pension scheme improved for everyone.

■ Especially if you're looking for improvements on **past service**, an AVCs scheme can cut the ground from under your feet.

Your argument that people with long years of service get pitiful pensions when they go will be countered by management saying, 'Well, if they mind so much they can always join the AVCs scheme.'

If, despite all this, you decide to go in for an AVCs scheme, remember that it is a useful savings mechanism and no more.

▪ Don't let management oversell it.

▪ Make sure the implications are fully explained to anyone thinking of paying in to the scheme.

▪ Make clear (and say it again in future years) that an AVCs scheme is no substitute for a good basic scheme, and its existence is not in any way going to change your views on the improvements needed.

There's no need to give a list of arguments for having an AVCs scheme. The only reason management will refuse one, if you decide to ask for it, is that it will be too much trouble to administer. If they can be persuaded to investigate they'll probably find that the insurance company or building society will gladly take on most of the administration (for a fee). Usually management will be quite willing to agree a scheme. It doesn't cost them anything, and the disadvantages for the unions are advantages for them.

The different sorts of scheme

The main types of AVCs scheme are:

▪ Insurance company, non-profit. These give you an absolute guarantee of what you will get, but it will be at a fairly low level, so that they are covering themselves if anything goes wrong.

▪ Insurance company, with profit. Again, you get a guaranteed rate, probably a little bit lower than in a non-profit scheme, but on top of this you *also* get a bonus, based on the profit the insurance company is making. This can't be guaranteed.

▪ Unit linked. Each, say, £5 of contributions buys a 'unit' in the scheme's investment, that is, in the stocks and shares they have bought, and when you want to get your money out you liquidate those units. If the stock market is high when you retire, you get all the profit. If it is low, you get only a low price for your units, and therefore may do very badly. This means that these schemes are dangerous for people who can't choose when they are going to retire, because they will lose if they happen to go when the market is in a bad patch.

▪ Building society schemes. They tend to give an interest rate linked to the mortgage rate, and therefore considerably better than they give the ordinary depositor, and you do better than you would as an ordinary depositor because of the special tax privileges. But you have no guarantee. If the mortgage interest rate goes down, your rate will as well. (Some insurance company schemes are also linked to the building society rate.)

The glossy leaflets provided by the various organisations selling these schemes can be overoptimistic, if not downright misleading. Given that they very much want your money, there would be nothing to stop the trustees, or a negotiating committee, arranging for a representative from the company whose scheme you are looking at (or more than one) to come to meet you and go over the whole thing in detail. If you employ a broker, s/he ought to do the shopping around for you (but remember s/he gets commission on the business). One of the questions you will want clear answers to, before committing yourselves, is what happens to people's contributions if they leave. Do they carry on getting bonuses and/or interest added, and if so at what rate?

5.

Permanent health insurance

Although this is not set up formally as part of the pension scheme, it is normally treated as part of it. It is closely linked with early retirement (often in fact the schemes will overlap), and it is usually administered by the same person in the company. This is why it is being covered here, rather than in the companion volume by Michael Cunningham, *Non-Wage Benefits*.

What permanent health insurance means

A group permanent health insurance (PHI) scheme is, in effect, a long term sickness scheme. It provides an income for anyone who is too ill to work, after a certain length of time, for as long as s/he is ill, even if the person is taken off the employing company's payroll, and even if the company goes out of business. Normally under a PHI scheme, the permanently disabled individual will be paid benefit until s/he reaches retirement age; then s/he will be transferred to the company's pension scheme.

The 'permanent' in the title means permanent so far as the **insurer** is concerned. Once an insurance company has accepted a contract for a PHI scheme, it has to go on providing the benefits so long as the employer is paying the premiums – even if the insurance company is making a massive loss on the deal. The premiums of course do not stay the same, so an insurance company wanting to get rid of an employer could push the premiums up and up. But the **insurers** may not cancel the contract (the employers can), and anyone already on their books for benefit would remain so.

What the Inland Revenue allows

These schemes are fairly limited (about ½ million people are covered) and are a recent import from America. The Inland

Revenue, therefore, hasn't quite taken them in, and has not set a maximum limit as it does on pension schemes. Whereas pensions have the Superannuation Funds Office all to themselves, PHI is dealt with by the ordinary taxperson who handles the rest of the company's affairs. It's possible therefore to get different rulings on tax treatment in different parts of the country but, if a peculiar ruling is given, the insurance company can generally sort it out with the Inland Revenue headquarters.

A PHI scheme is usually non-contributory for the employee. The *employer* gets tax relief on his premium.

When the benefit is paid, it can come in 2 ways:

■ via the employer, so that you are still on the payroll – it is then taxed as earned income under PAYE, and National Insurance contributions are also collected – or

■ direct to you from the insurance company, in which case you get a 'tax holiday' (you don't pay any tax on it), for the first tax year, and are then taxed on it as **unearned income**.

Typical arrangements

PHI schemes have developed in the last few years to a standard pattern, because in the absence of Inland Revenue restrictions the insurance companies have laid down their own. They are not regulations in any sense, but if you ask for anything different in your scheme, you're most unlikely to find an insurance company offering it.

The standard pattern is:

■ After someone has been off sick for a specific period of time (3 or 6 months are the most common periods), s/he will be transferred to the PHI scheme, which will pay a proportion of earnings as long as s/he is incapable of work. Some schemes define this as incapable of 'any work', others as incapable of doing 'your job'. The second alternative is more expensive (because it means people won't be transferred to alternative light work, so there will be more claims).

■ The proportion is often 50%, occasionally 66%, but *always* there will be a restriction that you may not receive more than 75% of your actual earnings before you fell sick – and in calculating this the benefit is added together with any State scheme benefit or income from any other source, such as an accident insurance scheme. This is supposed to encourage people to go back to work. The insurance companies say privately that it is management they tend to have trouble with, 'malingering', more than manual workers.

■ The benefit may increase annually by a specific percentage, or it may not. The premiums are higher if it does. A fairly typical figure might be 3% compound a year.

■ The scheme may pay the pension fund contributions in addition to the benefit paid out to the member, or they may be taken out of the member's benefit. Again, the premium will be higher for the first alternative.

■ Most schemes provide for 'partial disability' benefit – that is, if the person is able to do some job, but it is worse paid than his/her previous one, then s/he will get a reduced benefit to make up his/her earnings to the 'target' level.

■ There will be a list of 'exclusions'. That is, no benefit will be payable if the disablement results from, for instance:
* intentional self-inflicted injury,
* intemperance or drug addiction,
* war, invasion, riot or civil commotion.

When they first started in this country, schemes tended to have a long list of exclusions. Since then, experience has shown that most of them are more trouble to the insurers than they're worth, and many of them have been dropped. One that is still common is **pregnancy**. Some schemes exclude *any* illness or disablement resulting from pregnancy or childbirth; others impose an extra waiting period, usually of 3 months. A fairly standard wording would be.

> [Benefit will not be payable] in the case of a female member [incapacitated] from pregnancy or childbirth, unless incapacity continues for a period of 3 months after the conclusion of the pregnancy, in which case the deferred period for purposes of benefit shall be deemed to commence after the expiry of the aforementioned period.

■ A lot of schemes impose an eligibility period – that is, the employee has to be with the company a certain length of time before s/he qualifies. If the scheme doesn't impose it, the employer may.

Since PHI schemes are not technically part of pension schemes, they are not exempt from the Sex Discrimination Act or the Equal Pay Act, and it would be **illegal** to offer them only to one sex, or on different terms to men and women, or to offer different benefits (the pregnancy clause is a special case).

If you are trying to persuade your employer to start a scheme of this sort, there is a useful publication called *Permanent Health*

Insurance, published once a year by a magazine called *Policy Holder Insurance Journal*. It lists which insurance companies do PHI, and what variations there are between them. You need to be a pretty large company to have a scheme designed for you. An average sized one will have to take a scheme off the shelf.

If the insurance company doesn't want your business, either because it doesn't like the look of you or because it's overloaded with new work, it will tend to ask a very high premium to discourage you, rather than say no outright, so it's always worth shopping around. For some manual jobs, however, the premium will always be high because there is a specific risk.

The costs are comparatively small – between $\frac{1}{2}\%$ and 1% of payroll. A premium will normally be fixed in percentage terms for 3 years, and then revised up or down by the insurers in the light of their experience.

What should you look for in a PHI scheme?

■ A good level of benefit – 2/3rds of PAYE earnings if possible (given that you'll have to accept the 75% limit on earnings and NI benefits).

■ Regular annual increases – even if they are not very large, they will be better than nothing.

■ As few exclusions as possible – you'll have to accept some.

■ A waiting period that ties in properly with the sick pay scheme, so that someone can come off sick pay and go on to PHI without a gap. If your sick pay scheme is good enough, you will be able to accept a 6 months' waiting period, which reduces the PHI cost a good deal.

■ Coverage for *everybody* – if you have to accept a service qualification, it should be as short as possible (not more than 1 year) and any age limits should be as wide as possible. You probably won't succeed in getting part timers covered, but it's worth a try.

■ Pension rights safeguarded – the insurers should continue paying the contributions to keep your pension up to date.

What's the point of a PHI scheme, rather than good provision for early retirement due to ill health?

■ It caters for the long term sick who are eventually going to come back to work, as well as those who are not. The person who has had a bad car accident will eventually go back to work, though s/he may be away 18 months, and so s/he could not take early retirement, but needs more coverage than the ordinary sick pay scheme will give.

■ It does not 'write off' someone who does not want to feel his/her career is finished, as early retirement does.

■ While the individual being paid PHI benefit is still on the payroll, s/he has some protection against unfair dismissal under the Employment Protection (Consolidation) Act and therefore retains rights if s/he is ever in a position to seek reinstatement.

■ It will generally give a better level of benefit, except for long serving people who become ill a few years before retirement. To safeguard them, a good early retirement clause can also be included in the pension scheme, and the person transferred to whichever is better. The cost of this is very small.

If a scheme is introduced, you *may* find that the insurance company are tougher in their definitions than management would have been. They are likely at least to be equally tough to everyone, since they don't know the people and won't be motivated by office politics or friendship. But if you feel they are being unfair, ask for a 3-way meeting between the company, stewards, and insurers. If the company makes the request, the insurers are unlikely to refuse.

Possible arguments and responses

We are assuming in this that the company already provides decent sick pay. If it doesn't, then that ought to be the priority rather than PHI. Based on this assumption, the arguments you can use are:

■ More than 90% of sickness is over within 6 months. The PHI coverage therefore is for a very small group who are unlucky enough to be ill for longer, and who without this provision will be dependent solely on State benefit. PHI is therefore not expensive, but it is cost effective, as it will help those who need it most.

■ If someone whom the employer values becomes ill, the employer will be likely to make special arrangements for him/her – he may, for instance keep him/her on the payroll. A PHI scheme enables the employer to make provision for *everyone* in that event, without favouritism and without incurring a heavy financial liability.

■ If staff already have such a scheme, you can argue that the manual workers are just as valuable to the company as they are, and should be treated as such. There is *no* evidence that manual workers abuse such schemes.

Management's response may first of all be founded on ignorance – they may not have heard of the idea. Once they have found out about it, they may object on various grounds:

■ Cost – although these schemes are not really expensive. Get them to obtain a few quotes, without commitment, so you know what you are really arguing about, and can talk straightforwardly about money.

■ They may say that PHI is more expensive than providing the same benefits through the pension scheme. It is marginally more expensive than providing an early retirement pension *of a comparable standard*. But very few schemes do reach that standard. So if the employer starts using that as an argument, ask him to improve the early retirement pension to that level instead, to show his good faith.

■ He probably won't say it to you, but he may well be worried about the implications in employment law – that is, that he won't be able to sack sick people so easily. It may be worth bringing this out into the open and making him feel ashamed of himself.

■ If he says that he doesn't feel he can go 'out in front' of other employers, and that there are too few PHI schemes for manual workers for him to follow, it might be worth finding out about a few companies that **do** have PHI for their employees, in the same sort of industry and the same size. Try your Trades Council or your union's head office for information.

Finally, if you can once get him to the stage of having exploratory talks with the insurance company, they'll probably do the rest for you. Insurance salespeople can be very persuasive!

6.

Making a claim

Section 1: Effective negotiation

Essentially, making and negotiating a claim for pension scheme improvements is like making a claim for any other sort of benefits from the company. You put in for what you think is reasonable, you argue for a while about money, and in due course you reach a settlement which is the best you can get out of the company at the time. But there are certain *technical* problems that make pensions negotiations look different. For instance:

■ You are more closely bound up with a legal framework. No power on earth will persuade a pensions manager to agree to a change in the scheme that means it will lose its Inland Revenue approval, so it's not worth trying.

■ You're doing *very well* if you achieve the Inland Revenue maximum. In times of pay policy, unions became used to the idea that the 'maximum' was what everyone got. It isn't so in pensions – a scheme that reaches the Inland Revenue limits is a very expensive one.

■ There will usually be more involvement of 'experts' than in wage negotiations, on one or both sides. It's best to try to get the company experts – pensions manager, consultant, insurance company, and so on – actually *into* the meeting, rather than have the company refer back to them outside. They may well be on your side quite often – they want the business. *But* remember that the outside firms will want it at a profit – so you need to take care over what goes into the small print.

■ Pensions negotiations tend to take longer, and be conducted at a more leisurely pace than others. You don't get cliffhanging meetings going on till midnight, with beer and sandwiches being brought in, and anxious industrial correspondents standing on the doorstep. If things run on, you tend to adjourn till next time. There will frequently be homework to be done outside the meetings – getting the actuaries to recost a particular element, or drafting a form of words that covers all eventualities. Actuaries and lawyers can be very slow, so you may need to put pressure on them to get negotiations finished at all. Insurance companies can be even worse, unless they see a very straightforward profit coming out of it for them, as with a brand new scheme.

■ It is not easy to achieve a retrospective pensions agreement, partly because it's incorporated in a legal document, partly because all the time people are retiring, leaving, or dying and it will be difficult to treat them fairly in retrospect. So you need to start negotiating well before the 'anniversary date' when changes come into force and, if things drag on too long, you may find yourself forced to agree that you'll wait until the *next* anniversary date to see the changes put into effect. If the scheme is computerised, the deadline may be even earlier, to allow time for the computer programme to be amended.

There is one general point which, although very rarely spelt out, both sides are usually conscious of in negotiation. You don't have much muscle on pensions. People will very rarely take industrial action about the pension scheme. Sometimes it can be linked to other items, or annoyance about the management attitude on pensions will be the catalyst when a lot of other things have also gone wrong – but *never bank on it.*

This lack of muscle puts the unions in a permanently weak position, and the management in a strong one. You need to counter it by:

■ showing that you know as much as they do, if not more, on the subject;

■ appealing to their common sense; and

■ appealing to their 'public relations' sense. It is partly in order to prove what a good employer it is that a company will set up a pension scheme. If you can show that, on the contrary, it is showing them up as a *bad* employer because the scheme is misleading, or giving lousy benefits, you can go on to suggest that they are currently wasting the money they are putting into the scheme, and get much better value out of it by putting in a little more. (You don't need to *believe* this argument, so long as it works!)

Comparisons with other companies will often be useful. But there is a very wide gap between the best and the worst pension schemes, and there would be little point in comparing a struggling light engineering firm with ICI, for instance. When you are doing your research to start with, look at other companies

■ in your industry, and of roughly your employer's size,

■ and in completely different industries, but competing in the same labour market. You could argue, for instance, that a firm in Derby which tried to keep its wage rates comparable to Rolls-Royce's in order not to lose workers, ought also to keep its pension benefits comparable for the same reason.

As well as comparing staff and works benefits in your own company, it may be useful to look at senior management benefits, if you can find out about them. 'Top hat' schemes are usually kept pretty secret, for obvious reasons.

For **national** comparisons, the most useful publication is the NAPF *Survey of Occupational Schemes*, published every year by the National Association of Pension Funds. In 1980, when they published the 1979 survey, they left out some of the most useful information, on accrual rates, but even without that it is worth having, and has been used a lot in this book. You can get it from the NAPF, Prudential House, Wellesley Road, Croydon CR9 9XY.

The Government does occasional surveys on this, but although you can be sure they're statistically correct, they take too long to be published to be much use. The most recent was the *Government Actuary's Survey 1975*, published 1978 by HMSO, price £2.75. Organisations such as Labour Research and Incomes Data Services also do occasional studies on pension schemes. Various employers' organisations do their own surveys, often on a regional basis, which if you can get hold of them can be extremely useful.

It will also be helpful to have with you in any negotiations a copy of the 'Practice Notes' (see pages 260) from which you can quote if the company says something can't be done.

As with most negotiations, you're most unlikely to get everything you ask for, so in constructing the claim you need to think about what is really important and what is there in order to keep the issue open, but you don't really expect to win this year. As the different items cost very different amounts, it's useful to do a 'shopping list' which includes a mixture of high and low cost items. Some examples of *high* cost items would be:

■ improving the accrual rate substantially,

■ providing for past service at a reasonable rate,

■ reducing the retirement age by several years,

- providing automatic increases in pensions in payment, and
- removing the integration factor.

You would expect a worthwhile improvement in any one of these items to cost, broadly, 3% or 4% payroll (but remember, that's a very rough figure). If the company were to claim it cost a lot more, you should ask them to justify their figures in detail. There are of course *small* improvements in these items which would cost much less. Reducing the retirement age by only 1 year, for instance, would be a medium or even low cost item.

Moderately expensive items (roughly 1% or 2% of payroll) would include

- improving the definition of 'final pensionable earnings',
- improving the widow's pension from an accrued to a prospective basis,
- improving the leaving service provision, and
- giving a better deal for early retirement 'at the member's own request'.

Several of these will be more or less expensive, depending on what you start with.

Cheaper improvements, under 1% (often very much under), would include:

- giving better ill health early retirement provision *or* a PHI scheme,
- extending widow's pension to widowers,
- giving dependent children's pensions,
- giving an extra year's earnings as a lump sum death benefit, and
- improving temporary absence provision.

Extending eligibility costs money on a different basis – it brings more people on to the pensionable payroll. Introducing member participation doesn't cost anything, except time and energy. Additional voluntary contribution schemes normally only cost the company administrative time.

It's also useful to divide the items into those that stand by themselves, and those that have a 'knock on' effect, in improving others:

- Improving the accrual rate,
- providing for past service,
- removing the integration factor, and
- improving the final earnings definition

will all improve not only the pension, but also the early retirement pension, the spouse's pension and the life assurance. That's one reason why they are expensive items. The ill health retirement provision, on the other hand, will be very important for the person who has to retire early, but have no effect on anyone else. Again, a balance has to be struck.

Harmonisation of schemes

A common claim by manual workers is for a single scheme for both staff and works members. If the schemes are currently wildly different in quality, you may accept that it is not possible to move to this in one step, but nonetheless keep it as a long term aim. In that case, it will be important to ensure that no part of your claim is going to make this *more* difficult by taking the structure of the scheme in different directions. For example:

> The Whitecroft Group schemes for staff employees and works employees both give 2 times earnings as a death benefit. But the staff scheme gives a 1/60th pension, the works one 1/80th. The works negotiators here would be sensible to make an improvement in the accrual rate a priority, rather than improving the death benefit so that it was better than the staff scheme.

Finance

Normally in these discussions you will expect the issue of questions of cost to be part of the overall discussions of the package of changes sought. Occasionally, you will find an employer who:

■ is deciding to introduce improvements without putting in enough extra money to cover them; or

■ has been putting too little money into the scheme for a time, perhaps because of his own financial difficulties, perhaps because he thinks no one will notice. (See chapter 8 for a description of how schemes are financed). If you are pressing for details of costings at various points, this ought to become apparent; if you are suspicious you could ask for a meeting with the actuary to find out what's going on.

You then have two choices:

■ you can say that your first priority is to get the funding right, and that therefore before talking about benefit improvements you want to talk about money going into the scheme (which might mean forgoing certain benefits in the short term); or

■ you can take the same risk as the employer is taking: that he *won't* go bust and that in due course he will be in a position to make up the shortfall.

What you do depends on your judgement of the company. For instance, the British Rail pension scheme is now rather in this position, thanks to the Government tinkering with the funding rate in the 1980 Transport Act. But it is unlikely that British Rail will go bust, and if anything disastrous happened it's pretty certain that any government would have to bail them out. So the transport unions, although not happy, have been able to go along with the change.

> On the other hand, a company in the private sector was discovered by the GMWU recently to be paying substantially less than it should do. Although the rate was enough to pay pensions *already* built up, it did not cover the promise made for future pensions, and the position was steadily getting worse. The company was making no moves to improve it, and the actuary was not trying to make them. The union in this case strongly advised the shop stewards not to pursue a claim for improvements before the funding situation was right, on the basis that increased benefits on paper were no use unless there was cash to back them up. This advice was followed and the position is much improved.

It must be for those negotiating to decide if they are ready to take the risk. But if you feel you *are* taking a risk of this sort, you should insist on a very careful monitoring of the situation.

Section 2: A case study

This is an example of a pensions negotiation. It is taken from an actual one, but with some details altered to make things clearer, which is why the company's name has not been given. This particular example has been chosen because it has followed a formalised bargaining structure, unlike many others. It is **not** intended as a model.

Background: company XYZ is a British subsidiary of a foreign multinational. It has 5 plants in this country. Worldwide the company is in some financial trouble, because of taking bad investment decisions in the 70s, but the British plants were doing just about all right when the pensions negotiations started.

The **pensions negotiating body** is formally a working party of the company's National Joint Council. It has on it the national officers of the major unions. The GMWU and the EETPU regularly send their pensions specialists as substitutes for the national officers. The AUEW send along the national officer who also specialises in pensions, and the TGWU, who lead the negotiations, bring along their specialist as well. In addition, there is a representative from each plant. It was intended that the representative should be the convenor, but in several of the plants the convenor has got into the habit of sending along instead the local member trustee. The company send their industrial relations director and his deputy, plus the pensions manager and someone to take the minutes.

The main features of the scheme, at the beginning of negotiations, were:

■ a pension of 1/80th of final pensionable earnings – 'pensionable earnings' were defined as gross pay minus $1\frac{1}{2}$ times the State pension –

■ a guarantee that the annual benefit would never be less than 40% of contributions;

■ a widow's pension on death in service of $\frac{1}{2}$ the member's prospective pension, and a widow/er's pension on death in retirement of $\frac{1}{2}$ the member's actual pension;

■ a death benefit of $1\frac{1}{2}$ times gross earnings; and

■ pensions in payment were guaranteed to increase by 3% compound each year.

In 1977, when major changes were made because of contracting out, the unions agreed with the company a 3 year moratorium on negotiations. This was due to come to an end in 1980, so in the spring of 1979 moves were made to commence a new round of negotiations.

The **first step** was consultation in the plants. The convenors asked for views on important items and priorities from each plant, and the first working party meeting started with a trade union side, where the plants put forward their lists. Many things overlapped, but some were specific to one or two plants. For instance, one plant is on piecework, the rest on daywork, and in the **piecework** plant there is a problem in calculating the life assurance for anyone who was off sick before they died, which did not arise elsewhere.

Out of the discussions, a list of 10 items was drawn up:

1. Future negotiations to take place every 2 years
2. Death in service benefit to be on an equitable basis for members with sickness records
3. 5 year guarantee for pensions after retirement
4. Widow's pension to be broadened to a family pension of 2/3rds of the member's pension
5. Death benefit lump sum to increase to 3 times gross annual earnings

6. Minimum pension guarantee to increase to 50% of members' contributions

7. Inflation proofing of pensions in payment to increase to 5% p.a.

8. State scheme offset to be reduced to 1 times lower earnings limit

9. Previous scheme benefits to be credited at $\frac{1}{2}$ the accrual rate of the current scheme

10. Pension formula to improve from 1/80th to 1/60th of pensionable earnings.

At the full meeting with the company, the list was presented to them, and they agreed that their actuary would be asked to cost the proposals. No priorities were put on them at this stage.

At the next meeting, about a month later, the company returned with the list, and a 'price' in money figures and percentage of payroll terms, beside each one.

	% of pensionable salaries	£000s
Death benefit adjustment	.05	22
5 year guarantee – on a narrow definition	.05	22
on a wide definition	.25	107.5
Widow's pension improvement	.90	387
Death benefit increase	1.05	451
Guarantee of 50% of contribs.	1.25	537
5% compound increases	2.5	1075
Reducing State offset	(2.8)	1223
(As this changes the whole basis of calculating pensionable salary, it should not really be expressed in this way.)		
Past service credits	3.0	1290
Pension formula 60ths	3.75	1613
Retirement at age 60 for men	3.0	1290
Total cost, including wider definition of 5 year guarantee, but excluding the reduction in offset	15.75	6727
Plus *extra* cost of 'aggregation'	2.5	

You'll notice that:

■ The company have provided **two** definitions for the death benefit guarantee. The 'wide' one is that, when a pensioner dies, if his/her pension has not been paid for 5 years, the balance is paid as a lump sum to his/her dependants or representatives. The 'narrow' one is that the lump sum is only paid if there isn't a spouse to whom a pension will be payable.

■ An extra item has been added – early retirement for men. This came up separately from one of the plants to the wage negotiations, as part of the campaign against redundancies and for shorter working time, and the company had assumed that the unions would want to add it to the list.

■ There is an *extra* cost for 'aggregating' everything together – this is because some things have an effect on each other, like for instance the size of pension and the size of the integration factor.

■ The first item on the unions' list has been missed off altogether; this is because a request to change the length of the moratorium is not directly a cost item.

The company asked whether the unions wished to challenge any of the costings, but since they looked approximately right the unions felt they need not. They therefore had some discussion, as a side, on priorities, and adjourned, having requested:

■ one of the specialists present to write a paper setting out a possible list of priorities, and for this to be circulated to the plants; and

■ the plant representatives then to discuss it with their members and return with a view on the priorities.

The paper produced is below:

Draft proposals for priorities within the shopping list

1. How large a contribution should we seek from the company to begin with?

The joint contribution (company and member) to the **staff** scheme is about 4% higher than to the works scheme. It would seem reasonable to look for an increase to round about this funding level. Any past service commitment should be *in addition* to this because it is a debt from the past. They saved money by **not** having a good pension scheme then.

2. If we wish to improve the member's pension, what's the best way to do it? The various proposals have different effects, as below:

(a) going for 1/60th benefits everybody, but the higher paid more than the lower paid;

(b) reducing the State offset benefits everyone, but the lower paid more than the higher paid; and

(c) the 50% guarantee is of particular benefit to anyone whose pay record is shaky in the last few years, for instance because of sickness. We recommend selection of (b) and (c).

On the other items, there are several whose cost effect is so small that they can be added in with the major ones without any problem. We could for instance seek the death benefit adjustment and the 'wide' 5 year guarantee. We could also look for a *small* increase in the death benefit to 2 × salary, and a **modified version** of what we were asking for on the family benefit – keeping it at half the member's pension, but making it a family pension.

It is suggested therefore that there should be **two** lists of priorities – major cost items and minor cost items. The major items should be:

Priority
1. Past service credits
2. Reducing State pension offset
3. 50% guarantee
4. 60th pension
5. Early retirement for men
The minor items should be:
Priority
1. Death benefit adjustment
2. 5 year guarantee
3. Widow's pension becoming family pension
4. Death benefit at 2 × earnings

The next meeting again started with a trade union side. The priorities as set out in the paper were agreed on the major items, but it was decided that *all* the minor cost items should be pressed, without priorities. A claim drawn up on that basis was submitted to the company, who took this away, promising an answer in a few weeks. At the next meeting, they came back with a detailed response. They took the view that they wished their scheme to be not on a level with the best in the country, nor to be at average level with the country as a whole, but comparable to schemes in other companies of a similar size in broadly the same industry – what they called 'the community'. They said that, in view of their financial problems and the fact that they were very much on a level already with those with whom comparison was suitable, they wished to respond by offering (this is an extract from their minutes);

Lump sum death benefits
The company proposed that the lump sum death benefit should be increased to 2 times gross earnings in the 52 weeks before death or 2 times gross earnings in any previous tax year.

Death in service benefit
The company stated that it was prepared to discuss a formula for improving the position of those members with long sickness records. The company reminded the unions of its proposal to use holiday pay as a basis and stated that it was considering the use of sick pay as a basis for a formula.

Five year guarantee/Widow's pension
The company stated it was prepared to widen the current widow's pension to the same class of dependants as the staff pension scheme, although the pension would remain $\frac{1}{2}$ of the member's pension and not 2/3rds as claimed by the unions. The company was also prepared to guarantee pension payments for 5 years for pensioners with no

surviving spouse. The company believed that this was a logical approach in view of its offer to broaden the widow's pension to a family pension.

The unions replied by pointing out
■ that the items the company had chosen were the cheapest of those on the list, and even the cheapest alternatives where there was more than one, so the company were making an *extremely* limited offer;
■ in seeking comparison with 'the community', the company had selected their own group, so the unions had no way of challenging it; and
■ they had given, during the contracting out discussions, a commitment to 'move towards' a works pension scheme not less favourable than the staff's, and this offer gave no sign of their good faith on this.

The company were therefore asked to think again, and return for further discussions.

In the meantime, there were redundancies in one plant, and it became clear that there was considerable confusion over the provisions for leaving service. At the time of contracting out, the company had introduced, as they were obliged to do, a preserved widow's GMP for those who were leaving (see page 160 for an explanation of this). They had clearly intended to remove the previous rule that the dependants of a deferred pensioner received 5 times his/her contributions as a lump sum if s/he died before retirement. It had not, however, been agreed with the unions. The next meeting's first session, therefore, was taken up with 3 way discussions between the stewards of the plant (who had turned up in a body without authorisation, so that the company refused to meet them formally), the working party, and the company. An agreement was hammered out, giving *both* the widow's pension *and* the lump sum to deferred pensioners, but it was stated that it created no precedent for any other plant.

The position was further complicated by the fact that the company were trying to reduce their contribution this year, as their actuary had said that the scheme was overfunded, but were very anxious to reassure the unions that this was not a manipulation of the fund to suit their own financial position. The rest of this meeting was taken up with discussing the issue, and no progress was made on the claim.

At the subsequent meeting, however, the company came forward with a substantial offer, but it was
- phased over several years, and
- conditional upon the unions accepting that the company could reduce its funding for the year.

The offer was (from the unions' notes):

From April 1980: as previously offered
From April 1981: past service to be credited in scheme at 1/160th
From April 1982: past service to be credited in scheme at 1/120th
From April 1983: accrual rate to be 1/60th

To cover the discussions on deferred pensions, the company proposed that from April 1981, on the death of a deferred pensioner before retirement, pre-1975 entitlement would be paid as a lump sum of 5 times the deferred pension on the day he died. Post-1975 service would be paid as a widow's pension entitlement. Anyone leaving between April 1981 and April 1982 would have his/her pre-1975 pension calculated on the 1/160th basis, and anyone leaving after April 1982 would have it calculated on the 1/120th basis.

The company also stated that, on moving to the 1/60th rate, they would expect the manual workers to pay the 5½% contribution currently being collected from the staff.

After some agonising over the funding proposal, the unions decided to accept the offer – or rather, since they were only a working party, to recommend it to the NJC for acceptance. It was now very close to the date for the wage settlement, and a delegate conference was to be held in the near future. The company requested that the package should be put to the conference for their agreement, and that, if there was substantial disagreement, the wages and conditions package should be held up while further discussions went on. With some misgivings, the unions agreed to this. In fact the pensions package was agreed without problems, and the whole agreement was duly signed by the national officials.

The whole process took about a year, and ran up very tight against the anniversary date deadline. If substantial changes had been due in the first year of the phased agreement, there would have been considerable problems, but the unions were assured that the smaller changes could be dealt with easily by the computer. (The assurance came from the industrial relations manager; the pensions manager looked a bit doubtful.)

One of the most difficult items, which took up a tremendous

amount of time, was the definition of 'earnings' for life assurance purposes where a person has been sick for some time. Any formula that satisfied the piecework plant did not work for the daywork plants, and the company would not contemplate different arrangements for different plants. In the end, the formula below was agreed, more out of exhaustion than anything else:

> Where an employee dies in service his life assurance benefit will be based on 2 times the *greatest* of:
> (a) the employee's gross earnings in the 52 weeks before the date of death, or
> (b) the employee's gross earnings in any previous tax year, or
> (c) the 'rate of pay' as defined in the sick pay agreement, multiplied by 52 to provide an annual earnings basis.

Particular lessons that can be learnt from this case study are:
■ the need to start negotiations early enough;
■ the importance of consultation at plant level;
■ the importance of making clear agreements that dot all the 'i's and cross all the 't's – in this particular case confusion worked to the unions' advantage, but it doesn't always –
■ the usefulness of having *both* experienced officials, who know the company well, and pensions specialists on the negotiating body (though it's questionable whether so many were needed).

But this example is not put forward as a model – it's an illustration that you may want to discuss.

7.

Negotiating rights and member participation

Introduction

We are dealing with these two issues together, because they interrelate closely. While a member trustee is not in a negotiating role as such, the fact that s/he is there on the board of trustees is part of an extension of the scope of collective bargaining. Just as the job of a health and safety representative will often differ substantially from the job of a shop steward, so the job of a trustee, or a member of a pensions committee, will differ from that of a shop steward – but they are all part of collective bargaining in a broad sense.

There has been a tremendous growth in the number of companies with member trustees over the last 4 years, and there are also many companies which have set up 'advisory' or 'consultative' committees. Some of these are doing a good job: others are just talking shops, and were originally accepted by the unions either because it was the best they could get from the company or because they were new to dealing with pensions, and not too sure of the way to move. Now that there's been some time to test them out, and there is more knowledge and involvement in pensions among shop stewards, many of these setups need reviewing, and bringing more firmly within the control of the unions.

This chapter is subdivided into 4 sections:

Section 1: Trustees – what the job of a trustee is (and is not);

Section 2: Advisory and consultative bodies;

Section 3: Negotiating bodies; and

Section 4: Possible arguments and responses – both your own and those of the company.

Section 1: Trustees

A pension fund these days is almost always set up as an irrevocable trust. This means that it must have a trustee, or more than one, to control the trust.

Anyone can be a trustee provided s/he is capable of performing the duties and competent to carry them out. This means that the trustees must be UK residents, and they must not be minors or of unsound mind. A **company** can be a trustee.

The job of a trustee is too *look after* the fund in the best interests of all the members, *not* to negotiate changes in the scheme. (Wearing different hats, the same people who sit on the trustee board may also be negotiating on pensions, but when meeting as trustees they should not do so.)

In an average sized fund, the sort of items that might come to a trustee meeting would include:

■ deciding on investment policy, and monitoring its carrying through;

■ supervising the administration of the scheme;

■ satisfying themselves that the legal duties, for instance with regard to the Inland Revenue, are being complied with;

■ receiving and studying the accounts and actuaries' report;

■ taking decisions on what happens to discretionary benefits – death benefits, for instance – and

■ interpreting the rules, and deciding whether particular cases – for example requests to retire early – come within those rules or not.

So the trustees' job is **supervisory**: only in the smallest schemes will the ordinary trustee be actually signing the pensioners' cheques and arranging with the stockbroker what shares to buy. An average to large scheme will delegate its responsibilities to a paid person, most often the pensions manager.

Even so, the trustees have a legal responsibility, which they cannot delegate. It is always the duty of the trustees to check on what is happening, and satisfy themselves that things are going well, and take steps to put them right if they are not. It is as much the case with an **insured** scheme as with any other.

This is the legal theory, and if ever a case is brought to court for breach of trust (which is rare), that is the theory the court will follow. In practice, things have been rather different. There has been a great deal of negligent, and downright bad, trusteeship, and a good many skeletons are lurking in the cupboards of pension schemes to be pulled out. Some of them have been, in the newspapers recently, as well as in a forthcoming book by John Plender to be published soon by Macmillan, but there is undoubtedly more to come.

Given that the job is so limited, why do we want member trustees? There are divided views on the subject in the trade union movement itself. There is an argument that trade unions should refuse to get involved, because of the danger that, as with worker directors, we will get sucked into the system and start playing capitalism's game better than the capitalists. What are the counter-arguments?

■ **It's our money.** Since management bears some of the risk if things go wrong, because of the company commitment to pay 'the balance of the cost' it is fair enough that they should have some part in the administration, but we should have at least an equal share.

■ If you are going to take a 'more socialist than thou' attitude about pension fund money, the time to do so is before the scheme ever starts. Once there is a fund, which will probably be several million pounds, and growing fast, you can either ignore it or get involved in it. It won't go away if you pretend it's not there, any more than a piece of new machinery you don't like will.

■ *Someone* is going to control the funds, and with them economic power. If it's not us, it's management. The pension funds and other institutions are now the most important buyers and sellers of shares and government stock on the stock market and have taken it upon themselves to act to change Government policy – for instance by refusing to lend to the 1974–79 Labour government until it conformed to their views.

The appointment of member trustees is **no guarantee** that things will change. Many of those already appointed are simply acting as rubber stamps. But at least if we are in there we can try to change things.

The opposite arguments against having member trustees also come sometimes from trade unionists – that we ought to leave it to the 'experts', that it's management's job to manage, and that ordinary shop floor workers are not competent to do the work because they don't have the knowledge. Against that view, we would argue:

■ The 'experts' are not the trustees, they are the people the trustees *employ* – the pension fund manager, actuary, merchant bank, insurance company. There's actually a lot of evidence that these people haven't been very effective at doing their job (see John

Plender's book, for instance), and so no one need feel diffident about supervising them.

■ The trustee's job is to **supervise** and to be a **watchdog**. You don't need to be an expert yourself to see when the experts have got things wrong, *provided* you are willing to question sufficiently closely and not take things on trust. On that basis, an active trade unionist can do *at least* as good a job as someone from the personnel department, who is no more knowledgeable about pension funds than you are.

A lot of member trustees have not been sufficiently critical of what their advisers tell them, for understandable reasons. When you're sitting as an equal on the board with management, and people from the City, trained in public relations, are spending a great deal of time convincing you that their view is the *only* reasonable one, it is extremely easy to get sucked into the cosy world of pension fund management, and to find yourselves rapidly accepting the orthodox City view of what is in the 'best interests' of the member. There is not space in this book to go into the whole question of an alternative investment policy. All that can be said here is that there is no reason **in law** why speculative property investment should be acceptable and funding of a cooperative making socially useful products unacceptable, provided that trustees are able to show that they are likely to get a rate of return on either investment that is both reasonable and safe – which is what trustee law requires. The TUC has in fact called for a change in the laws governing trusteeship, but it is doubtful whether this is really necessary, since the current legal position gives a lot of scope for alternative policies, which has hardly been exploited yet.

The TUC have issued 3 pamphlets on this subject, which are worth reading if you're interested:

The Law of trusts and pension schemes: note of guidance (TUC Publications 1980) price 25p

The role of the financial institutions: evidence to the Wilson committee (1979) price £1.25

Occupational pension schemes: a TUC guide (revised edition forthcoming.)

The legal position

There is no legal obligation on companies to appoint member trustees. The Occupational Pensions Board recommended in 1975 that they should be appointed, on a voluntary basis, and the next year a White Paper was issued by the then Labour government, proposing legislation on the subject to make their appointment compulsory. The White Paper said:

> The Government are proposing that participation by employees in the running of occupational pension schemes should be achieved through the agency of recognised independent trade unions, and that they should have a right of appointment to 50% of the membership of any controlling bodies specified by the legislation.

This was however squashed by the pension fund managers and groups such as the CBI, who claimed that this proposal meant 'disfranchising' non-union members (who had never been enfranchised anyway). The Liberals also took up this cause, and one of the conditions of the Lib-Lab pact was that no legislation should go through in this form. It was clear from the outset that the Tory government elected in 1979, if it made a law on this question at all, would not do so in any way that gave powers to the unions.

The **legal power** to appoint trustees is usually with the company, because they are the 'settlors' of the trust. This is usually so even where there are member trustees. It is possible if you wish to add a clause to the trust deed spelling out that there are member trustees. For example, the British Leyland Hourly Paid Trust Deed, drafted in 1976, said:

> **Rule 25. Appointment of trustees**
> A. The statutory power of appointing a new or additional trustee or trustees shall be vested in the principal employer which shall have the power by deed to remove any trustee from office and appoint another trustee or trustees in place of any trustee so removed.
> B. The power vested in the principal employer by paragraph A of this Rule shall be exercised only after consultation with the relevant trade unions.
> C. (. . .) The number of trustees of the scheme shall not be less than 4 and the following provisions shall apply:
> a. those of the trustees who are participating members are . . . called 'member trustees' and those who are not participating members are called 'management trustees',
> b. the number of member trustees and management trustees shall be equal.

If you have a signed agreement, you can refer to this in the trust deed, or it can do instead.

The exact structure of a board of trustees can vary a lot, depending on what is set out in the trust deed. So too can the **powers,** and you need to be very careful that a company does not appear to be conceding member involvement while at the same time moving **control** away from the trustee board.

There are 3 main types of boards of trustees:

■ Groups of individual trustees, each appointed as a named individual, through a fairly cumbersome procedure. Each time a trustee is changed, there has to be a variation in the trust deed, which can take a long time. If member trustees are appointed in these cases, they will each sign a legal document, countersigned by a representative of the company, to give them their formal position.

■ Groups of directors of a **trustee company**.

For example, Turner and Newall (Hourly Paid) Pension Trustees Ltd is legally **the trustee** of the hourly paid pension scheme. It has 11 directors, 5 of whom are appointed from the members of the scheme and they then have their names added to the company's register of directors before they legally take up their position.

■ A professional trustee company. The banks, big insurance companies, and insurance brokers, run these. The company setting up the pension scheme buys the services of, for instance, Barclays Bank Trust Co Ltd, who then carry out all the duties of trustee for your pension fund, as well as a lot of others. The legal responsibility for doing the job properly then falls on them. In order to get member involvement here, if the company insist on maintaining this arrangement, you would need to have a 'management committee' with member representation, which has powers of decision formally delegated to it by the trustee company.

Boards of trustees **in themselves** may not be all that they seem; for example:

BOC Ltd has two pension schemes, called the No 1 and No 2 schemes, with identical trustee structures. The boards of trustees consist of 3 individual trustees from the company, and 3 from the membership (the member trustees are elected by the pensions advisory committee (the PAC, of which more later, in section 2 of this chapter, pages 211–13). **But** there is also a seventh trustee, BOC Pension Trustees Ltd, of which *all* the directors are directors of the company, and a representative of them sits also on each trustee board. *And*, to quote the annual report, 'the fund's investments are held by BOC Pensions Ltd and registered in the name of the bank's nominee company with whom they are deposited.

'The investment policy is laid down by a strategic investment committee which meets quarterly. The comittee comprises a director of BOC International as chairman; the chairman of the individual trustees; 3 partners of a firm of London stockbrokers; a director of a merchant bank; an investment manager of an insurance company; the pensions manager; and a PAC elected individual trustee attends by rotation.'

So each member trustee actually gets to a meeting which decides on investment once every 18 months, and the trustee board itself has no legal powers in this field (though the minutes of the strategic investment committee are given to them).

This is a good example of the sort of structure we should not be accepting and, where we have been trapped into it in the past, we should be seeking to change it. It means that power is diverted *away* from those who ought to control it.

TUC policy is 50% member representation on **all controlling bodies** of the pension scheme. However, this may not always be attainable. You may need to accept a compromise, with 50% of members other than the chairperson, so there would be a 3–4 or 5–6 split – and the chairperson would be a company appointee who had the casting vote. If you have to concede on this, try again in 1 or 2 years' time, when you're in a position to point out that disaster has not yet befallen the fund.

Another point which needs to be looked at closely is the method by which the people to be appointed are found. This will vary a lot according to the size and complexity of the company you're dealing with.

A **ballot** among all the members of the fund is one way. In a small company with only a few sites, where everybody on each site knows each other, this is the obvious method. You need to ensure, though,

■ that the unions can keep control of the ballot; and

■ that the people who go forward for election understand what the job of a trustee is, and especially that it is **not** a negotiating job.

In a large company you may need a very complicated electoral structure to get a fair balance between sites and employment groups. You may not be able to have as many trustees as you have sites, if the committee is to be of a workable size, so you will have to perform a balancing act between, say, the large site in Manchester and the small one in Gloucestershire, or between process and the craft workers, to make sure that they will all feel fairly treated. Including this in an electoral structure may be just too complicated.

As an alternative, you could have **indirect election**, perhaps via a delegate conference, or appointment by the combine committee, national joint committee or a special pensions committee if you have one. The people you appoint need not be members of the committee, though they could be. You'd need to get nominations from the plants, and perhaps to bring into your discussions someone with experience of appointing trustees – perhaps a union pensions specialist, if one is available, or possibly the consultant employed by the company on pension matters, if you are sure you can still keep *control* in your own hands.

The Lucas Industries works scheme has a central consultative committee, composed of nominated representatives from shop stewards' committees. The constitution says:

'**Representatives**

'1. Principles. The following general principles will regulate the nomination of Trade Union representatives:

(i) Each representative shall represent approximately 2000 members.

(ii) Each representative shall, if possible, represent members whose places of employment are in the same geographical location.

(iii) Each representative shall, if possible, represent members within the same manufacturing group of the Lucas group of companies.

(iv) Each representative shall be a member of the Lucas works pension fund.

'2. Nomination. Senior shop stewards' committee or the appropriate shop stewards' committee with representation constituencies shall choose their representative or representatives in such a manner and in accordance with such procedures as are applicable in those constituencies . . .

(. . .)

'4. Nomination of directors for Lucas employees of the Lucas Works Pension Fund Trust Ltd.

(a) There shall be three Lucas employee directors.

(b) The employee directors will be nominated by the members of the Lucas works pension fund consultative committee. To be eligible for appointment a person must be:

(i) a contributing member of the Lucas works pension fund and able to complete three years with the company before normal retirement date;

(ii) age 23 or over and have been in the employment of a participating company for at least 5 years and, during 4 whole years of such employment, have contributed to a pension scheme operated by a participating company;

(iii) a member of the Lucas works pension fund consultative committee;

(iv) supported in his or her nomination by 3 members of . . . the committee . . . and receive the votes of a simple majority of the entire number of such members of the committee.

(c) In the event of the provisions . . . above being inconclusive the final choice will rest with the members of the works pension fund, through a ballot.'

A third alternative, which has been very much used in the past, is **joint selection**, where appointment is done by interview by both company and union full time officials. Thus at Ransome Hoffman Pollard the procedure is:

Procedure for nomination and selection of trustee directors
Applications from scheme members will be invited at site level. Each application must be supported by at least 10 members. . . They will be vetted by site consultative committees and those considered most suitable will be forwarded for consideration to an appointments subcommittee which will interview a short list of applicants. The subcommittee will consist of the group industrial relations manager (chairman), the group pensions manager, a senior RHP personnel manager and 3 union officials. Those selected will be given training as appropriate, and they will serve for 3 years and be eligible for reappointment.

Many other examples do not include a 'vetting process' at site level.

The arguments that have been used for this type of procedure are:

■ It tends to be easier to obtain from the company than other procedures, and as any decision should be unanimous, they cannot put one over on you.

■ It means that you can appoint the 'best person for the job' who, since the role is not the same as that of a shop steward, might not be the one who would come up through election.

■ It enables you to do the 'balancing act' between plants, areas and bargaining groups, without needing to draw up a complicated electoral system.

But the arguments against such a procedure are stronger:

■ It goes very much against the democratic basis of the trade union movement, and the practice of electing (and recalling) the holders of other posts in the collective bargaining structure.

■ The joint procedure should apply to all trustees or none, and since the management trustees are never chosen this way, why should the member trustees be?

■ The trade union members of the selection committee will have their hands tied in the sort of questions they might want to ask (for instance, on political involvement) by the presence of senior company management.

■ There's a limit to how far you can find 'the best person for the job' in a 20 or 30 minute interview anyway.

There are some very good member trustees who have been appointed by a joint selection procedure; and there will be many cases where a company will not agree to anything else, and you have to compromise. But generally the principle that should be followed is that the appointment of member trustees should be under **trade union control**. Selection should not be ruled out. In a smallish company without a strong joint union committee, it may be the only practicable procedure – especially since the members themselves may not be sure enough that they know what pension trusteeship involves, the first time round, to feel confident that they will pick the right people. But it should be **union selection**, for instance by union pension specialists, not a joint procedure with the company. Before entering into it, you need to get clear agreement from the company that they will appoint whomever you select, and not use their legal powers to veto your choice.

Whatever procedure is adopted, there are certain other points to bear in mind:

■ Once trustees are appointed, legally they are all equal. All have the same powers and responsibilities. Member trustees should not allow themselves to be second class citizens. Management trustees should not have special places on the investment committee, nor should member trustees let themselves be pushed into a purely 'welfare' function. Any facilities given to management trustees – places at conferences, travelling arrangements for meetings or discussions with the 'experts' – should be offered to member trustees as well.

■ Training should be given, preferably before the trustees ever take up office. In-company training can be useful, as it will teach you about the details of the scheme you're working with, and the administrative procedures the company uses; but you should also ask for facilities to go on your union's course, if they have one. The TUC also sometimes runs courses.

■ Don't allow the company to dictate that the trustee should not be a shop steward, or that s/he must give up union jobs if appointed trustee. It's a matter for discussion with the members whether the trustee should be a shop steward or not. The advantage of having a shop steward is that s/he is already part of the union structure, and is in close touch with the members. The disadvantage is that stewards are generally overloaded with work, and they might find it difficult to step out of the negotiating role and into the administrative role.

■ You need to establish a mechanism, again under union control, for regular discussion of how the trustees are getting on. An occasional slot on a combine committee agenda, or a meeting with the unions' full time officials and the site convenors, are two possible ways to do it. If there is a pensions negotiating body, then the member trustees should either attend its meetings – though not take the lead in negotiating – or at least be kept in touch with what's going on.

Section 2: Advisory and consultative bodies

In addition to member trustees, many companies have set up pensions advisory committees or pensions consultative committees. They vary a lot in intention – and format – and are often set up outside, and with no proper connection with, the union structure.

> BOC has a pensions advisory committee of 28 drawn from its different divisions. The divisional management decide on the method of appointment; in the case of BOC Gases it's by ballot; in other divisions the procedure is not formalised.

Whether intentionally or not, these committees can be used by companies as a method of giving **token member participation** and defusing the demand for real involvement. Thus another company in the chemicals industry, faced with a request for negotiations on improving the scheme, said:

> Consultative machinery has been set up in the divisions, and a group pensions advisory council (GPAC) was formed, with trade union and other members from all the divisions. This body, which is chaired by a main board director, is free to discuss all matters concerning pensions, pensioners and the pension fund, and is enabled at regular intervals to put forward to top management proposals for change . . . We believe that the members of GPAC and of the pension scheme as a whole are well pleased with these arrangements.
> As you probably know, the pension fund trustees include trade union members.
> In view of the comprehensive and successful joint arrangements already in force we see no advantage in a further meeting at national level to discuss pensions.

In a large company, some sort of formal communication structure is going to be necessary if the trustees are going to have any hope of keeping in touch with the members, but you don't have to have a special committee. The work can just as well be done by the shop stewards' committees, if they feel they can cope. It should be a decision of the *unions*, not the company, whether they want to have a separate organisation for pensions.

The important point is to have a channel of communication both *up* and *down*. Members will feed in problems, queries, things they don't understand and points where they believe improvements are necessary. These will go up, according to what they are about, either to the trustees, for matters of administration, or to the negotiators, where a rule change is being asked for. From those bodies, in the other direction, draft scheme booklets, other written material, suggested rule changes and information on the progress of the fund, should be coming for comment. A consultative body at plant level can also send lay representatives to a central negotiating body. Thus, the Ransome Hoffman Pollard agreement says, for instance:

> **Consultative committees**
> To contribute to the effective participation in the running of the pension scheme there will also be established:
> 1. A local pensions consultative committee, membership of which is open to contributing members of the pension schemes who are also members of their appropriate trade unions. The nature of the representation and the number of members will be determined in detail by local agreement. In general it will reflect union membership at the location.
> The function of the local committee is:
> (a) to provide a forum for the election of 1 or 2 of its members to the central pensions consultative committee;
> (b) to provide such assistance to the central committee as the latter considers necessary for the successful conduct of their responsibilities;
> (c) to provide a channel of communication between members of the fund and the pension administrators.
> 2. A central pensions consultative committee. Membership of this committee will be drawn from senior management, local consultative committees, and the full time national officers or their nominees from the appropriate trade unions. Its function will be to play a major role in communication, consultation and negotiation of pensions matters. Changes in the pension scheme will be negotiated by the committee and not through the normal site negotiating machinery.

Incidentally, the member trustees sit in on these negotiations, but take no part when the company is there, although they *do* take part in trade union side discussions.

Again it is important that any consultative bodies are clearly part of the trade union structure. If one has been set up that is not, then at least clear links need to be made, even if nothing else in the structure is changed. A conference of consultative committee members, trustees, convenors and full time officials, on a regular basis, would be one method.

Even genuinely useful advisory bodies need to be carefully monitored to see they don't turn into mere bureaucratic talking shops, with everything interesting being referred somewhere else for decision. It's important to see, therefore, that

■ those on the local committees get some proper training, preferably from the unions rather than from the company;

■ if something goes up to the next level, whether it came from there originally for comment or was initiated at local level, a decision is reached reasonably fast and the local committee are *told* what it is (it is very frustrating to see your good idea disappear in a mass of paperwork, never to appear again); and

■ there is a mixture on the committee of people whose main interest is in pensions and people whose interest is in the more day to day problems of the workplace.

If it is clear the company *are* trying to make it into a talking shop, it may be better to threaten to pull out if it doesn't improve than to struggle on.

Section 3: Negotiating bodies

Over the last few years some companies have developed formal procedures for negotiating on pensions; others brought together a group specifically created for that purpose during the process of contracting out, and have had no national level meetings since. Even a good scheme may need renegotiation when conditions change, and the many poor ones certainly need fairly frequent discussions on improvements.

The argument for negotiating rights is that pensions are deferred pay, and should be subject to negotiation like any other item of pay. The *legal* position is that pensions are one item, under sections 11–16 of the Employment Protection Act, on which an independent recognised trade union may seek negotiating rights, and take the company to ACAS if it does not get them. These legal powers have rarely been used because of fears that, once the lawyers begin to argue, definitions may be so narrowed down that they are useless. The unions have tended to rely on activities other than court cases to get negotiating rights. (See *Rights at Work* by Jeremy McMullen, Pluto 1978, for details on recognition.) Chapter 6 above, 'Making a claim' deals with the differences between pension claims and other sorts of claims (pages 188–89). In this section we deal with specific issues of setting up negotiations, including

- the level at which you negotiate, and
- the role of full time officials.

It is one of the peculiarities of pension schemes that, however the company is organised, whether it is highly centralised or allows a great deal of autonomy at plant level, the pension scheme will almost *always* be centralised, and controlled by people reporting to the main board. The subsidiaries of a group normally have no independent powers to take decisions about the pension scheme. Even in the few cases where a group has deliberately broken up its pension scheme, and claimed to devolve control to local level, local management *still* rely on the 'advice' of group management, and follow policy made at group level.

> Wilkinson Match have 5 pension schemes, all identical, one for each of their divisions. They also have a central pensions manager, and it is clear that he would be fully involved in any negotiations that took place about the pension scheme at, say, their subsidiary Bryant and May.

In any pensions negotiations at plant level, therefore, local management can be no more than messengers back to the company. Even if the group pensions manager is himself present, major issues will usually have to be taken back to the group board for decision, and what happens will therefore depend partly on the views of other managers at other plants. Local negotiations on pensions, except on issues that affect **only** that plant, (such as the method of collecting contributions) are usually a waste of time. Central negotiations, at group level, with all interested unions involved, are far more useful.

This approach, however, runs counter to a lot of ideas, and may be resisted from several quarters:

- The **company** will often dislike it, because they fear that there are possibilities of a pensions negotiating body being the forerunner of a combine committee. Even if the unions give assurances that this won't happen the company would, probably correctly, assume that useful information would be swapped between stewards at different plants over lunch.

■ It is out of line with policy in a number of unions, especially the AUEW, which is also far from happy with any moves towards combine committees. In practice, the unions have generally accepted, at head office level, the need for centralised pension negotiations; but for them it tends to mean full time official, rather than shop steward, or convenor, involvement.

■ For this reason centralised negotiations are often viewed with suspicion by shop stewards as well, as they see it as a method by which power is removed from them on an important issue. So indeed it can be, if the procedure agreed allows it – which is why getting the *structure* right is important.

The problem you may well find when you get interested in your pension scheme, is that you know very little about pensions, and feel you must turn to your officials, or to your union's head office, for advice. Partly because of the mystique that surrounds pensions, people tend to be more conscious of their ignorance than on other subjects. You may be afraid of making yourselves look fools in front of management, and rely on the full time official or the expert, in situations where when dealing with other subjects you would be perfectly ready to handle the discussions yourselves. But your goal should be to build up member involvement in negotiations while retaining the expertise of the full timers for when it is needed.

This is not easy, especially since more than one union, and often quite a large number, may be represented in a company. So if you simply add lay members to a negotiating committee, you may find it getting so big as to be unworkable. Rather than leave it all to the full time officials, however, it might be better to set up a procedure whereby you elect a small number of representatives on to a negotiating committee, along with an arrangement for reporting back.

Associated Engineering, for instance, has a procedure agreement which says:

1. A pension scheme delegate conference will be established which will meet at least once per calendar year. Each of the operating companies will send representatives to this conference.
2. The employees' representatives will be chosen domestically via the existing domestic negotiating/consultative bodies so as to give one representative from each recognised union for each operating company. The representatives must be members of the general pension fund.
3. Executives nominated by Associated Engineering will also attend the

conference, and there will be an agreed number of full time trade union officials . . . present if they so wish . . . one for each recognised union with members in the pension scheme.

4. Items for the agenda of the meeting will be invited and these will be circulated to those due to attend, 3 weeks before the conference takes place.

5. The principal purpose of the conference will be

(a) initially to formulate an agreed mechanism for appointing a number of trustees from members of the scheme;

(b) to receive and discuss any reports of the trustees on the operation of the general pension scheme: such reports will generally be circulated with the agenda;

(c) to reach agreements with AE concerning the future operation of the scheme.

6. If no acceptable agreement to any proposed alterations put forward by members of the scheme is reached (either at the conference or within 4 weeks afterwards), a negotiating subcommittee meeting may be called by the national . . . officials or the nominees of AE to discuss further the issues in dispute.

7. The negotiating subcommittee will consist of full time national union officials and lay members chosen at the annual delegate conference, and nominees of Associated Engineering. There will be a maximum of 12 people present at this committee, of whom not more than 4 will be members of AE.

8. If agreed necessary, then at an appropriate stage the results of the meeting of the subcommittee may be reported

(a) to the operating Companies and hence their negotiating/consultative bodies in the form of an agreed statement;

(b) by the . . . national officials at the resumed meeting of the delegate conference (which would not be attended by representatives of AE) if they deemed such a meeting necessary.

9. (a) The cost and the responsibility for organising the annual delegate conference would be that of AE.

(b) In the case of a delegate conference called by the unions to discuss negotiations on changing the pension scheme . . . the travel costs of the delegates would be paid by the appropriate operating companies and the agreed paid leave of absence granted. The cost of any overnight accommodation would be the responsibility of the trade unions.

You wouldn't need this sort of elaborate arrangement in all cases, though. Where a combine committee exists, they can elect some of their members on to a pensions body; or if there are only a few sites, all the convenors or senior stewards could be involved. You could ask one or more of the experts from the larger unions' head offices on to the committee to provide specialist advice. If several unions represented in the company employ experts, you could agree among yourselves which to invite. If none is available, you *could* employ a professional from a firm of insurance brokers or pension consultants to do the job. You need to be very careful, though, because:

■ it is liable to cost a lot of money (find out how much first, before committing yourselves);

■ they may try to push their own pet scheme, rather than what you want (and be earning commission by doing so); and

■ they may know less than they think. Someone dealing with *individual* pensions may know very little about *group* pensions.

There can be difficulties in getting all the unions to sit down together, especially if you have long standing differences of opinion on other things. It is vital, though, that you work out a way of doing so on this subject, so far as you have a common pension scheme. Otherwise the company won't hesitate to exploit the differences for its own ends. If there are separate schemes – for instance, staff and works – there may not be any need actually to negotiate as one body, but you still need to keep in touch, so that you are not putting forward contradictory arguments. This will be particularly important for the works representatives, assuming the eventual aim is harmonisation, even if this is a very long way away. You'll need to make sure that you don't ask for an improvement in such a form that it takes you *further* away from the Staff scheme (see page 192 for more on this point).

On the management side, although you cannot dictate whom they bring along, you should try to get the people who *actually deal* with the scheme there, as well as those you normally negotiate with. The industrial relations or personnel manager is not likely to know much about the scheme, and you will waste a lot of time while s/he adjourns meetings, and goes off and gets advice from somewhere else. Try to get the **pensions manager** or, if the scheme is administered by a firm of consultants (there are several of these, mainly subsidiaries of big firms of insurance brokers), one of their representatives. You might also want the actuary (see pages 225–38 for an explanation of what s/he does) and, if the scheme is insured, someone from the insurance company as well, especially if you're being told you can't do things because of them.

In deciding what sort of structure you want for negotiations, the sort of points you will need to think about are:

■ The size of the company, and the geographical spread.

■ Are there too many plants for a representative of each to sit on a negotiating body? If so, how are you going to select the negotiators?

■ Is one plant much bigger than the others? If so, how are you going to stop the smaller ones from feeling left out?

■ How many unions are involved? The majority union will normally take the chair at negotiations. How will the others be represented?

■ The occupational spread. Ensuring that both staff and works are properly represented will usually be crucial in a joint scheme, but the same applies also with craft and process workers, or indeed people who may be in completely different industries, in a large conglomerate. Their terms and conditions may well be quite different, if they are decided by several Joint Industrial Committees, and this can make things complex, if, for instance, sickness is differently treated.

■ The role of officials. How far do you want them to be involved? If they are doing the negotiating, how can you ensure that there is an adequate reporting back mechanism?

Sometimes, rather than a cut and dried negotiating structure being worked out in detail and then put into effect, it will 'just grow'. If once you can get people together to talk to management about *something* on pensions, you can always find something else to talk about, so another meeting has to be convened, and a strictly 'one-off' delegate conference can make demands which involve reporting back to a further conference. Management itself may be engaged in an internal negotiating process, breaking down the desire for autonomy and fear of joint union action among local managers. Underlying local managers' resistance may also be their own ignorance, and a dislike of the unions getting to know about something, even the pension scheme, that they don't know about. Being pragmatic, rather than insisting on everything at once, may bring dividends. It all depends on your particular management.

Section 4: Possible arguments and responses

When the Labour government's White Paper came out on member participation (see page 205) all the big employers' organisations decided they were in favour of **participation**; what they were against was **trade union** involvement. It's that issue you've got to win on.

Some employers of course will say that they don't need

member participation anyway because the employees all know the scheme is wonderful – or, alternatively, that no one's interested. Against them, you could quote the National Association of Pension Funds. At its conference in May 1980, according to the *Guardian* of 16 May 1980,

> . . . recognising the difficulties of increased participation the NAPF Council nevertheless argues that it would improve employee relations and promote a better understanding of the workings of pension schemes.

It is *not*, however, union involvement which the NAPF supports, only member involvement; so you need to take care about how far you claim they support your point of view. Why do **we** believe it should be **participation via the unions**?

Because pensions are **deferred pay**. If the money wasn't going into the pension scheme it might be going into the pay packet, so you have as much right to negotiate on it, *and* be involved in the administration of it, as on any other item. While wages are a matter for joint negotiation, items like sick pay, bonus schemes, overtime and so on, are (or should be) matters for **joint negotiation and control**. Pensions are another item in this list (as the Employment Protection Act recognises). There's no hope of a group of un-organised people succeeding in negotiating or controlling anything – so it must be the union.

Management's response tends to be:

■ Since the scheme includes non-unionists, it would not be right for the unions to negotiate and/or be trustees on their behalf. This will be said particularly when the scheme includes senior managerial staff. You could answer that, firstly, all the non-unionists are free to join a trade union, and second, that the company and the non-unionists seem happy enough to allow the unions to negotiate on their behalf when it comes to wages, so why should they be suddenly concerned now? As far as senior staff are concerned, they will anyway be adequately represented among the management trustees!

■ It would be impossible to have proper negotiations, or trustee bodies, as there are too many unions concerned. It is remarkable how often management will produce this assertion, in all seriousness, believing that having more than one union makes them unique and that getting the unions to sit down together is therefore self evidently impossible. But that is certainly not true.

Most companies of any size in the UK have a number of trade unions involved, and many also have well developed negotiating and trustee structures that take this fully into account.

They may well then fall back on arguments about 'management's right to manage' and assertions that they do not consider pensions a negotiable item.

How far you want to push it, faced with this, must be up to you. You can take it to ACAS, or you can take some form of action. But people will not often take industrial action about pensions (as management are well aware: that's why they say this), so you may need to leave the question on the table and return to it later. If necessary, you might accept a body that has only advisory powers as a 'foot in the door'.

In talking specifically about trustees, you may find yourselves being drawn into a discussion about competence. *Don't* get put into a position where it looks as if you're criticising the existing management trustees, unless you have solid facts to go on – it will only put their backs up. The sort of line to follow is:

■ Trustees are not meant to be experts: they are meant to supervise the experts; and for that straightforward common sense, together with additional training, is the best quality.

■ Members will be given confidence that the problems that may arise on their death, for instance, will be considered by someone whose lifestyle is similar to theirs, and who appreciates what it would be like to live on State benefits, rather than by well off managers who, with the best will in the world, have got their experience in a very different environment.

You will also, inevitably, have to say reassuring things to the effect that

■ yes, you do realise that it is not a negotiating role, and that the trustees' responsibility is to act in the best interests of all the members, not only those in his/her particular trade union;

■ and you realise that it is a definite, and often quite arduous, legal responsibility;

■ and that there are certain matters which will have to be kept confidential, such as the personal circumstances of individuals.

One final point is that, when you've *won* on this issue in negotiations, the people appointed may well find themselves having to fight the battle all over again at the trustee board. Many of the people who sit on boards of trustees at the moment, the company secretaries and non-executive directors, will not often meet trade unionists and will frequently be quite naïve in their views. The unfortunate people appointed as member trustees will probably have to spend the first 2 or 3 meetings proving that they are human, so you should add patience to your list of the trustees' necessary qualities.

8.

Financing pension schemes

Introduction

Schemes that are approved by the Inland Revenue for tax purposes, in the private sector, are almost all **funded**. In the public sector, some schemes are **'pay as you go'**. The difference was explained briefly in chapter 4, section 15, 'Escalation' (pages 151–52), so turn back to that if you're unclear.

In this chapter we're looking at:

1. What funding means

2. How the cost of a pension is calculated – and the job of an actuary

3. What happens to the money

Section 1: What funding means

The **theory** of funding is that whatever money is paid into the pension scheme by you, or for your pension by your employer, is set aside for you, and invested so that it produces income, so that there is a lump sum available when you retire that can then be turned into pension.

MacGregor and Co agree to pay £100 a year for 10 years into a bank account for the employee Peter Rabbit's pension. P Rabbit adds £50 a year. Interest rates are steady at 5% a year, so the 1st year's £150 accumulates compound interest over 10 years and becomes £233. The 2nd year's accumulates over 9 years, and so on. In the end, when P Rabbit reaches 65, a lump sum of £1887 is waiting to be turned into pension.

(**Compound** interest means that each year interest is paid not only on the basic money, but also on the interest already paid in previous years. Thus the first £150 becomes £157.50 at the end of the year, and the next year's interest is paid on the £157.50.)

As P Rabbit knows the average life expectancy of a 65 year old male is 12 years, he decides he needs to arrange for his pension to last for 12 years. But this does not mean he must simply divide £1887 by 12, because the money that he draws out *last* will have been, again, accumulating 5% compound interest each year while it is waiting for him to draw it. So he can be a little more generous. He therefore decides to draw his money out at £170 a year to live on.

However, P Rabbit has a problem: 12 years is the *average* life expectancy, but he has no way of knowing whether he is going to match the average or not. He may live 1 year, or he may live 30. If he lives 1 year, there will be money left over; if 30, he'll run out of cash.

That is why the majority of pension schemes are **group** pension schemes. (The pensions you buy from insurance companies are too: the group is all the other people who've bought pensions from that company.) Though Peter Rabbit cannot be sure that *he'll* match the average, you can be pretty sure that, taken as a whole, a large group will. So the money that is saved on those who don't draw their pension for long can be spent on those who draw it for many years. In a group scheme, the money is put in not for any one person, but for the group as whole. In fact the **average** employer's contribution of, say, 10%, will cover a much higher contribution for the older person and a much lower one for a young person. Indeed, in actuarial terms – the way such matters are reckoned – there may be **no** contribution at all coming from the employer for the person under 30.

The basic framework of funding is made much more complicated by the fact that we have inflation. Very few schemes now pay in fixed sums of money; it would be far more likely that MacGregor's were paying in 10% of P Rabbit's salary and P Rabbit 5%, and that it was agreed that he'd get 10/80ths of his final earnings when he retired. His salary might be £1500 when he started, but, with 5% wage increases, it would be £2330 when he retired. With 10% increases, it would be £3890, and with 20% increases it would be £9280.

How does a pension scheme cope with this? What enables them to make promises that they can pay a pension based on *final* earnings is that, when inflation is high, normally interest rates are too. Historically, interest rates have averaged out at a percentage point or so above the rate of inflation. If inflation ran at 5%, for instance, you'd have expected interest rates to be 7% or so, so that people could earn a 'real' rate of return on their money – that is, so that the money they had in the bank was actually increasing in purchasing power, not simply in money value.

At times over the last few years, this hasn't been so. Interest rates have not kept up with 20% inflation. So money is sitting in stocks and shares actually losing purchasing power, even though it is gaining large amounts of interest in **money** terms.

Why then, bother to put the money away at all? There are a number of arguments on this; and certainly there must come a point, with the combination of inflation and recession, when funding no longer makes any sense. But the argument is that it is better to have *something* in the bank for the future, even if it is losing its value, than nothing. It has been compared with fetching water from a tap. If you have only a bucket with a hole in it, you'll have to make a lot more journeys to the tap than if there was no leak; but if you throw it away in disgust, you have no way of fetching the water.

The alternative would be to 'pay as you go', that is, to pay pensions to those already retired from the income being created today; and to rely on future workers to pay our pensions when we in turn retire.

The problems that arise on this, it is said, are:

■ What happens to pensioners if a business goes bankrupt?

■ What happens if a whole industry disappears, for instance because of new technology? In 20 years' time nobody might be reading printed newspapers any more, it might be all on the television screen – and where would Fleet Street workers get their pensions then?

■ People might rebel against paying high contributions and taxes for the benefit of pensioners.

These arguments have some force, but they'd have much less if the Government either took over the pensions industry, or regulated it more heavily, so that it acted as a backstop in cases of bankruptcy, for instance. Other countries which are more economically successful than we are manage without funding pensions in the way that we do – France and Germany, for instance.

It's an open question whether funding or 'pay as you go' is more beneficial. The one certain thing is that funding is deeply entrenched. Many pensions professionals react with near hysteria if someone suggests moving away from it. Changing it, unless done gradually, would cause a considerable upheaval.

Pension funds are now huge: at the end of 1978, there was £31 billion in the funds themselves, plus £38 billion of long term money in insurance companies (according to the Wilson report). It's been claimed that this means that British workers control large sectors of the economy, but of course this is not so. Control is vested in the hands of a small group of City institutions – merchant banks, stockbrokers etc, who manage the funds for many companies. Member trustees have in general hardly begun to wrest control away from the financial high priests.

Section 2: How the cost of a pension is calculated

Having seen what funding means, we need to come down to detail and look at how the cost of *your* pension scheme is calculated. This is the job done by a professional called an **actuary**.

Actuaries have a highly specialised mathematical training, although some people might regard their trade as closer to fortune telling. (They also have some of the toughest restrictive practices around.)

Going back to the example of P Rabbit, the actuary there would usually start by being told by MacGregor and Co what pension they wanted to give Mr Rabbit, and for how long. S/he would then work backwards, calculating compound interest, and could in due course tell them how much they and P Rabbit have to put in to get that answer.

When s/he is dealing with the real world, with larger schemes and problems about rates of inflation, the actuary will have a more difficult job. Instead of a straightforward mathematical calculation, s/he will have to make **assumptions** about

■ how many people are going to die before retirement and therefore get a lump sum, rather than a pension;

■ how many people are going to leave the company;

■ how many people are going to retire early, and therefore start drawing their pensions before they would normally be expected to;

■ how long people are going to live after they've retired;

■ how fast earnings are going to rise between now and the date people retire; and

■ what is going to happen to interest rates in the future.

How many people are going to die, and how long the pensioners are going to live, are things that can be estimated fairly accurately, because there are tables taken from the experience of many years, showing for any particular age group how many people can be expected to die in the year. For early retirements, and for leaving service, it's largely a matter of guesswork based on the 'feel' of the scheme.

It is the last 2 estimates that cause difficulty, because they involve making predictions about the political and economic situation many years from now. It is *possible* to make predictions which at least give you a basis to work on, for 2 main reasons:

■ The two factors tend to interrelate. Interest rates have usually been a little higher than the rate of inflation, and what matters most is the relationship between them. Thus, if the actuary decides that the rate of interest is going to be 11% and the rate of wage increase 9%, s/he is predicting a 2% 'rate of real return'. It doesn't matter very much if the rate of interest is 13% and the rate of wage inflation is 11%, as the rate of real return is still 2%. But it matters a good deal if the rate of interest is 11% and the rate of wage increases 10%, because that means the real rate of return has been drastically cut to only 1%.

■ But even if an actuary gets his/her figures wrong, the saving grace – which allows them to carry on in business is that any one set of predictions does not have to last very long. **Actuarial valuations** are exercises in costing pension schemes. In the past, they were usually done every 5 years. With earnings rising, this was not often enough, and so most companies have moved on to valuations every 3 years. Some in fact have annual valuations, but this is generally regarded as too often. Actuaries tend to stress in their reports that, if they get their figures wrong once, they can always correct them next time.

What does an actuarial valuation look like?

It's usually a bound pamphlet, anything up to 40 pages long, which the trustees will receive as a formal document. Pension scheme valuations can be written in any number of ways, and there is **no** standard or model form.

This section goes through some of the main items that are usually found in a valuation report, and also points to some of the questions to ask. If the report of your scheme doesn't contain all the items of information that are dealt with here, you ought to ask why not – but there may be a good reason, such as it not being available. All the quotes that follow are taken from one particular report, but it is *only* used as an example. The company name we've used is not the real one.

Before a valuation can start, all the information needed has got to be collected together, and checked for accuracy. This will be on the ages of the people in the scheme, their pension rights, and also on the scheme's holdings of stocks and shares and property. It will often take the scheme administrators a very long time to get all this together, and then when they hand it over to the actuary there may be further delay, as there are only about 200 actuaries in private practice and at busy times they tend to get swamped. So the information the trustees get is frequently out of date.

The report will be presented as 'the result of an actuarial valuation into the X fund *as at* 6 April 1981', or some other date. This is the 'valuation date', at which the values of stocks, shares etc are calculated.

The report will usually start with a brief history of the scheme – which may come in useful when you want to check on which subsidiary companies were brought in when – and also a brief summary of the benefits. This is really padding. It needs to be checked to be sure that it's right, but you don't need to spend too much time on it.

There will then be a statement of the membership of the scheme. Here is an example of one, for a largish scheme:

The following statement summarises the membership of the fund at the date of the investigation. The corresponding figures for the previous investigation of the staff pension fund are shown for purposes of comparison.

	30 September 1978		30 September 1975	
	Number of members	Annual earnings £000s	Number of members	Annual earnings £000s
Active members:				
Male	22,717	88,444	14,154	35,415
Female	5,369	14,228	1,228	1,865
Total	28,086	102,672	15,382	37,280
		Annual pension £000s		Annual pension £000s
Pensioners:				
Male	2,663	1,472.7	1,442	719.6
Female	669	137.8	314	50.6
Dependants	712	392.2	444	167.0
Total	4,044	2,002.7	2,200	937.2
Deferred pensioners (other than EPBs)				
Male	1,130	422.7	816	282.3
Female	131	34.4	78	11.4
Total	1,261	457.1	894	293.7
EPBs	6,612	89.7	5,374	67.1

(A **deferred** pensioner is a person who's left the company and has a frozen pension kept for him/her. It's quite usual to have a fairly large number compared to the number of pensioners. An **EPB** is a preserved pension under the old graduated scheme.)

The **information** on this will be obtained from the pension scheme's own records (and the employer). If the figures look different from what you'd expect, you should ask for an explanation. This is the basic material of the valuation. If something's wrong here, the whole thing will be wrong.

Sometimes the actuary will not have all the information, especially where schemes are amalgamating or new groups are being brought in. In that case, s/he ought to make an estimate, and say what the assumptions are. For instance:

> In some cases the terms of admission from previous schemes have not been finally settled and detailed information is not available in respect of pensioners and deferred pensioners entitled to benefit from these schemes. We have completed our valuation on the basis that the value of the liabilities relating to these schemes is equal to the assessed value of the assets transferred and have included a further provision in respect of possible underfunding in certain of the schemes. We are satisfied that the effects on the overall finances of the fund of these assumptions are not sufficiently great to call into question the results of the investigation.

Some reports will have a couple of paragraphs about the progress of the scheme over the years since the last valuation. Others will put the same information in a table, like this one:

	£000s	£000s
Amount of fund at 30 September 1975		41,188
Investment reserve at 30 September 1975		1,830
		43,018
'Normal' income 1 October 1975–30 September 1978		
Ordinary contributions by: members	10,567	
companies	12,706	
Dividends, rents, interest, etc, less investment expenses..	13,231	
Total		36,504
'Normal' expenditure 1 October 1975–30 September 1978		
Pensions and allowances paid by the fund	4,279	
Lump sum benefits on retirement	3,812	
Lump sum benefits on death	664	
Contributions refunded on withdrawal of members	2,000	
Total		10,755
Excess of normal income over normal expenditure		25,749

	£000	£000s
Special items of income 1 October 1975–30 September 1978		
Special contributions by companies to finance past service entitlements	406	
Capital funds of other schemes taken over:		
external	902	
former company schemes discontinued..........	9,411	
Contributions by Hungarian Lighthouses Ltd to fund awards to pensions payable from fund	1,447	12,166
		37,915
Capital funds transferred to other schemes		1,704
Net cash flow into fund..............................		36,211
Net profits on sale of investments		1,265
Adjustment to book value of fund for pre-1977 accrued income in managed fund...........................		1,512
Funds and reserves at 30 September 1975 (see above)...		43,018
Amount of fund at 30 September 1978................		82,006

The report ought specifically to say whether there are items that have been met by the company, such as special payments on a redundancy scheme, or increases in pensions in payment, as in the example below:

> Although no provision is made in the rules of the fund for regular increases in pensions in course of payment, reviews have taken place from time to time and awards of pension granted. The estimated capital cost of these awards has been met by the special contributions from Hungarian Lighthouses Ltd, as shown in the statement above.

Having dealt with this, the actuary may go on to summarise what the fund is invested in, and to explain how it is valued:

> The following statement summarises the assets of the fund as at the date of the investigation

	Book value £m	Market value £m
Property...	30.20	49.85
Fixed interest securities	3.48	3.49
Convertible securities...............................	1.74	1.83
UK equities	30.98	39.79
Overseas stocks and shares	1.27	1.11
Eldorado Life managed fund	11.41	13.42
Mortgage loans	0.01	0.01
Cash on deposit	1.75	1.75
	80.84	111.25

The properties held by the fund have been valued individually by the fund's surveyors, and the market value shown in the foregoing statement is derived from their valuation, of which we have been supplied with a copy. The report shows a current net annual rental income of £3.39 million, which would rise to £4.74 million in 1983 if rents falling for renewal in the next 5 years are renegotiated at yields corresponding to current market prices. The greater part of the portfolio is represented by freehold or long leasehold property with rent reviews at 5 yearly or 7 yearly intervals.

The company doesn't use the property itself: it lets it out as offices or factories. The fact that it was valued by the fund's own surveyors, who would have been the people who inititially recommended that it should be purchased, was one of the things the unions particularly criticised in this report. On the other assets of the fund, the report says:

As on former occasions, the assets have been valued by discounting the expected future investment proceeds whether by way of redemption monies, dividends, rent or interest on the basis discussed in the following paragraphs.

Financial elements of the basis
Valuation rate of interest. The valuation rate of interest at which the future cash flows are discounted to the date of the investigation represents the overall rate of return to be earned from new investments made in the future. On the occasion of the previous investigation we adopted a valuation rate of interest of $8\frac{1}{2}\%$. Rates of interest have remained generally high and on this occasion we have thought it appropriate to adopt a valuation rate of interest of 10% per annum. **Pay escalation**. Provision was made in the 1975 valuation for general increases in salary levels at the rate of 7% per annum, a margin of $1\frac{1}{2}\%$ below the valuation rate of interest. In conjunction with the increase in the valuation rate of interest we consider it appropriate to reduce this margin to $\frac{1}{2}\%$ per annum, thus making provisions for general increases in pay levels at the rate of $9\frac{1}{2}\%$ per annum. **Rent and dividend increases**. In discounting the future investment proceeds from the existing assets it is necessary to make some assumption regarding the future increase in rents and dividend levels. On the previous occasion credit was taken for 3% annual increases in rents and dividends; in conjunction with the increase in the other financial elements of the basis we have assumed that on this occasion, these increases will be at the rate of $3\frac{1}{2}\%$ per annum. This represents, in our view, a relatively conservative assumption in relation to the other elements of the basis, but to the extent that actual increases exceed the rate assumed, resources may be generated within the fund to provide for increases in pensions in course of payment, such

increases having hitherto been funded by additional payments from the employer at the time they are granted.

In the immediate future rates of pay escalation are likely to exceed those for which explicit provision is made in the valuation. We have made approximate calculations to satisfy ourselves that, based on current expectations, the additional liabilities thereby imposed on the fund should be covered by increased earnings from investments.

Some of the terms used in the examples above need explaining at this stage. (We aren't attempting to explain all of them, because it would take too long. Many of them are covered in *Your Employers' Profits* by Christopher Hird, Pluto 1975.)

■ **Managed funds** are run by insurance companies, and are halfway between insurance contracts and full self administration by the company which has the pension scheme. It is not worthwhile for a large company to hand over its investment to an insurance company, and when a few years ago the insurance companies realised they were losing income as pension funds got bigger, they set up these funds. They will usually give schemes that want to change their contract better terms if they will put some of their money into a managed fund at least for a few years. If you simply end the contract with the insurance company without doing this, you tend to get a very poor deal on 'surrender values', as you do if you give up an insurance policy as an individual.

■ The **book value** is the amount it cost to buy all the stocks, shares etc. The adjustment here is because the shares have increased in value, so that their selling price is greater. If the valuation was being done at a time when the stock market was low, the market value might be ignored, or a figure calculated in some other way might be used. If so, you would need to press for details of what the market value really was.

■ **Discounting** means working out the expected level of income from these various sources, taking into account the effects of reinvesting the compound interest, and then turning it into a capital sum. It is the same sort of exercise as we did with P Rabbit's pension on pages 222–23.

■ The **valuation rate of interest** is the level of interest that, over the long term, the fund is expected to earn on average. This does not mean that every investment is expected to earn this – some will earn more, some less. This is why a 10% rate has been thought appropriate, at a time when interest rates are actually far higher.

You'll see that, in the quote, pay has been assumed to increase at 9½%, which is low at current rates. But the important point is the *difference* between the assumed rate of interest and the assumed rate of pay increases. A ½% gap is what the Government Actuary uses for the purposes of working out the cost of the State scheme, and is about as pessimistic as most actuaries feel justified in being. If you go to a **nil** gap, or even a negative one, the calculated cost of the scheme rises a lot.

One other point is that not all actuaries value the increases in rents and dividends separately from the rate of interest. The reason this one does so is probably the amount of property the fund owns. It is interesting to see how low a rate of return is expected on this.

Having looked at the financial basis of the valuation, the actuary then goes on to look at the statistics used. Our example says:

> **Statistical elements of the basis**
>
> The statistical elements of the basis comprise the basic pay scale, excluding the effect of general increases in the level of earnings, rates of mortality, death before and after retirement, rates of retirement and withdrawal from service of active members, and marital statistics such as the proportions of members who are married and the ages of their wives. These elements of the basis can normally be settled on the basis of the detailed experience of the fund in recent years and the experience of other larger schemes of which we have details, making provision for any general trends indicated by the results of these investigations. On this occasion, the experience of the fund during the intervaluation period will not be an adequate guide in itself because for the greater part of that period membership was restricted to staff employees and our general experience is that most of these rates differ significantly between staff and hourly paid . . . We have therefore considered the experience of other schemes in settling the basis, and the majority of the assumptions differ from those made on the previous occasion.

What this means is that because the scheme has changed very much (by allowing in hourly paid people), the actuary is not able to use statistics drawn direct from the scheme. Instead, he has used *national* figures. A smaller scheme would anyway have to do so because there would not be enough information coming from the scheme itself.

The report then goes into detail on the various items:

> **Mortality**. We have modified the assumptions previously made in the light of general experience and in particular of an extensive investigation made into the experience of insured pension schemes generally. The resultant rates assumed slightly lighter mortality than previously

and a different pattern of rates by age, but the financial effect of the change is small. The same rates have been adopted for both current and prospective pensioners, but allowance has been made for somewhat heavier mortality for those members retiring on grounds of ill health.

Retirement on grounds of ill health. Provision has been made for a somewhat greater proportion of members to retire on grounds of incapacity.

Age retirement. It is necessary to make some assumptions regarding the proportion of members who will retire on full accrued pension within 5 years of normal retirement age. Although the experience of the last 3 years indicates the actual ages at retirement are slightly greater than those assumed on the occasion of the 1975 valuation it seems not unlikely that in the long term these ages will fall. We have, as a measure of precaution, adopted revised rates of retirement for men, leading to an average age at retirement of 62.3. The rates for women have remained unchanged, the derived average age at retirement being 58.5.

(This particular scheme allows people to retire on their accrued pensions after 60 for men, 55 for women. Not everybody does so, as the pension will be too small to live on, but the actuary has assumed people will start retiring earlier in the future, as a cautious approach to costs. This point was looked at on page 124, in 'Early retirement'.)

Withdrawal. Rates of withdrawal are commonly volatile and may to some extent be related to the general state of the economy. Although such rates would normally be greater amongst hourly paid employees, so that there would be some justification for adopting rather heavier withdrawal rates than previously, we do not wish to overstate any future release of liability from this source, and have therefore retained the relatively conservative rates previously adopted. The preservation requirement of the Social Security Act 1973 and the provisions to be made for contracted out members will reduce the release of liability on withdrawal.

This means people who leave the company, for whatever reason, including redundancy. In the past, the actuarial valuation usually assumed that very few people would leave, and this meant that a 'profit' was built into the scheme when they did, because they would take their own contributions and leave the company's. Today that doesn't happen, because of the preservation rules, but actuaries can't make any more allowance for this than they were doing already.

The next section of the report will draw together the statistics, and tell you what the result is:

Valuation result

The result of the investigation is summarised in the following statement, in which the emerging benefit outgo in respect of current members and pensioners is discounted to the valuation date and compared with the discounted value of (i) future joint contributions from the employer and the members, and (ii) the investment income from the existing assets.

What does this lot of jargon actually mean? What the actuary has done is calculate how much benefit is going to be paid out in the end, and then work backwards, taking account of the contributions that will be paid in and the interest earned, to see if enough money is going into the fund to pay for the benefits that are promised. It's the same procedure, but much more complicated because the fund is bigger, as with P Rabbit's pension on pages 222–23. Because it *is* complicated, this is where the actuary's special skill, which is mainly mathematical, is important.

Valuation statement as at 30 September 1978

	(B) £m	£m
Liabilities		
Present value of:		
Pensions and allowances in course of payment including those contingently payable to widows of pensioners		16.50
Deferred pensions prospectively payable to former members and their dependants		1.13
Provision for benefits in respect of former company schemes discontinued as at 31 March 1978		11.00
Benefits prospectively payable in respect of active members		
(a) retirement benefits	167.25	
(b) widows' and children's benefits on death after retirement	19.26	
(c) widows' and other benefits on death before retirement	17.71	
(d) lump sum on death in service	16.29	
(e) benefits on withdrawal	7.38	228.34
Total		256.97
Assets		
Present value of:		
Future contributions by the members and the employer		169.11
Expected future investment receipts from the present assets of the fund		98.99
Total		268.10
Surplus, being excess of assets over liabilities		11.13

Although this 'valuation statement' looks rather like a balance sheet, and is in fact sometimes called a 'valuation balance sheet', *don't* think of it as a statement about real money. All the figures are for annual amounts of income or expenditure a long way ahead, turned into capital by the use of a fair amount of guesswork. The surplus is not money in the bank; it is a theoretical amount.

In this particular report the actuary then goes on to look at what the results show, and then at whether or not the fund can afford **pension increases**. This is probably because s/he has specifically been asked to look at this, either by the company or by the trustees.

It will be seen from the foregoing statement that the future contributions together with the accumulated assets are more than adequate to meet the liabilities in respect of the current pensioners and members. At the date of the previous investigation the assets and liabilities were broadly in balance. The changes now made in the actuarial basis have not greatly affected the result. The experience of the fund during the 3 years under review has been favourable, the considerable enlargement of the liabilities caused by increases in the general level of earnings being more than covered by investment profits. The other factors affecting the financial progress of the fund have not had an appreciable overall effect on the surplus. The experience of the fund as regards the statistical elements of the basis has not differed so greatly from the assumptions made on the previous occasion as to affect the finances to any considerable extent: in particular, profits on withdrawal have contributed relatively little to the results.

No provision has been made in the calculations for future increases in pensions in course of payment. Such increases will clearly be necessary if the fund is to fulfil its aim of providing an adequate income in retirement. Hitherto, ex gratia increases have been granted at the discretion of the company and funded by special payments into the fund. In the light of the results of the current investigation, we have made supplementary calculations to determine whether the current contribution rate, together with the existing assets, is sufficient to support future increases at a level comparable to those granted in recent years. We find that this is not the case, so that additional finance will still be needed if such discretionary increases are granted in future. However, the current surplus will enable relatively substantial increases to be granted for some years. The conservative basis of valuing the existing assets may also provide further funds for this purpose. We would therefore recommend that no immediate action be taken in respect of the margin disclosed by the valuation, which represents only 4.3% of the value placed upon the liabilities. If over the period until the next actuarial valuation it is thought appropriate to grant further pension increases the cost of these may, after consultation with ourselves, be met from the fund.

This section is saying that there is enough money in the fund for increases in pensions to be paid out of it in the *short* term, but in the longer term the company would have to put more money in to cover this. The negotiators would probably ask that any increases should be paid for by the company, rather than swallow up the surplus, which is only a small proportion of the total. They would also be cautious about suggesting that very much of the surplus was used on improvements, given the uncertain economic situation.

In the next section, the actuary looks at whether the contributions are sufficient, and decides that they are:

Contribution rate

In the first place, we have investigated whether or not the current joint contribution rate of $14\frac{1}{2}\%$ of contribution pay is adequate to meet the liabilities for new entrants to the fund. We find that the theoretical joint contribution rate is a little under $14\frac{1}{2}\%$. We therefore recommend that this contribution rate be maintained unaltered by the employer, who meets the balance of cost of providing the benefits of the fund, should therefore continue to contribute at the rate of 8%, the members paying $6\frac{1}{2}\%$ in accordance with the rules.

If the actuary felt the contribution rate was *too high*, this is where s/he would say so, and recommend what should be done. S/he might well suggest that the company reduce its contribution. In that case, the unions would be likely to oppose it, and to ask for the extra to be used up on improving benefits, increasing pensions in payment, or building up a reserve (or all 3).

The next section looks at whether the fund is **solvent**, in the short term; that is, whether there is enough money already in the fund to pay for benefits already earned. This is a double check.

Solvency

The results of the investigation, as shown in the valuation statement, relate to the total prospective benefits of the current membership and credit has been taken for future contributions from the members and the employer. We have also investigated the extent to which the assets in the hands of the trustee at the date of the investigation provide security for the accrued liabilities based only on completed pensionable service. We find that the assets held were more than sufficient to cover the accrued liabilities, after making provision for the anticipated increase in these liabilities arising from future increases in pay. There is therefore a satisfactory level of asset cover at the present time. On a more restricted definition of solvency, the fund is fully solvent on a discontinuance basis, that is to say the market value of the assets would be more than sufficient to secure immediate and deferred annuities in respect of both current pensioners and active members equal to the current pension entitlement, in the case of active members based on current pay and pensionable service to date.

Discontinuance means what you would get if the fund was closed down tomorrow. A scheme should always be solvent on a discontinuance basis, even if on a 'going concern' basis (that is, assuming contributions will be paid in during the foreseeable future) it is not fully so because some newer benefits are being paid for gradually. If the actuary's report says it is not solvent on this basis, immediate action should be taken, which means putting in more money. Sometimes it is difficult to tell which basis is being used, in which case the actuary should be asked to explain.

Some actuaries value *only* on the discontinuance basis. This is not necessarily a sign that something is wrong, but you ought certainly to be asking questions.

If the scheme is *not* solvent on the 'going concern' basis, and there is no obvious reason like the fact that some improved benefits are being paid for gradually, then again action ought to be taken, because not enough money is going in. Often the company will claim that everything is all right because they are '100% solvent' or '120% solvent' on discontinuance. This means only that there is enough money in the fund to pay the benefits you have already built up, at *today's money values*, if the scheme closed down tomorrow (or if the company was taken over), so things are certainly not all right in that case.

Any report on a **contracted out** scheme must also cover the question of whether the liabilities under the Social Security Pensions Act are being fulfilled. This one says:

Social Security Pensions Act 1975
We are able to confirm, on the basis of our investigation, that the asset cover and current contribution rate are together more than adequate to enable us to provide for the Occupational Pensions Board the necessary certificate relating to the security of the priority liabilities in the event of winding up, to enable members of the fund to continue to be contracted out under the Social Security Pensions Act 1975. There have been no changes in the terms for contracting out since April 1978 and, in current conditions, we see no reason to reverse the decision made to contract out.

Finally, there would usually be a summary of the report, such as this one:

Summary

The results of the investigation, as described in this report, may be summarised as follows:

(i) The accumulated assets in the hands of the trustee, together with the continuance of the current joint contribution rate of 14½% of contribution pay, are more than adequate to meet the prospective benefits in respect of current pensioners and members.

(ii) If no further improvements in benefits are introduced and contributions are maintained at their present level there should be sufficient resources within the fund to enable some increases to be granted to pensions in course of payment as the need arises in the period before the next actuarial investigation. The position will then be reviewed but increases cannot be expected to be granted on a regular and continual basis thereafter unless there is an increase in the rate of contribution.

(iii) There is a satisfactory level of asset cover and the fund is fully solvent.

(iv) There is no problem in the continued contracting out of the members under the provisions of the Social Security Pensions Act 1975.

Often, it is only this summary that is published, sometimes as an attachment to the scheme accounts or to a 'simplified' report that is issued to every member. It is meaningless unless you know the assumptions behind it. Any group negotiating on pensions should always ask for the full report.

Section 3: What happens to the money

When pension fund money is collected in, it isn't just put in the bank. It is **invested** in stocks and shares, and anything else that is believed to provide a reasonable rate of return.

The legal responsibility for this will be with the trustees, or sometimes with a separate 'corporate trustee company', as in the BOC example we gave earlier. But only in the very small, or the very unusual, fund will the trustees themselves actually do this work. Usually they will give it to the **fund manager**, which can mean someone directly employed by the pension fund (or the company) to do the work, or it can be a contract with a merchant bank, stockbroker, consultant, or insurance company. Many schemes have a pensions manager who deals with the day to day running of the scheme, but hands all the money over to someone else to invest. Even when the pensions manager is doing the investment, s/he probably gets advice, on a fee paid basis, from one of these bodies.

There are many variations on the mechanics of dealing with

the money. Usually, whoever is doing the detailed work will report to the trustees every year or every quarter. It is for the **trustees** to decide the terms in which they report. If the body they are using to invest doesn't want to follow any restrictions placed on them, it's open to the trustees to change to another body.

Generally, trustees decide that they only want to discuss **policy**. That is, they do not want to decide whether they will buy 150 or 160 shares in company X, they want to look at broad questions like 'Should we put 50% of our new money into shares in the engineering industry?' Very often, they give guidelines to the manager to put, say, 25% of the fund into Government stocks, 25% into property, and the rest into shares in private industry ('equities'), but allow the manager discretion not only on how s/he carries this out, but also to go against the guidelines provided s/he has a good reason which s/he is prepared to explain and justify at the next meeting.

The pension funds, the insurance companies, and the people who handle their money like the merchant banks and stockbrokers are all part of what the newspapers call the 'financial institutions' or 'the City'. This is a very tightly knit world, in which a small group of individuals controls very large sums of money. It is hardly surprising that their recommendations tend to be very similar at any one time. There is no need to believe in a conscious conspiracy on this. It is simply that there is a 'magic circle' which controls the very large sums of pension fund money, and although people may reach different conclusions, they tend to think in the same sort of context. It is extremely difficult to get useful advice from anyone knowledgeable who is outside this 'magic circle'. Trade unions, for instance, will give only generalised recommendations, if they give any at all, even to trustees appointed by themselves. They do not feel they have the expertise, and they are afraid of the legal consequences if they are taken to court for giving wrong advice.

For a detailed look at the concentration of control of pension funds, look at *Pension Funds and British Capitalism* by Richard Minns (Heinemann 1980). The *Report of the Wilson committee* (*Committee to review the workings of the financial institutions*) (HMSO 1980), and the volumes of evidence given to the committee, also have some interesting information.

The duty of a trustee is to see that the funds are invested in the best interests of all the members. Trustees have a right to appoint whatever professional advisers they feel they need to assist them to carry out this duty. But, it is worth repeating, it is the trustees who retain the legal duty, and who have to decide what *is* in the best *long term* interests of the members. There is a lot of evidence that trustees, including member trustees, allow themselves to be used as rubber stamps for their professional advisers' doings.

The next section is a *very brief* description of the main areas of investment. It is *not* intended to cover everything – that would take another book. The book list on page 260 will tell you some books to read if you want to know more.

There are three main areas where it is standard practice for funds to invest.

- The UK market,
- Overseas, and
- Property.

Within the UK market, they can invest in

Government stocks. These are also called 'gilts' or 'gilt-edged securities', because it is assumed that there is no risk attached to them and they are therefore as safe as gold. This is money the Government borrows to cover a budget deficit, and also, along with other public bodies, to pay for capital spending. They issue 'stocks' which are essentially promises to repay so much in X number of years, and to pay X rate of interest meanwhile, and it is these that a fund can buy. The amount that the Government needs to borrow in this way, at any one time, is what makes up the public sector borrowing requirement (PSBR) which politicians and economists talk about. Any Government can normally rely on the financial institutions lending it any money it needs, by buying up all the stocks it offers. Every so often, though,the institutions will decide that the price is not right. Then they may refuse to buy stocks for a few days or weeks. When this happens, a Government that wants to carry on borrowing will be forced to adjust its price, and this will mean that the rest of its economic strategy will have to change. There is thus enormous power in the hands of the pension funds.

Equities. These are shares in companies. The larger companies have shares that are 'quoted' on the Stock Exchange, which means that on any one day you can find a published price for them, and a stockbroker who will sell or buy them for you. Then pension funds tend to concentrate on fairly large blocks of shares in the larger, well known companies, which means that it can be difficult for the smaller, less familiar company to find finance. Some of the largest funds have made special arrangements to invest in 'unquoted' companies (see Richard Minns' book for details), but only a very small proportion of total funds is used in this way.

Overseas investment has been growing in popularity since in 1979 the Tory government removed all exchange controls. Following this, a massive move into overseas investment was made – £490 million in the last 6 months of 1979 alone, by the institutions. Any type of investment that can be made by a fund in this country can now also be made overseas, although the funds might find themselves affected by tax laws elsewhere. Funds have bought property, as well as shares, abroad, for instance in the USA. Investment in South Africa is generally recognised as a 'hot potato', but it is less accepted that there are also moral and political, as well as commercial, aspects to a decision to invest in a repressive regime such as Chile, or an aggressively industrialising country like South Korea.

Property is also an area where there is a growing involvement by pension funds. The smaller funds will tend to invest in a 'property unit trust' (an investment agency which will do the work for them), if at all. You have to be quite large before you can buy up a whole office block at current prices. Some of the very largest funds are now investing in direct development, in partnership with insurance and/or property development companies. A number of pension funds got their fingers rather badly burnt on this in 1973–74, the days of the property boom and bust. One example of a fund more recently involved in this was the Electricity Council, which in 1980, after suspending 2 very senior staff, retired them because of rumours concerning a property company called Westmoreland.

There are a number of other things that funds invest in – forestry, farmland, commodities, gold coins, even paintings and sculpture. All of them are more or less speculative and a fund should not have much money in any of them. There are some things funds *don't* invest in – building society accounts, for instance – because the tax situation is wrong.

Pension fund accounts

There is no legal obligation on pension funds to publish accounts, as there is on a public body. A good pension fund does do so, and makes them easily available to its members, often both in complete form, for those who want them, and in a simplified 'special edition' that is provided to everyone. Often considerable care is taken with the presentation of these. But many other funds do not publish accounts at all, or say that anyone can see them provided they call at a specified time at the company's registered office in some obscure place – which of course makes access difficult. (There are **some** insurance companies which refuse to publish separate accounts for the schemes they control; this is one of the questions you should certainly be asking an insurance company before you give them your business.)

Below is part of a fairly typical 'employee edition' of one company's pension fund accounts; these come from Arthur Guinness & Co.

Main points from the trustees' report
Pension increases
Pensions were increased generally by 6.5% from 1 January 1979. The further general increase of 17% from 1 January 1980, which was announced recently, is of course not reflected in this report.
Investment strategy
The investment strategy adopted by the trustees is to invest in property, United Kingdom equities, and gilt edged securities, overseas equities and short term cash deposits.
Contributions
Member companies contributed for 1979 at the rate of 16.3% of eligible emoluments together with a lump sum payment of £251,000.

Financial facts
The growth of the fund at market value

1977	£23.0 m
1978	£25.6 m
1979	£28.9 m

Why the fund must grow
During the year ended 31 December, 1979 the value of the fund increased by £3.3 million. The fund's immediate liability is to pay the pensions of members currently retired and it has sufficient money now to pay these pensions. It also has to ensure that money will be available in the future to meet the costs of pensions for members currently employed. It is therefore necessary for the fund to increase over a period of time.

Where the money comes from and where it goes to

Income	£m
From: members – voluntary contribution scheme	0.1
company	3.1
	3.2
investments (including tax refunds of 0.4)	2.1
Total income	5.3

Expenditure

Pensions	2.0
Lump sums (a) commutation	0.3
(b) death benefits	0.2
Total expenditure	2.5

Growth of fund

Money available for investment (income £5.3m less expenditure 2.5m)	2.8
Appreciation in market values of investments	0.5
Total growth – Market value at 31 December 1979 £28.9m (1978 £25.6m)	3.3

Where the money is

		£m
Stock Exchange investments		20.8
Property		7.1
Total investments		27.9
Sundry debtors	0.6	
Life assurance policies	0.2	
Cash at bank	0.3	
	1.1	
Less liabilities	0.1	
		1.0
Total amount of fund		28.9

What we are investing in	£m	%
United Kingdom ordinary shares	10.5	38
Property	7.1	25
United Kingdom fixed interest securites	6.8	24
Overseas ordinary shares	3.5	13
Market value of total investments	27.9	100
Investment in ordinary shares (UK 10.5m, overseas £3.5m)	14.0	51

[Ordinary shares by percentage]	%
Financial groups	23
Consumer goods (non-durable)	21
Capital goods	15
Oil's	11
Consumer goods (durable)	6
Investment trusts	5
Other groups	19
	100

Negotiators, or members of any sort of pensions committee, would want a copy of the full version as well; and you'd also want someone involved in preparing them to come along to your meeting. The sort of questions you would want to see answered by the accounts might be:

▪ What is the company's contribution? Has it gone up or down in the last year, either in money terms or in percentage terms? Why?

▪ How does it compare to the members' contributions? What's the ratio between them? Has this gone up or down? Why?

▪ What is the money invested in? How is it split between the main investment groups, compared with other schemes? If it's different, why?

▪ Within 'equities' how many companies is the money invested in, and in what areas? Is too much concentrated in one sector? (If 50% of the investment was in gambling, for instance, and the police then closed the casinos down, the fund would do badly.)

▪ If part of the fund is in property, who decides what to buy and sell, and who values it?

▪ Does the pension fund own shares in the employing company? (This is called self investment.) There is no law against doing so, but it is not a good principle to invest much money – more than a few per cent of the fund – in your own company.

▪ Has there been a lot of *turnover* of stocks and shares in the last year? Buying and selling costs money because you have to pay commission – how much has been paid? Did the new purchases have a better rate of return *after* the cost of buying and selling has been taken into account?

▪ How is the fund manager paid? What are his fees and how are they worked out? They could be on a flat rate, a percentage of new money, a percentage of the fund.

▪ Does any part of the fund manager's income arise from the buying and selling of stock (which would give him an incentive to do as much as possible on this)?

▪ Where does the scheme come on the various 'league tables' prepared by stockbroking firms to show how well you're doing compared to others? How are those league tables worked out? (You shouldn't place too much faith in these, though. Many of them are very gimmicky.)

▪ Have the advisers, or fund managers, taken any part in **policy making**? For instance, have they agreed to sell shares in a particular company so that a takeover bid could go ahead? If so, on what criteria did they base their decision, and whom did they consult?

Many workers whose money is going into pension funds are beginning to ask questions about the use of their money in more radical terms – for instance how far it is being used for socially useful investment. Since this is intended to be a handbook, this is not the place to discuss these more definitely political issues, but several of the books included in the book list on page 260 cover them, and it would be worth looking at some of these for further information, especially if you have, or are trying to get, member trustees.

Pressure to obtain full disclosure of pension fund accounts, and then to have the right to ask searching questions about them, **and** get useful answers, is vital if unions are to assert real control over their deferred pay. But while many employers are happy to hand out nice simplified versions of their fund accounts, as public relations exercises, they will tend to react extremely defensively to requests for further information. Here, for example, is an extract from a letter from Maurice Oldfield, manager of the Allied Breweries pension fund (value in 1980 £250 million) in reply to an article in the *Financial Times* urging greater disclosure:

> As far as information to the public is concerned, a better comparison with companies is with a private company. Apart from satisfying the 'demands' of journalists, what would the public display of occupational pension fund details achieve? The parties to the trust deed, the trustees and the employers, have a responsibility to the members and the beneficiaries. If the members wish to make the details public they can do so but this is hardly the right course for the pension fund administrators.

It is this sort of attitude that the unions, and the ordinary members, are up against.

9.

Takeovers, closures and redundancies

Introduction

These events raise a lot of complex issues, and so we're dealing with them in this chapter, all together, rather than spread around the book. But you will probably still need to refer back to the other chapters quite a lot as you go along.

The chapter is divided into three sections:

1. Takeovers
2. Closures
3. Redundancies

Section 1: Takeovers

There are two types of takeover:

■ when a business takes over another business completely; and

■ when it takes over *part* of that other business.

Thus, ABC Ltd may buy enough shares in XYZ Ltd to give it control – this is the first type. Or it may do a deal with XYZ Ltd to buy its office equipment division, while leaving the rest of XYZ in existence as a separate entity – this is the second type.

Rights at Work by Jeremy McMullen, Pluto 1978, goes into the effects this has on redundancy pay. Here, we are looking simply at the **pensions** position.

If ownership of the business changes hands, then the pension scheme, as a separate fund attached to that business, goes with it, and the employees can stay in the separate scheme within the new company for ever, if that's the way things work out. A contracting out certificate needs to be varied, but only on the technicality of adding the new subsidiary's name to the list covered by the holding company on its master certificate.

Where *part* of the business is taken over, it's more difficult. The employees affected have to be withdrawn from the previous scheme, and put in a different one (assuming the new employer has one). Therefore the old and the new companies' contracting out certificates have to be changed, which may mean that 3 months' notice has to be given and consultation carried out.

So far as the **pension scheme** is concerned, the changeover may well mean leaving one job and starting another, so there may be an opportunity for refunds to be taken, although the Inland Revenue have been tightening up on this recently. The new employer **may** make entry into this scheme, on whatever terms, a compulsory part of the conditions of employment. Since so far as this is concerned you are new employees you do *not* have to be given a choice in the way that existing employees do (see page 59).

The Inland Revenue recognises that things are not usually sorted out very quickly, and so it will allow a 'period of grace' during which people working for the new employer are still technically covered by the old employer's pension scheme. This would not normally be for longer than 1 year, but if there are particular difficulties they will give you longer. The most common difficulty that arises is between the actuaries of the 2 funds, who will be unable to agree how much of the old scheme money belongs to the people involved in the takeover, and therefore how much money should go over from one fund to the other.

The first rule, in any takeover (and this doesn't just apply to pensions), is *keep copies* of any announcements that are issued to the workforce, any letters that are sent out by management. Keep notes of any meeting held by the old or new employers to explain what is going on. You may well need them in the future. Management will *often* make reassuring statements, or give assurances that 'nothing is going to change, your terms and conditions will be just the same' and then try to go back on it later. It's your responsibility to see that they don't get away with it. If management is *not* making this sort of statement, you should ask them – and try to pin them down in writing – as early as possible. If you get in as soon as something is in the wind, the sale agreement may not yet have been signed, and you might be able to influence it.

Your **legal rights** on takeovers, as far as pensions are concerned, are very weak:

■ Because of the section in most scheme booklets which says:

> X Industries reserves the right to change or terminate any part of the X plan described in this booklet. Such a step would only be taken after due notice to members of the plan and to other affected members.

or something similar, so long as the company take a little care about giving due notice, you have not got much of a case for breach of contract.

■ If the new company closes down the pension scheme, thereby worsening the conditions of employment, and you left *because of it*, you might have a case for constructive dismissal. But there have been very few cases on this (because people tend not to leave because of their pension scheme).

■ If maintenance of the scheme was in the sales agreement between the two companies, there may be scope for a civil action for breach of that contract. This would involve the old company taking the new one to court. However, if the new company maintains the scheme for a few months and then closes it down, it will be able to say that it is because of 'other factors', nothing to do with the sales agreement, and therefore the chances of success would be small.

So although threatening legal action, and the publicity that goes with it, may be a useful weapon, the chances of actually succeeding in court are small. It's usually better to rely on the force of the commitments made, and the need for the new employer to establish good relations with his new workers.

It must be emphasised that the legal protection given to your pension scheme in a takeover is *much weaker* than that given to other terms and conditions of employment. At worst, the employer can get away with freezing your past pension and not offering you entry into a new scheme at all.

If the takeover is really a rescue – if it was clear that your company (or your part of the company) was going to close down if it wasn't bought, or if the receiver had actually been brought in, and sold your plant off – then your position on what you can get is much weaker than if yours was a profitable plant bought as an investment. But what you should *try* to get will be the same in each case.

The essential principles to be followed are:

■ *Don't* allow your pension rights to be bought out by a cash sum, however attractive it may be. Pension rights are different from cash, and one cannot replace the other in that way.

■ Try to insist that any new scheme is so arranged that it is no worse, *not only* as a package as a whole, but also for *each individual*. If the new scheme provides a better spouse's pension, but a worse death benefit, the person who leaves no spouse will lose, so his/her rights must be safeguarded.

■ Try to insist that any benefits you get are based on the service you have done with both companies, and your final salary at the date of retiring or leaving, not on how far the money in the old fund will go. It's not your fault if the old scheme was not properly funded. It was for the new employer to find that out, and adjust the purchase price to take account of it. If he didn't do so, that's his bad luck, and you shouldn't be penalised. But if the new employer has made a mistake, it may cost him a lot to give this to you, so you will have quite a fight on your hands.

If the new company is one that has been expanding a good deal recently, it is likely to have a fairly rigid policy on how to treat new subsidiaries designed to cut down cost. In that case, you want to argue for that policy to be changed, because this is more likely to succeed than arguing for being a special case. Try to get in touch with any other recent acquisition (the new company's annual report should tell you about them) and form a common front. Try also to get in touch with stewards in the new parent company, and ask them to make clear that they don't want to profit at the expense of the new acquisitions.

What is the company doing for the pensions of the management people it has brought in? The chances are that it is giving them better terms – possibly even very generous ones, if there are people it wants to make sure will stay. So, assuming the new company has bought your company not *just* because of the management skills, but because of the workers' skills as well, surely they ought to treat the workers no worse than the managers?

Amalgamating schemes

Where a whole business has been taken over, it may well be some time before anything is done – often several **years**. Amalgamating the pension schemes will often come at a late stage in establishing a corporate identity, and doing it properly – ensuring that no one is made worse off and that the schemes are levelled up to the standard of the best scheme – can be expensive.

The company will generally have clear ideas as to *why* it's bringing everyone into a new scheme. It's a fairly laborious task, so they're not doing it for fun. Probably their reasons include:

■ the administrative costs of running a lot of small schemes are high;

■ the board don't feel that local management are making a very good job of running the individual companies' schemes and they want to bring them all under the control of one professional pensions department;

■ they feel they're getting a bad service out of the insurance companies, and could do the job more simply and cheaply themselves;

■ they want to establish a stronger 'corporate identity' and make you feel you're working for Universal Grand Magnificent Ltd, not Small Miserable Ltd its subsidiary.

It is therefore important to *them* to get as many people as possible into the new scheme, and for that they do *need* the union's recommendation. This means that you're in a fairly strong bargaining position, and it's worth trying to exploit it. Ultimately, however, the new company still has the power to close down the old scheme, although it cannot in these circumstances force anyone into the new one, if there has been a time lag between the takeover and the tidying up, and you are now an existing employee. So if you can't get what you want in the new scheme, but it is nonetheless reasonable, you'd have to think pretty seriously before recommending people not to go into it.

As there are so many different circumstances, we can't go through them all, but here are a few case studies that may help you to see what can be done within your company.

1. Wimpey Waste Management was sold by Powell Duffryn to Wimpey's. This was a **partial takeover**. Wimpey's have no pension scheme for their manual workers, and wanted to buy out the Powell Duffryn membership, who were in the PD contracted out scheme, by giving them a cash lump sum in return for freezing the pension. The members refused to accept this. After considerable negotiation, the company set up a special scheme, restricted to this group of employees, which was contracted in but included a guarantee on the pension and the dependants' pensions. For the latter, this reads:

> In the event that the aggregate benefits payable to the dependant under the scheme together with any pension or other related benefits payable by the State as at present accruing (if any) should be less than the pension equivalent of the

following benefits payable under the PD RBS [the Powell Duffryn retirement benefits scheme] in the event of death in service, the company will make up the difference so as to ensure that benefits as favourable as those that would have been received under the PD RBS would be payable. **This undertaking applies to the complete period from 6 April 1978, or the date of joining the PD RBS if later, to the date of retirement or earlier withdrawal.**

The PD RBS benefits referred to above are as follows:

(i) Death in service lump sum payment of 1 times earnings.

(ii) Widow's pension (subject to reduction if she is more than 10 years younger than her husband).

(iii) Children's allowances (payable until the child's 19th birthday, or the date of cessation of full-time education if earlier).

A dependant may elect to take part or all of the benefits payable as a result of the death of the member in cash, subject to Inland Revenue regulations.

So the ex-Powell Duffryn employees are now a small group, within a large conglomerate, with a special pension scheme provided just for them, which safeguards each individual's rights under the previous scheme.

2. Thomas Tilling Group sold Volkswagen (UK) to Lonrho. The Thomas Tilling scheme was contracted out. A new, contracted out Volkswagen scheme, which was different in some ways from the previous scheme, was set up. The booklet states:

Pensionable service means the complete and continuous years and months of your contributory membership while a member of this pension scheme, or the Thomas Tilling scheme in which the company participated.

Employees who were members of the company scheme before 6 April 1978 are guaranteed that their pension, calculated under the new rules, will not be any less than the pension that would have resulted using the method of calculation under the rules in existence before that date [i.e. under the Thomas Tilling Staff Scheme rules].

So these employees now have full credit for their Thomas Tilling service in the Volkswagen scheme, and a 'no worse off' provision.

3. WGI Ltd, who have a 1/100th 'ride on top' contracted in scheme, took over entirely Cawthraw's Ltd, with a 1/60th contracted out scheme. To complicate things further, the Cawthraw's scheme was non-contributory, and the WGI one contributory. The company closed the Cawthraw's scheme, and offered members transfer into the WGI contracted in scheme, on the basis of a 'once for all' pay increase of 2.35%, which was enough to cover the cost of paying contributions. Full credit for past service would be given in the WGI scheme. Thus, if an individual worked 10 years for Cawthraws and then 10 years for WGI, at retirement date s/he would have 20 years' credit for pension from WGI. The company also agreed that they would carry out a 'no worse off' exercise for anyone retiring in the next 5 years – that is, they

would calculate the pension on the old and new bases, and pay the better.

So in this case they went from a contracted out to a contracted in position, with a safeguard for their previous service but no residual special provision within the new scheme. This is not as good a result as the previous example, but better than many.

4. Associated Biscuit Manufacturers took over Smiths Food Group as a complete business. ABM proposed that existing members of the Smiths plan would have the option of either staying in that plan or transferring over to ABM terms, but that new employees would have to join the ABM scheme. The assets of the Smiths plan would be transferred to the ABM fund, under the ABM trustees (who included members).

After strong objections from the shop stewards' committees in Smiths Foods, and a number of meetings, it was agreed that while the two funds should be merged, Smiths would have proportional representation on the trustees, and the Smiths scheme would remain open for future Smiths employees as well, so that there would be no option to transfer at least for the moment.

Here the two schemes were, as packages, fairly similar in quality. The unions' anxiety in Smiths arose from the fear that ABM would use the Smiths *fund* to strengthen their own, and they were therefore concerned to keep things separate. The final agreement in fact strengthened the Smiths members' position over what it had been, because they had previously only had a consultative committee (which has continued to meet) and they now also had member trustees.

Note: all these are examples of more or less successful agreements. There are many unsuccessful ones. If you can't succeed at the time of a reorganisation of pension schemes after a takeover, don't despair. If you end up with a frozen pension, for instance, it may still be worth returning to the issue in a few years' time, especially if it has remained a 'festering sore' and is leading to continuing bad feeling between component parts of the company.

Section 2: Closures

By this we mean companies that go out of business altogether, whether by voluntary liquidation or compulsory bankruptcy. Closure of one site by a company that remains in existence is dealt with in the next section, under **redundancy**, as in principle it is no different from the much smaller redundancy of a few people in a department.

On a closure, the scheme will be wound up, and the rules governing this come into force.

In a contracted out scheme, if there is not enough money to go round, then any benefits payable under the Social Security Pensions Act, and the premium needed to secure them, **must** have priority.

The **Inland Revenue** says that, on a winding up

■ benefits must not exceed the normal Inland Revenue maximum; and

■ if, after all the other claims have been met (including increasing benefits in payment, if the scheme rules allow that) there is a surplus in the scheme, then the rules must provide for that to be returned to the employer, who will then be liable to tax on it. Winding up is the only circumstance in which the employer can directly obtain money from the pension fund.

If the scheme is winding up, and therefore going out of business, the pensions due to people cannot be preserved within it. So either

■ there must be a **transfer** to another scheme of the money that's built up for your pension, or

■ the money must be used to buy a deferred annuity from an insurance company, and they will keep this for you until you retire.

The duty of the person put in by the creditors, the receiver, in a liquidation, is to get as much money out of the company as possible to pay the debts due to the creditors. His duty to the pension fund members, therefore, is to give them only the **minimum** under the rules, so that the maximum is left over.

In the dying months of a company before a liquidation, there may well have been a period during which the contributions to the scheme were not being paid; perhaps they were being collected by the employer but not handed over to the insurance company. Under the Social Security Pensions Act, any employees' contributions deducted but not passed over for the last 4 months, and any employers' contributions for the same period are a preferential debt in liquidation. That is, they rank with the tax people and the DHSS, and before any business creditors.

If there is not enough money even for this, then in the last resort the Redundancy Payments Fund will make up the difference, but *only* for the GMPs.

When the scheme suddenly stops, because the employer has gone into liquidation, the following points are important:

■ Move quickly. You'll have a lot of other things to think about as well as your pension rights, but they are important too. If you think a crash is coming, make sure that you have all available information about the scheme, including a copy of the rules, and check what they say about discontinuance. You'll usually find that section at or near the end of the rules. Turn back to page 175 for details of what they *should* say.

■ If a receiver has been installed, arrange a meeting and ask him/her what the position is. Is there going to be enough money in the fund to pay all the benefits, or will there be a shortfall? If s/he says s/he doesn't know, because no proper actuarial review has been carried out, ask how long it will be before this is done, and ask to be kept informed.

■ You may then have to wait some time for things to be sorted out. The company's documents ought to include a list of the members' names and addresses, but since they may be in some chaos, *make your own*, give a copy to whoever is actually dealing with the winding up, and then hang on to your own copy. You should also include on your list the members' dates of birth, marital status, and how long each one has been in the scheme. Make sure the full time union official, or the legal officer, has a copy of the list too – all the shop stewards may have emigrated by the time it is finally settled.

Keep in touch with whoever is doing the work. It may be a bank, or a local solicitor, or the pension fund manager. Often tying up the ends will take 1 or 2 years, but don't let them forget you're waiting for news.

Ultimately, the ex-members should be sent individual notifications of the amount of benefit that they have frozen for them, and the name of the insurance company with whom the policy has been bought. Check that this has gone to everyone; this is why keeping a list of those involved is important.

In this situation, there will be no question of *negotiating*. You won't have any option about what you get – you'll simply have to accept the division of whatever there is in the pension fund, as a frozen pension. But that shouldn't stop you arguing if you think there's been a mistake – if, for instance, someone has been left off the list, or if the insurance company say the scheme was wound up when you were still paying contributions to it.

Once you are sure all the facts are straight, there is no point in trying to get a better deal that would cost the failed company money. The receiver's responsibility is to the creditors, not to you. The ex-employees' pensions come a very long way down his/her list of priorities.

There are some cases where although a receiver is put in by the creditors, the company is given permission to continue trading and parts of it, at least, are then sold off as a going concern. In that case, although you might not be able to do anything with the existing company, you might be able to persuade the new company to treat you reasonably. See section 1, 'Takeovers' (pages 246–52, for information on this.

Section 3: Redundancies

The third area of difficulty is redundancy, either of a small group or of everybody in one part of the company. There's been a tendency in the past to leave pensions until last, or indeed to forget them altogether. This is partly because people think there is nothing to be done about getting a better pensions deal when redundancy strikes, whereas in fact there is quite a lot.

Not many schemes have specific provisions on redundancy. It was not covered by recent NAPF surveys, so it is not possible to give figures. The only major group of schemes is in the public sector. For example, the British Gas scheme says:

> If your job becomes redundant and you have
> (a) completed 10 years' service
> (b) reached age 55 (50 for women) or over
> you will receive an immediate pension calculated as for normal retirement but subject to the minimum pension calculation as in ill health [which gives some credit for prospective service].
> If however you have completed 10 years' service and are compulsorily retired because of redundancy between the ages of 50 and 55 (45 and 50 for women) you have the option to take a reduced deferred pension payable at age 55 (50 for women).

One company in the private sector that has a section on redundancy written into its scheme booklet is BOC, which says:

> Voluntary early retirement: you can retire on immediate pension up to 10 years before normal retirement age provided you have completed at least 10 years' pensionable service . . . If you retire within 5 years of normal pensionable age you are entitled to a full pension based on pensionable service completed. However, if you retire between 5 and 10 years before your normal retirement age your pension (based on pensionable service completed) is reduced by $\frac{1}{6}\%$ per month or part month between your date of retirement and your 60th (man) or 55th (woman) birthday.
> Redundancy: if you are made redundant, in circumstances in which

> you would qualify for an immediate early retirement pension . . . and
> you have completed 20 years' pensionable service, any reduction
> referred to [above] will be waived. The company and the trustees may
> waive the reduction if you have completed only 10 years' pensionable
> service.

Other companies, such as Delta Metals and Tube Investments, have policies on how the pension scheme deals with
redundancies, but do not publicise them except at the sites where the
issue arises.

Many companies say that they prefer to deal with the issue
when it comes along. This has the same drawbacks in the pension
scheme as it does on severance or redundancy pay in general. If you
don't get the broad framework at least set out in advance, you tend
to be in a much weaker bargaining position when redundancies
actually turn up.

Proper redundancy provisions in a pension scheme are
expensive, and they tend to fall on the company all at one time, if for
instance there is a plant closure. But part of the point of them, as
well as looking after the individual better after s/he loses the job, is
to deter the company from making people redundant without
serious consideration.

There is however an opposite view, that having any sort of
scheme in existence gives management an easier ride. The viewpoint
you take must be a matter for *your* decision.

If you decide not to negotiate until there is a redundancy,
then, given the length of time anything to do with pensions takes,
you *ought* to start negotiating on the pensions deal very soon after
the principle of the redundancies has been accepted – at the same
time as talking about the redundancy money, but separately.

The guidelines below are drawn up with negotiating *in
advance* in mind. But you can also use them if you're negotiating at
the time of the redundancy.

The sort of points you need to look for are:

■ Anyone over 50 made redundant should be allowed to take
an early retirement pension without any loss of rights under the
redundancy scheme, and should be allowed to commute the
maximum amount the Inland Revenue and the Occupational
Pensions Board will permit (the GMPs must remain as a pension).
This will often give a better lump sum than a refund of contributions
would, where that is available. If there is any doubt, the company

should calculate what is available and give the member a free choice of the options.

■ There should be no minimum service qualification for an early retirement pension.

■ Early retirement pensions should be calculated on the same basis as for ill health early retirement, that is, taking into account actual *and* prospective service. If you can't get this, then *at least* there should be no reduction because of early payment. (See page 119 for the Inland Revenue view on this.)

■ Life assurance should continue for everyone made redundant, whatever their ages. (The company can arrange a group life assurance scheme, which is not expensive.) It may be necessary to agree that a person taking other pensionable employment will stop being covered.

■ If the pensions being paid to the ordinary pensioners are increased at any time, the early retirement pensions should be too.

■ Deferred pensions for those too young to take early retirement must also be looked at, and preferably given on better terms than usual. This is dealt with in chapter 4, section 16, 'Leaving Service' pages 156–65, so turn to that section.

■ None of this should be offset against the ordinary redundancy money, and people should not be asked to choose between one or the other.

Under the Redundancy Payments Act, the employer is allowed to reduce the statutory redundancy pay of people close to retirement (see Rights at Work page 350). But he doesn't have to do this – so don't let him.

Information to those being made redundant is also important. As early as possible, people should be given an estimate of

■ what their deferred pension would be;

■ what their early retirement pension would be;

■ how much they can commute into a lump sum; and

■ what refund of contributions, if any, is available.

Final details will not usually be available until after they finish work, but should be passed on as soon as possible after that. Everyone should have the chance of an interview with the pensions administrator, or a consultant, several weeks before they go, preferably on site, and *in the company's time*, to go through the options. It should not be a sales job for one particular option, or for any particular use of the money.

The extra cost of these provisions, even if it is only 1 or 2 people who are affected, should *not* be met by the pension fund, but by the company making a special payment into it.

Possible arguments and responses

Management objections to redundancy provisions within a pension scheme will be on grounds of **cost**. If you're negotiating in advance, there may be a fear of making a commitment which, if there were a large number of redundancies, they would find difficult to sustain. Once an item is written into the pension scheme, it can't be repudiated by the management. It's then up to the scheme administrator to do what the rules say.

Management may say:

■ It would be unfair to treat one group of employees more favourably than others. They may suggest that this would be 'at the expense of the pension scheme'. But, as we said before, the cost of these provisions should be met by the company, *not* by the scheme, so this argument is quite unreal.

■ That they wish to retain their freedom of action, and that if you make the cost of a future redundancy programme too great, you might find the company being liquidated completely. What weight you give to this sort of argument will be up to the people who know the company. Are they trigger happy types, threatening closure every 10 minutes, or do they only say things when they mean them?

If you're negotiating when the actual redundancies are happening, management will, almost certainly, be balancing the cost of any special provisions they make against the cost of other parts of the redundancy package. They may argue that it is more cost effective to put money into other parts than into improving the pension provision. This would not often be the case, because of the tax advantages of pension schemes – but it could be, for instance, if the scheme is very bad, so that even increased pensions would be very small.

The company may argue that what they provide from the pension scheme doesn't matter anyway, because people will go out and get new jobs. You should point out that, even when unemployment was not so high, people over the age of 50 or so found it very hard to get new jobs; today, with unemployment rising, it's much *more* difficult.

You could also add that, since the Tory government came to power, the unemployed are now being treated worse than ever by the Social Security system. They have seen the rate of benefit cut, in real terms, and however long they remain unemployed, they are always treated as short term claimants for supplementary benefit, and are therefore on a *lower* level of benefit. As we've said before, the reason employers often give for having a pension scheme at all is to fill in the gaps left by the State, and this is one of them.

Management may say, however, that although they feel sorry for these people, what happens to the unemployed is not their problem, it's a matter of general social policy. This is *not the point*. These individuals would not be unemployed, if it were not for management's past and present actions, and management must accept a continuing responsibility.

Finally, if you do achieve something in this area, and especially if it is an agreement at local level,

■ let stewards at other plants in the same company know,

■ let stewards in other plants in the same area know, and

■ tell your union's head office.

Anything that can be used as a precedent in this field is useful to other negotiators.

Book List

You may find the following books helpful in negotiations, or in thinking more about pensions. This is not an exhaustive list.

Official Publications
(*The Publisher is HMSO unless otherwise stated.*)

Social Security Act 1975
Social Security Pensions Act 1975
Finance Act 1970 and *1971*
Occupational Pension Schemes: Notes on Approval under the Finance Act 1970 (referred to in the text as 'Practice Notes'), published by the Board of Inland Revenue Superannuation Funds Office.
Occupational Pension Schemes 1975: Fifth Survey by the Government Actuary 1978
Equal Status for Men and Women in Occupational Pension Schemes: Report of the Occupational Pensions Board, 1976
Report of the Committee to Review the Functioning of the Financial Institutions (Wilson Committee), 1980
Joint Memoranda of Inland Revenue Superannuation Funds Office and Occupational Pensions Board – series available from Joint Office, Apex Tower, New Malden, Surrey.

Specialist Books on Pensions

Occupational Pension Schemes: a TUC guide, TUC 1981
Tutt and Tutt, *Private Pension Scheme Finance*, Stone & Cox 1971
McKelvrey, Round and McArthur, *Pension Schemes and Retirement Benefits*, Sweet & Maxwell 1977

Harry Lucas, *Pensions and Industrial Relations*, Pergamon 1977

Harry Lucas and Suc Ward, *Pensions Bargaining*, WEA 1977

Law of Trusts and Pensions Schemes: Note of Guidance, TUC 1980

Survey of Occupational Pension Schemes 1979, NAPF 1980. New edition published annually

NAPF Year Book 1980 (updated annually). Lists pension schemes, consultants, investment advisors etc. who are members of the NAPF

Guide to Pension Schemes, Incomes Data Services 1980

J. S. D. Seres and J. W. Selley, *Pensions: A Practical Guide*, Oyez 1980. A book written mainly for solicitors dealing with pension schemes

Michael Barnes and Ronald Spill, *The Pension Scheme Trustee*, Guild Press 1978

Pilch and Wood, *Pension Schemes; A Guide to Principles and Practice*, Gower Press 1979

More General Books on Funding etc.

The Role of the Financial Institutions: TUC Evidence to the Committee to Review the Functioning of Financial Institutions, TUC 1979

John Hughes, *Funds for Investment*, Fabian Society 1976

Bristow and Dobbins, *The Growth and Impact of Institutional Investors*, Institute of Chartered Acountants 1978

Sue Ward, *Controlling Pension Schemes*, WEA 1978

R. Minns, *Pension Funds and British Capitalism*, Heinemann 1980

Index